plowman's folly

and

a second look

CONSERVATION CLASSICS

Nancy P. Pittman, Series Editor

With the Conservation Classics, ISLAND PRESS inaugurates a new series to again make available books that helped launch the conservation movement in America. When first published, these books offered provocative alternatives which challenged established methods and patterns of development.

Today, they offer practical solutions to contemporary challenges in such areas as multiple-use forestry, desertification and soil erosion, and sustainable agriculture. These new editions include valuable introductions from the leaders of today's conservation movement.

The inaugural titles in the series are:

BREAKING NEW GROUND
by Gifford Pinchot

Introduction by George T. Frampton, Jr.

PLOWMAN'S FOLLY
and
A SECOND LOOK
by Edward H. Faulkner

Introduction by Paul B. Sears

TREE CROPS
A Permanent Agriculture
by J. Russell Smith

Introduction by Wendell Berry

ISLAND PRESS
WASHINGTON, D.C. ∞ COVELO, CALIFORNIA

plowman's folly and a second look

BY EDWARD H. FAULKNER

ISLAND PRESS

Washington, D.C. □ Covelo, California

Reprinted by special arrangement with the University of Oklahoma Press.

Library of Congress Cataloging-in-Publication Data

Faulkner, Edward H. (Edward Hubert), 1886-1964.
Plowman's folly ; and, A second look.

(Conservation classics)
Reprint. Originally published: Norman : University of Oklahoma Press, 1943. (Soil conservation)
Reprint. Originally published: Norman : University of Oklahoma Press, 1947. (Soil conservation)
1. Tillage. 2. Tillage--United States. 3. Tillage--United States. 4. Soil management--United States. 5. Plowing. 6. Plowing--United States. 7. Soil conservation. 8. Soil conservation--United States. 9. Soils. 10. Soils--United States. 11. Plows. 12. Harrows. 13. Conservation tillage.
I. Faulkner, Edward H. (Edward Hubert), 1886-1964. Second look. 1987. II. Title: Plowman's folly. III. Title: Second look. IV. Series.
S604.F38 1987 631.5'1 87-82036
ISBN 0-933280-43-2 (pbk.)
ISBN 0-933280-51-3 (cloth)

Manufactured in the United States of America
10 9 8 7 6 5 4 3 2 1

plowman's folly

CONTENTS

FOREWORD

ON A LATE afternoon in the early 1940's, Savoie Lottinville, like a proper director, had waited to close up shop himself at the University of Oklahoma Press. On his way to the rear exit, passing through the mailing room, he noted a manuscript left to be packaged and returned to its author with the usual regrets. Glancing at the first few pages, he was immediately impressed and later settled down to a careful reading during a railway trip to New York. The manuscript, called *Plowman's Folly*, had to do with a vital, too-often neglected resource regarded by many as merely "dirt": the *soil* and the effect upon it of the modern plow.

At the other end of the line from Oklahoma was Oberlin, Ohio. Nearly half a century has passed since I was visited there by Edward H. Faulkner, a personable gentleman from the neighboring town of Elyria who explained his theory to me, and mentioned that his manuscript—a critique on the damage done to farm soils by the use of the modern version of the old crooked stick known as the moldboard plow—had been rejected by a succession of publishers.

He told me that years as an agricultural agent in the upper Ohio and Erie basins had awakened him to the fertility of newly-cleared land as compared to the "worn-out" farms that followed cultivation.

At that time, I was becoming familiar with events in the grasslands of interior North America that had culminated in the great dust storms of the 1930's. I had also learned that a similar process had taken place in regions as diverse as Neolithic Denmark and modern Guatemala. As far as I could find out, fertility was only restored by allowing the land to return to its natural state for a time. The sad truth seemed to be that both forest and grassland soils all too often failed to remain fertile under human management.

Faulkner's concern with a problem vital to Man's survival on this planet led him to search, through observation and experimentation, for ways to care for the Earth's dark carpet we call soil. Starting with the common knowledge that good soil is generally dark in color due to the decomposition of organic materials, Faulkner observed that where trees and grass grow, such stuff piles up and decays on the *surface.*

Faulkner's genius was to question the very basis of agriculture itself—the plow. He began to see that the curved moldboard of the modern plow, rather than allowing organic matter to be worked into the soil by worms and other burrowing animals, instead buries this valuable material *under the subsoil* where it remains like a wad of undigested food from a heavy meal in the human stomach.

This is the essential message of *Plowman's Folly*, along with its simple remedy, a more general use of a machine called a disk plow. This device cuts into pieces and works into the upper layers of the soil weeds and other green manure along with dead plants and animal wastes. Here sufficient air and water allow their conversion into what are known as organic colloids, whose peculiar function is to organize mineral particles into a "crumb-structure." These crumbs hold mineral nutrients as a bank holds its deposits, subject to demand from the plant's roots. This process is remarkably like respiration in plants and animals—the free movement of oxygen, carbon dioxide, and water essential to the continuance of life.

Savoie Lottinville didn't need me to tell him to publish Faulkner's book, sensitive as he already was to the problems of natural resources. His perspicacity was rewarded, too, as the sale of the book, published in 1943, was reliably reported to be a million and a half copies, including translations.

To the pleasure of reading his book and the reflection on its meaning, I leave to the reader.

Paul B. Sears
Taos, New Mexico
July, 1987

Paul B. Sears is the author of *Deserts On The March*, soon to be republished by Island Press in the Conservation Classics Series.

INTRODUCTION

SURELY, IF THERE ever were a single, perfect symbol for the American ethos, it would be the moldboard plow. The virgin American land was made for this plow; manifest destiny was achieved with it; the wealth of the nation depended on it.

Thomas Jefferson, like many farmers of his day (and this), loved to plow. The plow was, he thought, "like sorcery" and was "the most useful of instruments known to man."

Accordingly, in 1837, a thirty-three year old blacksmith from Rutland, Vermont, came to the Illinois prairie to set up a smithy. His name was John Deere, and he eventually developed a means to produce steel moldboard plows inexpensively. There is a theory, and it may well be correct, that John Deere's mass-produced steel moldboard plow changed the history of the nation, for now a plow was light, affordable, and would last. With a stout team, a man—any man, not just a wealthy landowner like Jefferson—could cut deep into black bottomland soils and zip open prairie sod that had formerly been unplowable. These new plows meant the opening and plowing up of the vast agricultural heartland of America and beyond—into what was known as the Great American Desert, a fragile ecosystem that many now believe should never have been plowed at all. Here was a natural resource that seemed endless and inexhaustible when John Deere's steel plow was introduced. But exactly one hundred years later, during the time of economic depression, the Dust Bowl had become so overused that it was a chief cause of national agony.

One agronomist living and working during the 1930's in Ohio decided that the agony of soil erosion and agricultural depression was not foreordained, could have been avoided, and even now was remediable, if only farmers would give up the moldboard plow. The agronomist's name was Edward H. Faulkner, and there ought to be a great, green statue of him in front of the Department of Agriculture's building in Washington, D.C. Hardly likely. In fact, Faulkner had to resign from the department in order to pursue his theories.

The theories appeared, after many years of experimentation, in the 1943 bestseller, *Plowman's Folly*. But the book, and its author along with it, are all but forgotten by a new generation of government and academic agricultural experts, many of them of the hidebound sort that Faulkner would probably be doing battle with were he alive today.

In 1943, the United States was in the middle of a war that no one was yet entirely sure it would win, or at least win hands down. The Dust Bowl droughts were gone, but not forgotten; tremendous pressure was placed on agriculture to produce more and more for the boys at arms and for starving allies. Food rationing was in force, and forty million victory gardens had been established on the home front by patriotic American families. Interest in the science and art of agriculture was at its highest point ever, even among those who hadn't given it a second thought before.

This was the context in which Edward Faulkner, with a kind of cool daring, made these assertions in the opening paragraphs of *Plowman's Folly*:

> Briefly, this book sets out to show that the moldboard plow, which is in use on farms throughout the civilized world, is the least satisfactory implement for the preparation of land for the production of crops. . . . The truth is that no one has ever advanced a scientific reason for plowing. . . . The entire body of "reasoning" about the management of the soil has been based upon the axiomatic assumption of the correctness of plowing. But plowing is not correct. Hence, the main premise being untenable, we may rightly question the validity of every popularly accepted theory concerned with the production of any crop, when the land has been plowed in preparation for its growth.

This remarkable book is, in every important respect, the theoretical cornerstone of what is now called "conservation tillage," currently practiced on nearly a third of our cropland. In conservation tillage, which began on a commercial scale in the early 1960's, the moldboard plow is never used; organic residues, as Faulkner insisted, are left on or just below the surface of the soil in order to reduce erosion, conserve soil moisture, and retain essential nutrients. Clearly, this is one of the most significant changes in the ten-thousand year history of agricultural technology. And yet, the book in which it was first proposed very nearly did not get published.

Here is how it happened—or almost didn't happen. One day, at Malabar Farm, the thousand-acre Ohio establishment owned by Louis Bromfield, millionaire novelist, experimental farmer, and soil conservationist, a "smallish, graying man with very bright blue eyes" presented himself to the well-known author, who had been visited already by a procession of cranks proffering endless horticultural panaceas and was wary of such encounters. "He said his name was Faulkner," Bromfield continues, "and that he wanted to talk about a new theory of cultivation that did away altogether with the conventional, long-accepted moldboard plow." Bromfield listened to Faulkner's explanation for a while, mumbled something perfunctory, and bade his visitor goodbye, hoping he might never see him again. Undaunted, Faulkner returned several times, insisting that Bromfield pay attention. Finally, he did. "I had never thought about the evil the moldboard plow might do," Bromfield confessed, "until I listened to Ed Faulkner."

In due course, Faulkner presented Bromfield with a long manuscript for a book and asked for help. The proprietor of Malabar Farm had his own literary projects to attend to, but he sent Faulkner to, among others, Paul B. Sears, author of the 1930's classic, *Deserts on the March.* Sears looked at the manuscript, and after offering it to five publishers who turned it down, finally persuaded Savoie Lottinville of the University of Oklahoma Press to take it on.

What happened next is a fascinating footnote in publishing history. Oklahoma published a much-shortened version, owing to the wartime paper shortage, as well as to literary considerations for a book that was, after all, quite technical and unlikely to get much attention from either the general public or agricultural authorities. As it turned out, Oklahoma went through eight printings in scarcely more than a year. Then, out of paper, they turned to Grosset & Dunlap, a major New York trade publisher, who printed 250,000 copies in 1944, an astonishing number for a book that ordinarily might be expected to sell no more than 5,000 copies. But the book was a hit from the very beginning. Articles about it were published in magazines from *The New Yorker* to the *Saturday Evening Post*. Bromfield himself wrote some of them and was accosted (if that is the right word) by two Hollywood actresses in a Chicago hotel, who asked, "What is all this business about *Plowman's Folly*?"

To report that his ideas were greeted by skepticism in the agricultural scientific community of the time is a massive understatement. Had his book not been a bestseller, it would have been ignored. But it was a bestseller, and so Faulkner was branded a "nut," a "crank," and a "fanatic" whose basic theory of natural soil dynamics was dismissed for subsidiary reasons. Indeed, some of these subsidiary elements had less universality than Faulkner originally claimed for them, and in 1947 he wrote another book, called *A Second Look* in which he modified some of his suggestions.

Also in *A Second Look* Faulkner tells of attending a major scientific meeting on soils. After listening to all the speakers, he bitterly concluded: "It seems certain that none of these men believes the soil can be self-sufficient. Each speaker assumed just the opposite in fact. To this extent, therefore, the thesis of *Plowman's Folly* has no standing with this group." The scientific community had unfortunately confused Faulkner's basic ecological theory—among the most percipient ever advanced in agricultural science—with his assertions of potential subsidiary attributes.

The big issue was, and still is, weeds. Faulkner's "plowless farming" was thought impractical in humid areas simply because there was no obvious way to control weeds except by plowing them down in the fall and again in the spring with a moldboard, and then cultivating betweentimes. While some of his techniques could ameliorate the weed problems, they could never really eliminate them, and soon Faulkner was forgotten. His star waned almost as quickly as it had risen. Instead, it became the agricultural chemist's finest hour.

Purdue University soil scientist William C. Moldenhauer recounts this period in the history of conservation tillage. "When herbicides came in and you could control the weeds without having to till hell out of the ground, we began to have more confidence in our ability to leave some residue on the fields."

Herbicides were, and still are, essential in moving the concept of conservation tillage from a set of theories into actual practice in American agriculture. But in the long run, seeing conservation tillage simply as the substitution of herbicides for tillage is a too-simple view of a complex of technical factors that come into play. For one thing, a whole new approach to tillage machinery design has been developed, which lagged behind the development of herbicides. Moreover, new rotations, new ways of planting, new fertilizers and fertilizer-application techniques, even new crops must be part of a conservation tillage "system." When all these factors are in place, then the theoretical debt that conservation tillage owes Faulkner becomes plainer, and some scientists are beginning to recognize this. On the matter of soil capillaries, for example—the "wicking action", as Faulkner described it—soils expert William Moldenhauer perhaps speaks for more scientists than himself when he says, "We're back to that now. We didn't pay attention, and we should have."

And so the mad theories which found their origin in the work of Edward H. Faulkner have finally been accepted by respected scientists like Moldenhauer, and have been put into practice at field scale by conservation tillage farmers all over the country, whether or not they have heard of the "smallish, graying man with very bright blue eyes" who started it all. Perhaps the best way to honor Edward Faulkner is not with a statue, but, in his own words, with "the self-sufficiency of the soil." What a remarkable, and permanent, monument *that* would be.

Charles E. Little is the author of *Green Fields Forever*, (Island Press, 1987) from which this introduction is adapted.

to my late father, JOHN WESLEY FAULKNER, JR.
who did for the land as regular routine
much of what farmers now are paid to
do as compensation for past errors

Acknowledgments

I have had much help in this work; much of it was unintentional. There is not space to thank all of those who have helped in some way or another. A few who have helped voluntarily and to whom I am especially indebted are:

Professor Paul B. Sears, Head of the Department of Botany, Oberlin College; Russell Lord, Editor of *The Land;* Garet Garett, Special writer for the *Saturday Evening Post;* Peter Vischer, Editor and Publisher of *Country Life;* Ollie E. Fink, Curriculum Supervisor, State Department of Education, Columbus, Ohio; Charlotte Brooks, Assistant Librarian, Elyria Library; Merritt Powell, Manager, Lorain County Farm Bureau Co-operative, Elyria, Ohio.

E. H. F.

1

THE MARGIN OF ERROR

BRIEFLY, this book sets out to show that the moldboard plow which is in use on farms throughout the civilized world, is the least satisfactory implement for the preparation of land for the production of crops. This sounds like a paradox, perhaps, in view of the fact that for nearly a century there has been a science of agriculture, and that agricultural scientists almost to a man have used and approved the use of the moldboard plow. Nevertheless, the statement made above is true and capable of proof. Much of the proof, as a matter of fact, has come in left-handed manner from scientists themselves. The truth is that no one has ever advanced a scientific reason for plowing. Many learned teachers have had embarrassing moments before classes of students demanding to be shown why it would not be better to introduce all organic matter into the surface of the soil than to bury it, as is done by the plow.

The entire body of "reasoning" about the management of the soil has been based upon the axiomatic assumption of the correctness of plowing. But plowing is not correct. Hence, the main premise being untenable, we may rightly question the validity of every popularly accepted theory concerned with the production of any crop, when the land has been plowed in preparation for its growth. That brings virtually all of our soil theories up for critical examination; so, in this book, the whole gamut of theory we have evolved concerning the growing of crops will be brought into focus for examination in the light of the discovery that plowing is wrong.

The discussion will be undertaken in language common to the layman, so far as this is possible, and throughout the text footnotes will be introduced to explain whatever may be perhaps out of range of the thinking of the average reader. The nature of the reasoning upon which this entire study is based makes it unnecessary to resort to any but the simplest of scientific terms. Moreover, there are few ideas which are not common knowledge—strange as that may seem. The vast amount of technical language created by scientific agriculture, as a result of an early and fundamental mistake, has produced its own confusions. Indeed, the mistake originally made might justly be called the basis for most, if not all, of the technology connected with present-day agronomy.

An agricultural experiment station has its uses, but these obviously would not have embraced the problem presented in this book, if those who work the soil had not got off to a false start in the matter of plowing. In brief, if a way had been found to mix into the surface of the soil everything that the farmer now plows under; if the implements used in planting and cultivating the crop had been designed to operate in the trashy surface that would have resulted from mixing rough straw, leaves, stalks, stubble, weeds, and briars into the surface—crop production would have been so automatic, so spontaneous that there might not have developed what we now know as agricultural science. Actually, we would scarcely have needed one. From one point of view, we have been creating our own soil problems merely for the doubtful pleasure of solving them. Had we not originally gone contrary to the laws of nature by plowing the land, we would have avoided the problems as well as the expensive and time-consuming efforts to solve them.

That we would also have missed all of the erosion, the sour soils, the mounting floods, the lowering water table, the vanishing wild life, the compact and impervious soil surfaces is scarcely an incidental consideration. We have really had a fling at scientific agriculture. The fling, in fact, appears to be the scientific counterpart of what our grandfathers used to call "sowing wild oats." It is time we sobered up and began to apply to the growing of farm crops the same basic science we have for so long been using in the factories, mills, and workshops of our reasonably progressive civilization.

We have equipped our farmers with a greater tonnage of machinery per man than any other nation. Our agricultural population has proceeded to use that machinery to the end of destroying the soil in less time than any other people has been known to do in recorded history. This is hardly a record to be proud of. It gains nothing in attractiveness, moreover, when we consider that our Chinese friends and the often despised peasantry of the so-called backward countries of the world can produce more per acre without machinery than the American farmer can with all his fine equipment. Any reasonably well traveled person will confirm this statement.

One of the persistent puzzles has been the fact that an ignorant, poverty-stricken Egyptian who stirs his land with the ancient crooked stick can produce more per acre than his British neighbor whose equipment is right up to the minute. The explanation is that the poor farmer can't afford the equipment that would make it impossible for him to continue growing such high yields per acre. The full import of all this will be explained in due course.

There is double meaning in the statement that all of the trouble in producing crops seems to lie in the farmer's fields. The uncultivated fields and woodlands surrounding his land do not show any signs of trouble. Even the crops growing in the fence rows seem to thrive through droughts as well as in fine weather. Would that observation justify us in wondering whether the manner in which farmers handle their land might be responsible for the way crops grow under tillage? Certainly we should not overlook the possibility that a clue to the farmer's trouble might be found by a comparative study of cultivated and virgin soils.

Our conventional ideas of growing processes are due for drastic revision. Much thought and experimental work have been devoted to studies of plant growth, but there has been comparatively little consideration of the part played in plant and animal growth by the actual transfer, more or less directly, of previously used plant food from a lifeless body to one that is living.

We often think and speak of growth as if it were a building process—which indeed it is—but we are likely to assume without sufficient thought that the best growth would result from the use of materials not previously used in organic tissues. We think of our farm crops as getting a mineral solution from the land; and we think of that solution as originating from soil minerals directly, or from the fertilizers the farmer applies. We do not give much consideration to the biochemistry of the matter. We know that anything covered up in the soil is subject to rather prompt decay, if it is at all decayable, but we do not reason from that point to acceptance of the decay products as choice building material for crops growing in the immediate vicinity.

In our material civilization we have rightly learned to be suspicious of anything constructed of cast-off materials. Few people would buy an automobile that was assembled from used parts. And a suit of clothes made of shoddy material would not bring a very high price. Our basic distrust carries over into our thinking about the materials essential to the development of a plant. This would not be true if we did some critical thinking on the subject; but we have not done so. We have left the whole subject to our scientific men. They have learned the facts, and in many instances have published their findings in books or pamphlets which anyone who cares to do so may read; but few have cared to wade through the technical language in which such studies usually have been expressed. Such writings seldom make the headlines or the front pages, so we don't bother to read them. This may be distinctly bad for us.

Much of our knowledge of nutritive relationship is what might be called academic: pigeonholed after discovery and never developed into practical usefulness. Particularly is this true of our knowledge concerning plant nutrition. We know, of course, that no animal can subsist solely on mineral solutions in simple, inorganic form. We do not take our lime as lime water, or our iron as tincture—at least not to any great extent as a matter of nutrition. Our present knowledge indicates that the human race and the whole animal kingdom would disappear completely from the earth if deprived of that organic storehouse known as the plant kingdom. That being true, it is highly important that we have a thoroughly practical understanding of the nutritive relationships between plants and the earth; for those relationships are necessarily fundamental to animal well-being, including, of course, the human race.

For purposes of this discussion, it will simplify our reasoning if we think of inorganic solutions, such as those that occur in the soil where water is in contact with mineral crystals, as *new,* or primary plant foods; and the inorganic solutions that originate in the decay of plant or animal tissues as *used,* or secondhand plant foods. These are distinctly not the technician's terms for such concepts, but it will be shown herein that they are useful for the layman in understanding how plants may be made to grow best. It should be said, too, that in practice we would almost never find in the soil any organic solution entirely devoid of inorganic compounds. This is because the water which assists in the decay of organic tissues already carries a load of inorganic compounds when it is absorbed into the organic material.

The chief trouble with our farming is that we have concerned ourselves increasingly with the difficult techniques of supplying our farm crops with *new* materials for growth, when we could easily take full advantage of the almost automatic provisions of nature for supplying plants with complete rations in *secondhand* form. We have made a difficult job of what should be an easy one.

Several circumstances have conspired to distort our point of view on the nutrition of plants. Thirty years ago, farmers had not become so familiar as they are now with the possibilities offered by inorganic minerals as fertilizers. But, as they have learned about them, and as the costs of such fertilizers have been reduced from time to time, it has been progressively easier to use mineral fertilizers. Meanwhile the means of restoring organic matter to the soil has seemed at the same time to become progressively more difficult. The net result is that technical attention to the inorganic mineral supply has been more and more necessary; and the organic possibilities have simply vanished from consideration.

The last few paragraphs outline the basic nutritive concepts involved in this book. No new technical discoveries are to be aired here. The discussion is concerned wholly with reducing to practical terms, employable in anybody's back yard or on any farm, the scientific information possessed for decades but hitherto not put to any extensive use.

Green manures have been known and recommended for decades. For those to whom the idea is new, green manures are simply crops of any kind grown for use as decayable material in the soil where grown. Farmers have been advised for years to make frequent and regular use of green manures to supplement the always inadequate supply of animal manure. In keeping with this idea, county agents as early as thirty years ago urged farmers to make the plowing down of green manures the basis of their soil improvement program for very thin land. Then, when the results of those early attempts were reported, trouble loomed. Plowing down great masses of green manure proved such a colossal boomerang that subsequent attempts to improve growing conditions for plants have been cautious expedients rather than bold attempts to imitate the perfect example set by the natural landscape. It seems never to have occurred to anybody to question the effects of the universally approved moldboard plow.

The prevalent and generally accepted doctrine concerning green manures has accordingly been modified to two comparatively ineffective recommendations: (1) plow down the green manure crop early, before it has become woody and difficult to rot, and (2) if the crop gets out of hand and becomes woody before it can be plowed in, apply nitrogenous fertilizers to the crop itself before plowing it down.

Even these recommendations have always been recognized as makeshift procedures. It is only too obvious that tender rye or other green crops must contain less minerals than the same plants would if allowed to reach their full growth. And, while the second recommendation is of more recent origin and is supposed to be more advantageous, it has a fundamental weakness for which there is no completely effective remedy in nature. The purpose of adding the nitrogen fertilizer is to hasten the decomposition of the mass, thus removing the organic matter as a bar to further rise in the soil of water from deep in the earth. (It should be mentioned here that the plowing in of great quantities of absorbent material results in exhausting the water from the overlying soil layers.) The decay is hastened by this trick; but the decay products released are necessarily subject to being leached out of the soil by the first rains that fall after their release. A relatively small percentage of such nutrients can be retained by colloids—in soils which have enough colloids that are not already holding all the plant nutrients possible. The rest must inevitably be lost, unless by lucky chance insufficient rain falls to carry them away before roots arrive to salvage them. It must be remembered, too, that in most soils few roots ever reach the plowsole to do salvage work. The net effect, then, of this treatment is likely to be almost nil.

Later it will be shown that such use of nitrogen—any purchased nitrogen, in fact—is sheer waste of money, since nature is perfectly organized to supply the right amount of nitrogen to every plant. Later, too, the universal use in nature of the principle of direct transfer of organic compounds from the decaying dead to the growing living will be exemplified by illustrations from small-scale test work, supplemented by later field work, done during the past decade in a city back yard and on leased land in the country.

Most scientists probably are mentally unprepared to accept, without official tests, an idea apparently so new. An exception is Paul B. Sears, who in *Deserts on the March* has pictured plant nutrition as follows:

> The face of the earth is a graveyard, and so it has always been. To earth each living thing restores when it dies that which has been borrowed to give form and substance to its brief day in the sun. From earth, in due course, each new living being receives back again a loan of that which sustains life. What is lent by earth has been used by countless generations of plants and animals now dead and will be required by countless others in the future. . . . No plant or animal, nor any sort of either, can establish permanent right of possession to the materials which compose its physical body.[1]

Thus, pointedly, Sears brings to our attention a principle of plant growth which has not hitherto been sufficiently utilized, though most scientists have been aware of its academic existence at least. He says by implication that life necessarily depends upon the snuffing out of other lives—of enormous populations, in fact. We dislike thinking of ourselves as murderous, but the fact that we must be, if we are to live, is difficult to refute. As civilized beings, so-called, we keep the slaughterhouse out of sight of the dining room; but, unless we are vegetarians, our very existence depends upon keeping

[1] *Deserts on the March,* by Paul B. Sears (Norman, University of Oklahoma Press, 1935), 1.

that slaughterhouse busy. Even the strictest vegetarian must snuff out many lives—those of plants—if he is to retain his own.

Such suggestions may sound like bits of philosophical quibbling; however, the ideas involved are so pertinent to the subject in hand that they need to be brought sharply into focus in our thinking. We have always accepted theoretically the interdependence of every form of life upon other forms; we have not so easily progressed to the thought that dead tissues contribute their substance to new living forms. This is the solemn, necessary truth; and the earlier it becomes a part of our thinking, the more quickly can we plan intelligently the necessary work of recreating the soils on our farm lands. We have been too squeamish to visualize dead tissue being transformed into living, though with every mouthful we eat we demonstrate precisely that fact. Let us be practical, even if being so proves painful to our stomachs.

Plants establish intakes, in the form of roots, for nutritive materials in the decaying fragments of last year's plants; and, left to themselves, they will use without loss every atom of the material that previously had been used in the dead plants. As farmers, we have not left the bodies of last year's plants where the roots of this season's crops could invade them. Instead, we have buried those decaying remains so deep that few roots could reach them. We have, by plowing, made it impossible for our farm crops to do their best. Obviously, it seems that the time has arrived for us to look into our methods of soil management, with a view to copying the surface situation we find in forest and field where the plow has not disturbed the soil. No crime is involved in plagiarizing nature's ways. Discovering the underlying principles involved and carrying them over for use on cultivated land violates no patents or copyrights. In fact, all that it is necessary to do—if we want a better agriculture—is to recharge the soil surface with materials that will rot. Natural processes will do the rest. The plant kingdom is organized to clothe the earth with greenery, and, wherever man does not disturb it, the entire surface usually is well covered. The task of this book is to show that our soil problems have been to a considerable extent psychological; that, except for our sabotage of nature's design for growth, there is no soil problem.

Science now knows that several times more plant food is carried away from farm land in the streams that drain the various watersheds than is absorbed by growing crops or grazed off by animals. Most of this loss is in invisible form, that is, dissolved—an especially important consideration because it is in the only form in which plants are able to take their food. The undissolved (visible), eroded portion of the loss makes the news, simply because it is visible; but it is relatively unimportant as a loss, since beneath where it lay there is an inexhaustible stock of the same material. The chief damage done by erosion is the filling in of stream channels, reservoirs, and natural lakes, along with the burial of downstream lands under a quite inert layer of miscellaneous mud. Fortunately, the necessary technique for preventing erosion is precisely what is required to make the land most productive. By restoring the conditions which prevailed upon the land when it was new, we will cure erosion and restore productiveness in a single stroke.

For years scientific men have been aware that losses by leaching were in progress, but until the report of the National

Resources Board was made in 1934, few had any conception of the staggering scale on which our mineral resources were going out to sea. To arouse general interest in this matter, the U. S. Department of Agriculture included on page 99 of its 1938 *Yearbook* a condensed table of the various kinds of losses. To clarify further the seriousness of our land waste, the department hired Russell Lord, an able agricultural writer, to advertise the government's efforts to stop erosion by co-operative watershed demonstrations in various sections of the country. In his report Mr. Lord gives this concrete resumé of the figures in the report of the National Resources Board:

> Leached plant food is that part that percolates down through the soil and is lost by way of underground waters. . . . Of mineral losses (nitrogen, phosphorus, potash, calcium, magnesium, and sulphur) crops and grazing take off a total of 19,500,000 tons a year, while erosion and leaching whisk away nearly 117,000,000 tons.[2]

Incidentally, Mr. Lord became so impressed by the urgency of the situation reflected above that he wrote *Behold Our Land,* in which he presented further interesting material, and published it the same year.

Most of the dissolved plant food that escapes down the streams originates from the decaying material plowed in. This seems an inescapable conclusion from the known facts. This being true, by salvaging this waste, even though no other measures were taken for soil improvement, we should be able to realize greatly increased production from the land. So long as plant food continues to get away, both land and

[2] No. 321, U. S. Department of Agriculture, *To Hold This Soil,* by Russell Lord (Washington, Government Printing Office), 21.

people become poorer and poorer; and people become more and more subject to ailments which we now know are caused by insufficiency of some essentials in their diets. The drain tile and the moldboard plow, therefore, become suspect of complicity in robbing our people of their birthright of vigorous health—by stealing away vital elements from the plowsole before plant roots are able to salvage them. So logical does this inference seem that it is difficult to understand why it has never been investigated officially.

It seems a bit humorous, too, to suggest a need for investigating whether men could grow healthy crops if they copied the soil conditions which prevail in nature where crops are universally healthy. It is a good deal like suggesting to the mother of a new-born baby to investigate the possibility of feeding her child naturally rather than by bottle as conventionally is done. In neither case is experiment necessary. We already know—by incontrovertible example—that wherever man does not interfere crops grow spontaneously. It follows of necessity that if man duplicates in his farming the soil conditions which in nature produce such perfect results, he will be able to grow similarly perfect crops on cultivated land.

So, I introduce to you something so old in agriculture that it may justly be considered as new. The whole thesis is perhaps so clearly obvious that we have universally failed to see it. Seven years were required for me to break away from conventional ways of thinking about soil. Like all others trained in agriculture, I had vainly tried to piece the puzzle together, in order to make of agriculture a consistent science. Then I discovered, through certain tests, that the trouble lay in the operation which preceded all of the tests, namely plowing. It was as if one tried to assemble a picture puzzle with the pieces upside down. By simply correcting the basic error—by incorporating all of the organic matter into the surface of the soil—the difficulties all disappeared as if by magic. The tests by which these conclusions were reached are briefly described in the pages that follow.

2

WHAT IS SOIL?

THE WORLD'S first agricultural station was established in England nearly a century ago. At that time its only aims were to learn why England's soils would no longer grow as good crops as formerly, and to discover remedies. Since this beginning, similar institutions have been set up in most of the other countries of the world. There are more than fifty experiment stations in the United States. Some states support more than one, each independent, though all are under the same government. All but a few of these clinics have as a major objective the study of soil problems, and some of them have carried out soil experimental work which shows the effect of given treatments for as long as fifty to seventy-five years.

Such an array of long continued organized effort to determine the facts about the soil makes it seem improbable that we should need to inquire at this late date as to what soil is. Yet, like electricity and a number of other very important and familiar things, the soil has never been adequately defined. Nor is it expected that it will be defined now. It is hoped to arrive in this chapter at a more practical understanding of the soil than we have hitherto had. It certainly is true that, if we could not manage electricity any better than we manage our soil, we could never enjoy the long periods of uninterrupted service that we now do. As it is, we do so completely know how to manage electrical energy that it almost never disappoints us. Soil, by contrast, seldom ever comes up to our expectations, even though experts have been trying for generations to solve its problems.

It should be remembered, too, that knowledge of electricity is a comparatively modern thing. Edison first made his lamp glow a little more than fifty years ago. Consider what has happened since. Electricity has become the ideal servant of man; it is the only one that obeys an order instantly the order is given. The merest touch of a button or flip of a switch, and your servant is there on the dot. This satisfactory harnessing of electrical energy has been accomplished since the beginning of Edison's experiments.

Compare this amazing progress with the almost complete lack of basic progress in agriculture. Considering that hunger first urged men to activity, we know that man began to cultivate his own food plants as soon as he wearied of the arduous travel and search for them where they grew wild. This happened necessarily quite early in the history of the race. How early, nobody knows, for history could not be written by hungry men; and until a dependable agriculture had been established, hunger at times was inescapable. Soils had been cultivated, worn out, and blown away long before historic times, if we may judge by the tier on tier of buried cities in what now is desert. The establishment of a city anywhere presupposes an abundant food supply near by; so, when archeologists stumble upon the buried ruins of cities built one on top of the other, we know that the local soils at one time supported a considerable population.

You naturally would expect an art as old as agriculture, and as fundamental, to be developed to a fine state of perfection. At least, it would be expected to be far ahead of so recent an art as the use of electricity. Yet the history of agriculture has been a continuous series of disappointments. No race of people ever remained to solve the problems of the area it had worn out. Instead, as fast as the race had harvested the cream of fertility from one area, it sold, or just left, the land to its successors and moved on to richer fields. The following quotation, written at the time of the California Gold Rush, is interesting in this connection:

> Some pains have been taken in this report to prove that one thousand millions of dollars, judiciously expended, will hardly restore the one hundred million acres of partially exhausted lands in the Union to that richness of mould, and strength of fertility for permanent cropping, which they possessed in their primitive state.[1]

This testifies eloquently to the fact that soil deterioration had made great progress in America nearly one hundred years ago. Many of our best informed experts on soils would agree that, for all our effort of the past generation, we have barely held our own. The average yield of most field crops for any decade that may be selected will not be much larger than the average for the decade of 1870–80. We ought to have done better, surely.

Everybody agrees, of course, that we should have done better; and everybody would be glad to be told how—if anybody knows. The antiquity of our agricultural lore should have been an advantage, but it appears not to have been, because nobody ever actually conquered the problems of the soil he happened to occupy. People instead ran away from those problems and proceeded to create the same problems in a new place. Americans, as a people, did not, there-

[1] Report of the Commissioner of Patents, 1849 [quoted in *The Land*, Vol. I, No. 3 (Summer, 1941), 277].

fore, really set out seriously to study the situation until the supply of squatter territory was exhausted. In consequence we have no valuable inherited lore of the soil.

In addition to the advantage of time, the farmer has had another advantage of obvious value which he has never used. He has had before his eyes in every wooded country a perfect example of soil maintenance. And it is said that seeing is believing. Yet, the farmer has seen but he has not believed. He has seen the soft green foliage of the nearby woodland unaffected by the droughts which damaged his crops. He has seen the horseweeds actually topping the fence that surrounded his corn field while his corn was suffering for lack of water. The same weather prevails in the woodland and in the fence rows as prevails in the farmer's fields; yet neither the wild crops of the woodland nor the weeds along the fence show any sign of thirst.

This example of the unplowed field, this evidence that trouble stops where the plow stops, has been almost universally overlooked. Note this masterful description, by an early American, of the untouched forest:

> The soil we passed over this day was very good. Charming valleys bring forth like the land of Egypt. Grass grows as high as a man on horseback and the rivers roll down their waters to the sea as clear as crystal. Happy will be the people destined for so wholesome a situation, where they may live to the fullness of their days with much content and gaiety of heart.[2]

Unless cleared, or cut over, the forest continued its lush, rank growth. It was busy making lumber. It was converting

[2] Colonel William Byrd (a Virginia planter) writing in 1728 concerning surveying in the Dan River Valley, Virginia [quoted in *The Land*, Vol. I, No. 1 (Winter, 1941), 60].

into the finest imaginable walnut, gum, oak, cherry, maple, and pine the rotting leaves and other debris that lay on the ground just above the tree roots. In terms of today's living, the lovely woodwork of your floors, stairs, door frames, and in other parts of your house is made largely from reconditioned material—from rotted leaves, rotted wood, and all manner of decayed material. This fact will bear remembering as you read further. It is important.

Almost everyone has had the pleasure of walking through a forest. Did you note uprooted trees? And did you wonder why the roots seemed to bring up chiefly a layer of surface soil? The reason the uprooted tree disturbs only the surface soil is that the feeding roots are necessarily deployed in this zone. The deep roots of the tree provide anchorage against the wind, but it is the tiny, tender feeding roots in the surface layers of soil that do the real business of finding food for the tree. They need not go deep, for the water deep in the soil is brought up to them by capillarity in any case—just as the lampwick brings fuel to the flame. And the food supplied by these roots is chiefly the reconditioned material released when fallen leaves rot on the forest floor. Some new material, dissolved from the rock deeper in the soil, is included, of course; but much the greater part of the minerals used by plants of any kind growing in such an environment must be "secondhand" minerals. It is difficult to believe, when you study the beautiful grains of woods, that they are assembled from "scrap" materials. But in reality that is the way things are done in nature.

This, then, is the shining example of successful soil maintenance which has always been observable by the farmer, if he would do so. Perhaps because it was so near and so obvious, he has been unable to think of it as a lesson from which he should profit. There is more than a little of psychology in the failure of man to profit from the forest's demonstration—or the equally significant showing made by the grasslands which supported myriads of animals and yet gained fertility momentum year by year. To appreciate fully this psychological background will require time, for it involves the underlying reasons that caused plowing to achieve its popularity. Aside from that, there are curious human factors almost inherent in the makeup of man himself.

Not the least of these inherent human traits that have served to perpetuate error in the farming business is the incorrigible feeling on the part of people that they can be of assistance to plants in their growth. The statement appears at variance with our basic thinking, but, actually, there is nothing that anybody can do to assist a plant that is growing in its natural environment. And when we grow plants in an artificial environment, the best we can possibly do is copy as closely as possible the essentials of the natural environment. You know how you swell with pride when you succeed handsomely with your flower or vegetable garden. You imagine you have really helped the plants to grow—and, in a sense, you have. Yet, probably you set them in an unsuitable environment, then proceeded to further sabotage (unconsciously) the natural provisions for the welfare of plants. You are perhaps not peculiar in this respect. Everyone else does essentially the same thing and feels just as proud as you do, in spite of the error of his ways.

The reader will find it difficult, perhaps, to believe some of the facts I am going to recount, for they reveal how truly we humans stand in our own light in attempting to grow plants. What I have to tell, however, is true in all respects and will illustrate adequately my present point.

Some years ago our family spent a holiday foraging the woods for ferns to set in a shaded corner of the house wall. We found ferns, and we found a seedling hemlock actually sitting atop a very flat stone, its roots covered with leaves. There was no connection with the earth. Admiring this tiny tree, I picked it up, literally, since it had no roots in the earth to resist, and brought it home to transplant. Because its root system was a perfectly flat arrangement, I took a spade and patted down a flat area of soil, set the young tree on this spot, covered its roots again with quite a lot of leaves brought in for the purpose, and considered it transplanted. It stands in the same spot today, having grown quite from the start. To my knowledge it has never been supplied artificially with any water, except during one very dry period the first summer. The tree began to show signs of trouble then, so I poured one pail of water about its roots. Since it has become well established, nothing whatever has been done to assist it.

In mid-May or early June, 1941, my wife took a fancy to a maple tree three feet tall which she saw growing in a friend's yard fifty miles from our home. It was in full leaf, of course, so transplanting would present, supposedly, a difficult problem. The friend dug it for us, and we packed it in the trunk of the car. Next morning when we first saw it, its leaves were badly wilted, though still as green as ever. I first set the roots into the pool until a hole could be prepared. This hole was dug in the driest kind of place. There was no sign of moisture even at the bottom of the eighteen-inch space dug out. Because of this extreme dryness, the hole was filled with water. Into this water the tree was then placed, and the dirt removed from the hole was slowly settled about the roots. The work was done slowly in order to avoid causing the water to overflow the sides of the hole. When the hole had been filled in again, the tree was set. Throughout the summer its leaves showed no sign of ill effects from the transplanting experience. I should add that its treatment was not as fair a test as that of the hemlock, for my wife could not resist the temptation to water the maple occasionally. However, it is true that it went through many dry, hot days without being watered.

It has long since become axiomatic among scientists that the data supporting a given statement must not only be accurate but must be extensive enough to eliminate, within reasonable limits, the possibility of error in generalization. My next experiment involved operations on a much larger scale—the planting and care of an acre of tomato plants in each of the years 1939 and 1940. More than ten thousand plants were used during the two seasons, and the stand of plants was virtually 100 per cent for each season and each acre field. Soil moisture conditions were quite different for each of the two seasons, but the success of the plants was very similar. The experiment established to my satisfaction, at least, the importance of two principles: first, that the naturally settled, tight condition of the soil (before we start to get it ready for transplanting operations) is desirable; and second, that such soil should not be disturbed if transplanting can be accomplished without disturbing it.

At the outset, the soil was disked thoroughly in order to destroy whatever vegetation was at that time growing on it. In the spring of 1939, there was little but a scattering stand of weeds. In 1940, rye fully three feet tall—a fair stand all over the surface—had to be disposed of. The disk harrow so completely mixed in even the rye crop that little sign was left of any vegetation cover. Following the mixing in of this decayable material, the land was marked off in rows. To do this marking, a specially designed implement was used which simply "tramped" over the field—behind the tractor, of course—firming the soil together again at points where plants were to be located. By exerting considerable pressure at each such point, this implement reconnected the capillary contacts which the disking had broken up. (To visualize the effect of pressing the soil together again, just recall what would be the effect of snipping the lamp wick above the oil level; then later sewing the pieces together again.) The natural wicking action of the soil—destroyed temporarily by the disking—was restored *in the vertical column of soil just under the point where a plant was to be set.* That this actually was the effect of this pressure we have plenty of evidence. Even though the soil surface was dry and the weather hot in 1939, the bottom of a great many of these "tracks" showed moist even in the middle of the day. Unless the capillary connection had been restored, this could not possibly have been true.

Transplanting was done in the simplest possible manner. The roots of each tomato plant, after being freed of all clinging soil, were laid in the prepared track, covered with as mellow earth as could be found near by, and firmed in place by tramping. No attempt was made to place the plants upright. That is something that nature will attend to. Thus, the plants were left lying flat on the ground; but they did not lie there long. By late afternoon every plant set in the forenoon was pointing its tip toward the sky; by the following morning every plant without exception was standing upright. No water was used in transplanting, or afterward. Capillary water already in the soil was brought in from below—through the compressed column of soil beneath the site where the plant stood—and provided a dependable, continuous supply of moisture. No watering that could have been done at transplanting time could possibly have equalled this inherent natural supply. So, instead of going through a wilting period after transplanting, these plants (even though in some cases they were wilted when set) straightened up and never again, regardless of dry weather, showed signs of trouble from lack of water. And, which is additional proof of the validity of the method, blossoms which were on the plants when set often produced fruit. Any experienced gardener will recognize this as unusual.

In 1940 the entire acre was set in one day by an eleven-year-old boy and me, assisted by my daughter, who removed the plants from the flats for us. Moisture conditions were so different in 1940 that even less care was required, so we cut the work as short as possible. The boy literally dropped and I covered. He placed the plant roots in the proper space; I laid on a hoeful of as mellow earth as I could find in soil so soggy that we barely could walk over it without sinking in. For about five weeks after transplanting, this soil was too wet to be stirred. Several times, indeed, it was flooded. The plants in such wet conditions became purple, or purplish green. Yet, despite this extremely wet condition so long continued, this acre was later spoken of by neighbors as the finest field of tomatoes in the neighborhood. And the plants produced without interruption from the appearance of the first fruit until frost. Some of the very finest fruit was on them when frost came.

This description of the transplanting method used should show conclusively that it pays not to disturb the natural provisions for supplying plants with their needs; and that, if those arrangements must be disturbed, they should be restored to normal before transplanting is done. It was necessary to dispose of the rye that was growing on this land in 1940. Had custom been followed, it would have been plowed in; and in all probability tomatoes could not have been started successfully in it for a long time, if at all. As soon as it was disked in, the plant-setting could have followed immediately behind the marker. However, owing to the danger of late frosts, the actual placing of the plants was delayed until a week later.

In view of the extensive writings available on the proper procedure to be followed in transplanting, the method used with these plants will seem the rankest of carelessness. One of my neighbors thought so in 1939. He is a retired farmer and had learned something of the new theories upon which I was working. In general, he approved the ideas; but, when he saw the strange equipment (the marker) being used and observed the plants being set in so unorthodox a manner, he offered a friendly warning that they would never grow. It was with a broad grin that he came to the field later on, when we were picking the fruit, to say that we had the best stand of plants he had seen all summer.

What he had mistaken for carelessness was instead my full confidence that the soil unassisted would take care of the plants if we did nothing to prevent it. He had always assumed toward transplants (as did everybody else) an attitude similar to that of the broody hen toward her unnatural brood of ducklings. The hen is frightened when the day-old balls of down slide easily into a pool of water. People are similarly astonished to find that plants can get along without the customary care given them by the human race, provided only that they are placed in their proper element. We were trying to put these plants into an exceptionally correct environment. The decaying rye was to be reconstructed into fine red tomatoes; and the necessary water for accomplishing this transformation was to be conducted from below to the roots of the plants, without the customary interruption at the plowsole some six to eight inches under the surface of the soil. (This interruption, something which does not exist in nature, consists of the blotter-like layer of organic matter which the moldboard plow sandwiches in between the subsoil and the disturbed upper layers.) We were copying as closely as possible the natural environment in which plants always seem to thrive; but our behavior was so odd to anyone schooled in the customary ways of managing crops that it became disturbing to observers.

Much more might be said in support of this new conception of soil and the proper handling of it, but the reader will perhaps realize by now that Browning was right.

"God's in his heaven—
All's right with the world."

There is nothing wrong with our soil, except our interference, deliberate though unknowing, with the natural provisions for growing plants. Nothing is more obvious than the vigorous way in which nature takes over when land has been abandoned by farmers. All through the South, farmers have for generations "rested" their land for a number of years between periods of cropping. This practice used to be criticized severely as an evidence of laziness, but agriculturists have discovered that it really has merit, and that soil so treated is considerably rejuvenated and will again produce satisfactory crops. The benefits to be derived from allowing land to lie idle are directly proportionate to the abundance of wild plants that spring up. Southern farmers of the old school never kept their crops so free from weeds that there would not be plenty of seed to germinate on any land that was left to itself for a season or two. The second and third seasons' growth of weeds registered, by their increased height and vigor, the benefit the new plants received from the decaying material produced the previous year. The longer the fields lay idle, the more completely they were restored to normal productiveness. If many years intervened between plantings, however, a young forest might have to be cleared off the land again, so farmers usually renewed cropping after three or four fallow seasons.

Such processes of soil renewal really should not be construed as idleness for the soil. In reality the so-called idle soil is working vigorously to re-establish a non-erosive surface. If there are enough weed seeds in the soil when it is abandoned, only a few years will be required for the surface to be properly "nailed down" again, so that runoff water will not be so plentiful or so effective in moving the soil minerals.

Many of the ills of the soil are those which we humans have induced. We could have avoided all of the trouble we have had with the soil. But that we should have made precisely those mistakes which are now part of history is logical, when it is considered that the plow—now the worst curse of the land—was at the time it was invented a lifesaver for the population. The reverential regard we have for it stems from those early days when people escaped the starvation then threatening only because the plow enabled them to handle larger areas of crops. This is more fully discussed in Chapter 4. It should be understood, however, that, while this book condemns plowing without reservation, it is in no sense an indictment of the men who have recommended it throughout the years. The motives back of such recommendations were as deeply rooted in their natures as are the religious teachings of one's youth. It was my own good fortune to be compelled to make soil where none existed. The solution of this problem pointed unmistakably to the solution of most of our soil problems.

It is safe to say that if the invention of the disk harrow had preceded that of the moldboard plow, and if planting and cultivating equipment had been designed to operate in the trashy surface it would have left, there would never have been a moldboard plow. It should be clear that the immaculately clean material we now have on most of our farms cannot be called soil except by the most liberal literary license. Our ideal of the soil includes of necessity that it must be easy to work, free from obstructions. It must be tidy. The fact is that untidiness to an extreme—a surface covered or filled with abundance of decaying trash—is really the proper condition. We must, therefore, revise our ideas as to the nature of the material upon which we can depend for sustenance. We certainly can not depend upon the almost white soils we now cultivate with the plow.

3

SOIL DOES NOT ERODE

In a very important sense, soil does not erode, for the more or less pure minerals that are left after all the organic matter has disappeared from the land are not, properly speaking, soil at all. They are merely the raw materials from which soil was originally made and from which it can be made again. Erosion begins only after the soil surface has become virtually non-absorbent—a condition induced by the compactness resulting from the loss of highly absorbent, cellular organic matter present in nearly all undisturbed soils.

In native meadow or forest, rainfall—even the most torrential—strikes the spongy mass of humus and is held, with little or no runoff. Wherever there is runoff, the movement is retarded and ultimately halted by the successive areas of absorbent organic matter over which the water moves. In a tight soil, free from organic matter, erosion is almost inescapable because the very tightness of the soil defeats the gravitational movement of water.

Equally, a soil surface nicely charged with organic matter—decayed vegetable growth, trash, and dead and still living roots of all kinds—is poor field for the forces of wind erosion which have been so destructive in certain western states. But a soil which has been impoverished of organic matter is all too often gone with the wind.

Human generations are too short for us to have actually

witnessed the complete cycle from virgin to eroded soil. William Byrd,[1] the Virginia landsman of the eighteenth century, described the portion of this cycle that most people today have never seen. The following account of corn planting by a farmer of the early days is quoted from Ben Ames Williams' *Come Spring:*

> He early cleared a patch of land and planted corn as soon as he had done his burning. The green wood was not consumed by the fire, and charred carcasses of trees lay everywhere; but he did his planting among them, poking a hole in the ground with a sharpened stick, dropping in two or three kernels, brushing earth into the hole with his foot.[2]

By great good fortune, I have witnessed the planting of a number of fields of corn in our own time by much the same method as that given above. Prodigious crops can be produced by such apparently careless methods in such an environment. Two hundred and fifty bushels per acre are an easily possible yield. *Farmers' Bulletin No. 400,* issued by the United States Department of Agriculture but now long out of print, describes a corn yield in South Carolina that measured up 239 bushels per acre. It is certain that even this yield is well within present possibility.

Such highly productive land did not erode. It could not. There was no clean, smooth surface such as we now know. The entire depth of soil, perhaps ten to fifteen inches of it, was filled with visible organic fragments or was stained with the fine black smudge which represents the final stages of organic decay in the soil. This material was highly absorbent,

[1] See page 20.

[2] From *Come Spring*, by Ben Ames Williams (Boston, Houghton Mifflin Company, 1940), 111.

to the last black stain. Such substance would scarcely permit a single drop of an ordinary rain to escape over the surface. There was too much empty space to be filled within the organic matter itself. Indeed, little water drained down through this material until it had taken in all it could hold. The depth of the black zone and the amount of water it already held determined how much additional water could be absorbed. In periods of very heavy rainfall most of the water would go on through this mass, of course. There could be no runoff water, except in long-extended wet periods. Even then the runoff water would not be stained with clay. It would be as clear as crystal—quite different from anything we see today. The surface drainage from cultivated lands in our time is always the color of the land.

It will perhaps be objected that when this mass becomes frozen solid no more water can get into it than can penetrate any other solid mass. This is true—if the mass becomes frozen solid. But it is difficult to freeze such a mass solid enough that water can not penetrate it. There are two very good reasons for this: (1) The water retained by fragments of organic matter is held within the fragments, leaving open spaces between them. Examine a saturated straw pile. There is no water between the straws, though the straws themselves will be full. Even when this water is frozen, there still is plenty of open space throughout the mass. (2) Such a mass of organic matter is so perishable that decay processes are continually in progress, except when there is too little heat or too little moisture. To some extent these fermentation processes provide their own necessary heat. (Remember in this connection that gardeners depend upon the heat of fermenting manure to keep up the temperature of their hot beds.) This ability to maintain higher temperatures, even in wintertime, shortens the period during which a highly organic soil can be frozen.

There are other influences that conspire to prevent tight freezing of a soil that is chiefly organic matter. A covering of snow is the best kind of insulation against the much colder upper air. Soil will often remain unfrozen through a long, cold winter in temperate latitudes, provided it is covered by enough snow. It is well known that snow falling on weeds or any other kind of organic matter is more apt to remain snow than it would if it fell on moist, unfrozen mineral soil. When snow falls on the latter, it immediately dissolves, much as it would if it fell into water; yet at the same time, that which falls on grass, boards, rail fences, roofs, or any other dry substance may accumulate rapidly and remain undissolved. Soil which is highly organic in character, similarly, accumulates snow more readily, because it always presents a drier surface. It is reasonable to believe that throughout the winter it retains a thicker blanket of snow than the pure mineral soil; and with the coming of spring the heat of fermentation within the soil will more quickly thaw out any frozen layer that might exist near the surface. This improves internal conditions for water penetration.

It has long been known that relatively little water escapes from a forest floor as runoff. Just why this is true has been a matter for conjecture, though part of the explanation at least was advanced earlier in this chapter. A commonly held theory is that the organic matter hinders the progress of the water over the surface of the minerals in the soil, thus allowing more time for the minerals to soak it in. Doubtless there is some such effect. It may be more important than I think.

It certainly is true that much of the water soaks directly into the leaves and other trash which are found on the ground. And we know that the entry of moisture into leaf tissue is much easier than into mineral soil.

It may not be generally known that when water penetrates mineral masses it does so by finding its way *between* the particles. The tiny particles of clay, silt, or sand are almost completely exclusive. Water can not enter them. It can only cling to their outer surfaces. This is extremely important information to keep in mind in a study of soils, for organic matter, by contrast, literally pulls liquids *into* itself. Volume for volume, then, organic matter can hold many times as much water as can any kind of soil mineral; for organic matter is chiefly open space internally, while minerals are dense, solid crystal; a fateful distinction where water relations are concerned.

The idea is abroad that man is the lord of creation—that he dominates the earth. In certain minor respects this may be true, but in the main it is the purest propaganda; as ineffectual, when we examine the facts, as whistling in the dark. Consider the single example of erosion. The alarm of thinking men today, when they consider the plight of coming generations starving on eroded soil, borders on panic. What would they think if there were immediate prospects of a renewal of the worldwide erosion which originally sculptured the present features of the earth's surface? That was erosion with a vengeance—millions on millions of years of it. Mountains were buried in the sea by the tearing down of the original fire-formed stone of which they were composed, and the removal of the debris by the unhindered waters and winds which shuttled back and forth across such continents as then existed. Geologists still puzzle over the wreckage, trying to piece out the story.

That original large-scale erosion was finally curbed. But it was not done by that self-advertising animal called man. It was done by vegetation—plants. Plants, the conquerors, had to start from nothing but powdered rock. Some structural materials they extracted from the minerals themselves, some from the air and the rays of the sun, and the rest from water. The porous architecture they were able to create from these materials is still the wonder of existence, though so commonplace as not often to be even an object of curiosity. A casual glance at a bit of onion skin, or a few strands of algae, under a microscope is a revelation to the uninitiated, even though no further thought is given to it. If it is considered that this delicate, lacy network of cells could not be possible except for the presence in infinitesimal amounts of such chemicals as phosphorus, iron, sulphur, calcium, potassium, and magnesium, the miracle of life becomes apparent. To know, then, that world-wide erosion was curbed in the beginning by stuff similar to that on the microscope slide should give us a healthy respect for all plants and for their disintegrating remains; for, down to the last black colloidal remnant of the dead plant or animal tissue, organic nature continues to fight erosion by the trick of absorption. By eternally coaxing water to enter, organic tissues keep it under control. Hence the importance of having the organic tissues where the water can reach them the instant it hits the earth as rain.

Plants are the real masters of the earth. Independent of human management, since they antedated the race, plants came spontaneously from the sea and threw a restraining influence over the unstable surface of the land, quieting its restlessness. Botanists explain the process in detail and with plausible reasoning, allowing eons for the lapse of time from the first single cells to the giant sequoias, and other eons for suitably equipped plants to complete the vegetative mantle over the earth. Moses offers a different story, of course, but be that as it may, we can be sure that man will master the rest of creation only as he comes to terms with plants, the real masters. They hold the key to his food supply.

Admittedly, we have serious erosion to contend with now. Much of our land is again in almost precisely the condition all land was in before plants arrived. It is bare, and it is in movement. Yet the present situation is immeasurably more favorable than the earlier one. The same destructive forces of wind and water are at work now as then, but the forces of plant opposition are now fully organized and mobilized. Alone, unless interfered with by man, plants can reclaim wayward land in an infinitesimal fraction of the time that was required eons ago, before they had adapted themselves to such work. Even so, such a reclamation period, when measured in terms of human lifetimes, may be excessively long. We are likely to get hungry waiting for natural forces alone to stop erosion and restore soil to the eroding mineral surface. Men must lend a helping hand.

The processes by which vegetation accomplishes a new cover where the previous cover has been destroyed are neither secret nor mysterious. All botany texts and a variety of other scientific treatises discuss the influences that determine the development of plant communities. These factors have been so ably discussed elsewhere that there is no necessity for my doing so here. It may be pertinent, however, to introduce some of the underlying principles which determine the nature of plant successions as they occur.

Important among the life factors that occasion the growth of one plant as against another in a given location are the requirements of the species for water and for heat. Although the temperature of the air is influenced to a certain extent by the soil, we may pass it over, because it is not of major concern. Water, being literally managed by the surface upon which it falls, becomes the key factor to be discussed. Moreover, the manner in which the supply of water available for future plants is increased or decreased from year to year as a result of changes wrought by successive generations of plants on the site is an important consideration for us.

The earliest plants to occupy an area are composed of a more or less spongy tissue capable of absorbing and holding water for future need, in addition to that being used currently. This reserve water is supplied to the active plant tissues as required, and saves the plant from extinction when its roots have exhausted the supply of water in the soil. Such are the lichens and mosses. Their remains, unless whisked away by the wind, accumulate from year to year. In a few years the soil itself will necessarily have become intermixed with these spongy remains, so that many times more water will be retained in the soil than could be held by the pure minerals in the beginning. This additional water makes the living lichens thrive, which in turn further increase year by year the accumulated sponginess in the soil itself. If there were no other kinds of plants in the world, it is easy to conjecture that these pioneer plants might develop to giant sizes, like the cacti of the desert.

Miles away from this hypothetical spot where the lichen-moss drama has attracted a better water supply, another spot is covered by plants that could not possibly have endured the conditions through which lichens and mosses lived and prospered. As if by magic, seeds of these less hardy plants arrive by wind, bird, or animal. Presently the new plants annihilate the pioneers by the simple procedure of growing taller and robbing them of their essential sunshine. So the plants that prepared the way for these interlopers have to find another bare spot on which to make a new start. Later, the newcomers in their turn are driven away by other kinds even less hardy for which they have paved the way. In this evolution of plant populations on a given spot, the indispensable condition to a thriving community is increasing ability of the soil to retain rainfall.

The availability of water, while a prime consideration, is no more important than other requirements of plant growth; but it may prove the key factor in determining the degree to which a given species is provided with or exposed to other needed conditions. Thus water availability, by developing more expansive tissues, necessarily creates light limitations for low growing plants, so that water, not the unavailability of light, becomes the primary factor in crowding out a species which fails because of lack of light. It would not be surprising to find that the presence or absence of water is the real key to situations supposedly created by other factors.

In any case, each successive stage in the laying down of an absorbent mat on the earth's surface removes one step further the possibility of runoff and erosion. It is not for nothing that writers have referred in literary contexts to "the earth's carpet," for in a very practical sense it is the carpet which covers and protects the landscape. Consider the fallen autumn leaves: snow will billow high upon them in the winter months, melt in the sunshine of spring, and yet the leaves in the center of a heap will be dry. It is the humus below which has profited, as the winter moisture has filtered slowly down, to be caught and held by the sponge of true earth.

Conventional thinking about erosion so far has centered about the idea of securing greater infiltration into the mineral soil, since that is about all that is left on many farms. We have given almost no thought to the idea of providing volumetric space in and on top of the soil into which the rainfall would be helplessly snatched as soon as it fell, thus halting erosion at its source. Two reasons have favored such thinking:

1) It has never been thought possible for planting and cultivation to be done except on a smooth surface. Hence, nobody thought to try or suggest the possibility of growing cultivated crops without first disposing of whatever trash littered the surface. Such trash was always disposed of by plowing.

2) Farmers and scientists have long known that the chief need of soils is organic matter, but that need was supposed to be met by plowing the organic matter into the soil to a depth of six to eight inches. Nobody seemed to realize that this procedure actually robbed the following crop of virtually all the substance of this buried organic matter.

By such hapless reasoning we have preserved for generations a system of soil management which should long ago have been revised to conform to the known facts. Planting can be done in a trashy surface. It had to be done so when the land was first cleared. Doubtless, it is easier to manage land which has nothing on the surface to be caught and dragged along by the sliding equipment we use for planting and cultivating. But, if the crop planted in such smooth land must necessarily produce a smaller yield because of the purity of the minerals (freedom from decaying organic matter), it seems logical to suggest the wisdom of trying to devise implements which will negotiate the trashy surface. Equally, if crop yield is greater from a trashy surface, as has been proved by official tests at the Nebraska Experiment Station, the desirability of the necessary equipment is beyond question.

We emerge with two highly important objectives well within our grasp: improved crop yield, which is immediate, and arrested erosion, which is long range but closely related to our ultimate welfare. Both are attainable by the simple procedure of abandoning the ancient practice of plowing organic matter under and substituting instead the effective practice of leaving the matter on the surface or working it in from the top. The organic sponge on top precludes erosion and provides the substance for maximum plant growth. That which has been plowed under leaves a denuded and tight surface ideally suited to the processes of erosion, while the nutriment for plants lies six to eight inches below their incipient roots, out of reach and therefore ineffectual for the principal purpose at hand.

It can be said with considerable truth that the use of the plow has actually destroyed the productiveness of our soils. Fortunately, however, this result may be said to be temporary. With surprising suddenness the soil which is supposedly ruined will respond with bumper crops, providing it is supplied plentifully with organic matter properly incorporated into the surface. This generous response by soil thought to be "worn out" shows that our farmland has not been exhausted by cropping but has been rendered impotent by inept management.

Our faults are oftentimes excused on grounds of necessity. Plowing, however, can summon no such defense: there is simply no need for plowing in the first instance. And most of the operations that customarily follow the plowing are entirely unnecessary, if the land has not been plowed. It is possible to farm land without a smoothing harrow, without a cultipacker, without a drag, without a roller, without a single implement which is ordinarily used after plowing—in preparing the seed bed. The single exception to this is the disk-harrow, which is used to incorporate the trash into the surface as fully as possible. If the land has been disked without previous plowing, there are no clods whatever; consequently there is no need to use the customary smoothing equipment.

"Soil conservation" is a phrase which has been widely used but little understood. There is undoubtedly an important sense in which we must save soil losses, must prevent dissolved plant food from escaping down our streams; but that is only a minor part of the task ahead. The main job is to activate and to put into biological circulation minerals that, since the beginning of time, have been locked in the crystalline structure of rock of the earth's surface. Our failure to solve that problem generations ago resulted in our adding commercial fertilizer to land, not because the land holds none of the minerals contained in the fertilizer, but because we had not found a way to dissolve those minerals so that crops could use them. We now know how to perform this trick; so the future of soil conservation work is destined to be concerned more with releasing additional minerals from the soil rock than with saving losses which by comparison are relatively light.

Fortunately, however, the same practices which result in prying more minerals out of the rock result also in maximum saving of the previously dissolved minerals. Whether we call the method "conservation" or "proper soil management" is immaterial; but it is important that we consciously imitate the natural soil profile which always and everywhere leaves *all* the organic matter on or mixed into the surface.

Since plowing cannot leave organic matter on or in the surface except under such conditions as the pioneers found when they first cleared the land (when the entire soil mass often was black with intermixed organic and inorganic materials to a depth of a foot or more), plowing, as it is now done, is definitely out as a means of breaking the land surface.

When plowing is stopped, erosion will stop with it, for the organic matter mixed into the soil surface will cause that surface to appropriate the rain as it falls, thus removing the flow of water which is essential to the processes of erosion. Therefore, the cure for erosion is automatic when soil is again created, for soil does not erode.

4

TRADITIONS OF THE PLOW

THE ANSWER TO THE QUESTION, *Why do farmers plow?* should not be difficult to arrive at. Plowing is almost universal. Farmers like to plow. If they did not get pleasure from seeing the soil turn turtle, knowing the while that by plowing they dispose of trash that would later interfere with planting and cultivation, less plowing might be done. Yet farmers are encouraged to plow. Deep plowing is approved; or, in lieu of deep plowing, farmers are advised to cut deep into the subsoil in every furrow. Such advice comes from farm papers, bulletins, county agents, and a long list of other sources from which farmers commonly welcome suggestions and information. There should be clear-cut scientific reasons to justify a practice so unanimously approved and recommended.

If there are such reasons I have failed to find them in more than twenty-five years of search. As early as 1912, when my classmates and I were taking courses in soil management and farm machinery, we brought up the subject, quizzing professors as to why plowing, rather than a method of surface incorporation, should be the generally accepted practice in breaking the soil. A number of answers were offered, none, however, of a scientific nature; in the end some embarrassed instructors had to admit they knew no really scientific reasons for plowing. They suggested that the most important justifications for the practice might be that it "turned over a new leaf" for the farmer by the complete burial of preceding crop residues, thus leaving the land free from obstructions to future movements of planting and cultivating machinery.

Our experience was not unique. The editor of one of the leading American farm papers has this to say in a letter written to me on August 5, 1937: "It is a subject I became interested in about eighteen years ago. I made a two-thousand-mile trip among soil specialists and farmers and everywhere asked the question: Why do you plow? I was rather amazed at the unsatisfactory answers I received. Apparently farmers do not really know. When I summed up the answers it seemed that they had only one good reason for plowing, and that was to get rid of weeds."[1] That there may be good reason to doubt whether the plow does even that is indicated in an article in the January, 1941, issue of this same publication, in which one writer points out that plowing may preserve for future germination more weed seeds than it destroys.

In all truth, the ultimate scientific reason for the use of the plow has yet to be advanced. My own position, however, has already been advanced in earlier pages of this book. If I were advising farmers on the subject of plowing, my categorical statement would be *Don't*—and for that position there is really scientific warrant. A brief review of the reasons frequently given for plowing will give opportunity to point out the error involved in each.

An administrative officer in the department of agriculture of one of the New England states suggests in a letter that plowing is designed to allow oxygen to reach the roots of plants; he suggests, too, that plowed soil will not dry out

[1] Philip S. Rose, then editor of the *Country Gentleman*.

so rapidly as unbroken soil. His reasons seem to cancel each other, indicating that he had not considered these two suggested effects simultaneously. Letting air into the soil is an efficient way of drying it out, particularly that portion which is disturbed. Since the roots of crops must develop first in this inverted (and necessarily dried) section of soil, it seems that my correspondent really gave a good reason for not plowing.

This idea—that it is necessary to let oxygen into the soil—has been in circulation for many years. It seems that those who pass it on do not pause to examine its implications. In a world organized as this one is, air is all pervading, except where something else fills the space. There is considerable space throughout all soils from the surface down to the level of ground water. Part of it is filled with capillary water, which clings to the rock fragments themselves; but since the spaces are too large for capillary water to fill them completely, air must fill the rest. When the water table[2] rises, this air is forced out of the soil; when it recedes again, the air re-enters.

It might be objected that more oxygen is required in the soil than can enter the undisturbed mass. Perhaps. In that case we should study the undisturbed forest floor. The surface of the soil where the giant sequoias grow was suitable for their needs a thousand years before the moldboard plow

[2] Water table is the name given to the level of water below the surface of the ground. The level rises and falls in response to seasons of great or little rainfall. This ground water is the source of supply for perennial streams and springs. It is literally filtered water, since it has to pass through several feet of soil before reaching this low level. Streams supplied entirely from the water table are, therefore, clear at all times. Farm wells must be dug deeper than the lowest level to which the water table ever falls, or they become dry during long continued droughts.

was invented. It is not thinkable that such giants could have developed in the absence of an optimum amount of oxygen in the soil. It must be, then, that growing plants do not require more oxygen in the soil than naturally enters it in the absence of water. There may be extreme situations, for example, where the soil has been excessively compacted by the trampling of animals or people, requiring special treatment. It is not clear, however, that plowing would be the right treatment. The freezing and thawing of soil in winter usually assists a well tramped path to grow up in vegetation the following season, unless the use of the path is continued.

Ordinarily the publications of the government and of the various state institutions can be quoted freely. The information they carry is designed for public use, and wide distribution is desirable. Ohio State University's *Agricultural Extension Bulletin No. 80* is the only exception to this rule I have seen. It was copyrighted in 1928 and reprinted in June, 1940, still retaining the copyright. The reprinting of this bulletin justifies the assumption that its contents are still considered correct. Significantly, along with other government and state publications as well as the books on soils of the last decade or two, it takes for granted that the farmer knows *why* he plows. The text then proceeds to describe "good" plowing as the complete burial of all trash—so complete that none is exposed even between the furrow slices. This, therefore, may be taken as the more or less official point of view.

Various books on agricultural subjects published around 1910 do give what may be considered hypothetical reasons for plowing. Most of them are vague enough to be interpreted in a number of ways. Here is a list:

a) Soil structure is made either more open or more compact.
b) Retention and movement of water are affected.
c) Aeration is altered.
d) Absorption and retention of heat are influenced.
e) The growth of organisms is either promoted or retarded.
f) The composition of the soil solution is affected.
g) The penetration of plant roots is influenced.

This list was compiled from a single paragraph of a well-known soil text which was written in 1909. Though the authors did not realize it at the time, it is a bit of literary gumshoeing around a highly dangerous subject. The intent, apparently, was not so much to give information as to indicate in what various categories the student might expect to find it. The implied assumption is that plowing improves the soil as environment for plant roots. The practice could scarcely be justified otherwise. Just how this improvement is accomplished is left wholly to the bewildered student's imagination. And while he is trying to rationalize this puzzle he is likely to conclude that, if plowing really does improve the soil as a site for plants, the vegetation growing so lush on unplowed land must be to some extent underprivileged. Of course, even an astute student may miss that angle. It is obvious that most of us did.

Assuming plowed land to be better for plant growth, we should find grass growing more freely on plowed land than on similar unplowed land near by. Weeds, too, should show preference for plowed land. Volunteer growth should take over and develop more rankly after land has been plowed than before. Is this so? Observation is that, until plowed land has subsided again to its former state of firmness, plants develop in it quite tardily, if at all. When dry weather follows the plowing, it may be weeks or even months before either natural vegetation or a planted crop will make normal growth. The fact is that "bare" land, which notably erodes worse than soil in any other condition, consists almost wholly of land that has been disturbed recently by plow or cultivating implement. The only other bare land is that which has been denuded of top soil by erosion or other forces. There is significance in the fact that erosion and runoff are worst on bare land, and that bare land is defined above.

Take a casual glance at the landscape. Not only does the unplowed land continue to support its growth nicely while the plowed land is recovering its ability to promote growth, but even the margins of the plowed field itself continue to support their growth. Such evidence causes the argument that plowing produces a better environment for plant roots to backfire. The loosening up, pulverizing, and inversion process seems a first-rate way to make good soil incapable of performing its normal functions in plant growth. The explosive separation of the soil mass wrecks temporarily all capillary connections; the organic matter sandwiched in further extends the period of sterility of the soil because of dryness. Therefore, it is not strange that plowed soil is bare. Before it is plowed, grass, weeds, and other vegetation grow normally because there is unbroken capillary contact from particle to particle, extending from the water table to the surface. After plowing, this source of water is completely cut off until the organic matter at the plowsole has decayed. Hence the soil simply takes time out from its business of growing things until its normal water supply is restored. There is no mystery about it. It is only the working out of natural law. Wishful thinking is peculiarly ineffective in preventing this undesired outcome of plowing.

Another objectionable feature of plowing is the merciless troweling administered by the moldboard to that portion of the furrow slice which is brought from the plowsole and exposed to wind and sunshine. The effect is not noticeable, and probably not damaging, if the soil to the full depth of plowing is dry enough to crumble; but in these days, when all soils seem to become more troublesome to handle, it is seldom that spring plowing can be done early enough, if the farmer waits for the wet spots to dry out to a sufficient depth. Too often in his haste to get the year's work started, he rushes into the plowing while the soil glistens as it leaves the moldboard. Some men even plow when water follows them in the furrow. Such management of the soil certainly is playing fast and loose with resources which the soil might contribute to crop growth.

Plowing done when the furrow slice is plastic creates clods; every clod is so much soil mustered out of service for the season. The tremendous pressure necessary to separate the furrow slice from its base compresses effectively any soil that is moist enough to be plastic; and a moderate amount of clay in plastic soil serves to harden the mass upon drying so that adobe-like clods result. Smoothing implements may reduce the size of these lumps, but as clods they are likely to remain aloof from the rest of the soil throughout most of the growing season.

Such evidence of damage done by the moldboard has passed unnoticed by farmers as well as by most other people. Several reasons may be given to account for the public's blindness to obvious faults of the moldboard plow.

To begin with, conditions such as modern farmers face were remote indeed when the plow was first used with a crude moldboard attachment. That was two hundred years ago. The English countryside at that time was chiefly unbroken forest. The land that had been cleared of trees still was not very well subdued, for it was a hopeless task to try to keep the soil free from competing weeds and shrubs while a crop was growing. The forest was forever trying to recover the lost ground, and the only really effective tools farmers had against encroaching saplings, perennial weeds, and other unwanted growth were crude hoes, mattocks, and spades. Such plows as they had threw the soil both to the right and to the left. They did not cover trash very well, much less uproot permanently the wild growth which cumbered the ground. The "bull tongue" plow of the South is of somewhat the same design as most of the plows which preceded the moldboard.

Into such an environment the moldboard was introduced. It was a godsend. Pulled by an ox, or even by men, this plow would actually lift and invert the soil. This made it possible, by careful work, to eliminate completely the perennial weeds and some of the smaller shrubs. And, what was more important, the farmer who previously could manage only a few square rods now could raise food on an acre or more. Such an invention at a time when England was never far from actual starvation captured the imagination of rural people everywhere. It was electric in its effects upon contemporary thought. The population now could eat regularly and well, provided enough farmers could have moldboard plows.

Inventions did not occur often in the early eighteenth century. New aids to living were rare indeed. The moldboard plow, destined to revolutionize the living conditions of world populations, marked the beginning of a new era. So completely did it fill the greatest material need of a poorly nourished mankind that it was accorded a place in people's thoughts such as is usually reserved only for saints and priests. The plow had saved humanity almost literally.

The farmer of that day, in both England and America, had more trouble keeping unwanted things from growing than in getting his crops to grow. For him, then, the use of the plow was excellent strategy, because temporarily, at least, conditions were created which made it impossible for the weeds to grow. This gave the farmer time to get his root and grain crops started before the wild vegetation recovered from the setback caused by the plowing. Once his crops were well started, the incomparable richness of the black, loamy soil kept them well ahead of the weeds. Now that the black loamy soil has completely disappeared from most land in the United States, our proper strategy may well be the exact opposite of what was advantageous then. His plowing, even though it covered a lot of organic matter, could not create for him the sandwich, organic matter profile (OMP), for there was too much depth of blackness in the soil.

The earliest crude moldboards could not be favorably compared with the burnished products of today's factories. Hammered out by hand at forges erected at or near the ore mines, they could become smooth only through much use. They were designed by guess after many trials and did not become stabilized to dependable shape until a century after farmers began to use them generally. Despite its shortcomings—much easier to appraise from our perspective than from that of the contemporary farmer—the plow was, even in its crude state, the greatest invention of the age. It dispelled hunger as the first oil lamp dispelled darkness. Aladdin's lamp could not have been more wonderful.

When a century later the first experiment station was established at Rothamsted, England, no one seems to have raised a question whether the neat work done by the moldboard plow might be responsible for the trouble farmers were beginning to have growing crops. The men of science who manned that first station, as well as those in charge of the state experiment stations later established in this country, inherited an unquestioning reverence for the plow. The doctrine of the Divine Right of Plows passed down from generation to generation, so that the possibility that the plow might account for the waning fertility of the soil never seriously occurred to anybody along the line. For decades, to my own personal knowledge, men have sensed that the plowing in of a layer of organic matter at the plowsole must of necessity interfere with capillary movement; but the subconscious feeling that The Plow Can Do No Wrong apparently prevented anybody from doing anything about it. The result is that, although we have had experiment stations in this country for more than three-quarters of a century, no one of them conducted tests, before 1937, designed to compare directly the effects of plowing, on the one hand, with the surface incorporation of all organic matter on the other. Failure to do this has definitely handicapped the development of basic soil information which might easily have prevented the debacle toward which American soils have been drifting.

The failure to harmonize the implications of ordinary observations with really scientific information may be the result of historical lag, or an attitude of mind, or mere carelessness, or, finally, a combination of all three. If we consider the published recognition given to the importance of organic material in the soil surface, especially since the opening of the present century, it is difficult to avoid assessing blame, on the score of carelessness, against those who did not look beyond their immediate data to the established data gained from plowing. This is almost implicit in the following:

The *Yearbook* of the United States Department of Agriculture for 1903 carries this statement on page 284: "Decayed organic matter, by itself or in combination with mineral soil, absorbs moisture much more rapidly than soil containing little or no organic matter; hence, the greater the amount of leaf mold and other litter, the more rapidly will the rain be absorbed. Rapidity of absorption is also influenced by the degree of looseness of the mineral soil. In the forest the mulch of leaves and litter keeps the mineral soil loose and in the best condition for rapid absorption."

If such a statement seems sufficiently old for its validity to be questioned, compare it with the following, taken from pages 609–10 of the *Yearbook* of the same department for the year 1938: "Forest litter—the carpet of dead leaves, twigs, limbs, and logs on the forest floor—serves in several ways. Water falling as rain on bare soil dislodges silt and clay particles by its impact. These are taken into suspension and carried into the tiny pores and channels between the soil particles as the water makes its way downward. Very shortly the filtering action of the soil causes the openings to be clogged by the particles; water can no longer move downward through the soil, so it flows over the surface carrying with it the dislodged silt and clay; and erosion is actively under way. A protective layer of litter prevents this chain of events by absorbing the impact of the falling drops of water. After the litter becomes soaked, excess water trickles gently into the soil surface, no soil particles are dislodged, the water remains clear, pores and channels remain open, and surface flow is eliminated except in periods of protracted heavy rains."

I can detect no significant difference in the meaning of the two quotations. The latter gives a more intimate picture of the processes involved, but it fully confirms the less graphic description in the earlier statement. Moreover, every intelligently conducted experiment so far undertaken in this direction confirms the truth presented.

A paragraph from a letter dated February, 1940, should be interesting in this connection: "The Department of Agriculture has long been interested in developing new methods of soil treatment which will maintain and build up the organic matter content of the soil. Studies carried out by the Soil Conservation Service at a number of locations have already produced unusually outstanding results along this line. At Statesville, North Carolina, for example, it has been found that several inches of pine needles spread over the soil surface reduced the loss of soil by erosion to a point almost beyond measurement. There was also a considerable increase in the organic matter content of the soil and indications point to a worthwhile increase in crop yields. In Nebraska subsurface tillage, which leaves straw and other litter undisturbed on the soil surface, has proved remarkably effective in reducing soil and water losses and in preliminary experiments has led to a material increase in the yield of several crops tested." This was signed by the Assistant to the

Secretary. It may be said that my letter, to which this was the reply, had mentioned and asked for comment on the fact that the moldboard plow had never been put to test for validation. No mention of the matter was made in the official reply.

The fact that no advance whatever is apparent, when the statement of 1903 is compared with those of 1938 and 1940, indicates that effort to implement the earlier findings into general farm practice has been neglected. The statements from the yearbooks refer to forest soils, of course; but that fact must not obscure the larger fact that the findings discussed concern principles of universal application. Principles which are valid in the forest are valid in the field, always; so it seems that researches into the importance of organic matter on the surface of crop land should have been started as soon as the earlier announcement had been made. If any such work was begun earlier than 1937, I have been unable to find any record of it.

5

"RESEARCH"

Unsponsored . . . Unconventional

In strict honesty, the heading of this chapter must be enclosed in quotation marks, for I am not a research worker in the conventional sense of that phrase. The work that originated the theories of this book is called research only for lack of a better name. It did, however, give the necessary direction to my thinking, and that is a chief function of any research.

It all began as an attempt to grow vegetables in soil which, as I discovered too late, was better suited to brick-making. Thousands of people have made equally futile attempts, but they have had sense enough to quit when their corn stalks refused to exceed the diameter of a lead pencil or the height of a man's knee. I couldn't quit, for to quit would have left us with two thousand square feet of our back yard without grass and full of weeds, with no easy means of getting it back into lawn again.

It had been our custom always to have a vegetable garden. When we bought our home, it soon became apparent that the grass in the back yard was largely yellow dock. That fact gave excuse for digging up this section of the lawn, growing vegetables in it for a few years while we got rid of the weeds, and then either continuing the vegetable garden or putting the area back to grass. What actually happened was something far different.

A man was hired to do the necessary spading, while I went about my commercial business. When I returned later and paid him off, I discovered that what had been exposed in the spading was nothing but the toughest of white clay. The clods when dry were as sharp and firm to the touch as so much broken stone. I had had experience with several widely different kinds of soil, but this was an extreme condition which I had never before seen. Eventually the story came out, but not before we had tried for a year or two to grow something edible from that pure clay.

Our house, it appeared, had been the last one constructed on our street. The site had been low—some three or four feet lower in places than the general level to which the surrounding lots had been graded. The owner had invited the contractors to dump on this lot. So, above the original soil that had been there lay three to four feet of plain clay of the heavy character that prevails in this former lake bed. It was just "cellar dirt," with no discernible sand, silt, or organic matter to relieve its harshness. It was so hard when dry that I could put my full weight on a sharp spade without making any perceptible impression on it. Ordinary highway traffic could have traversed it without leaving a track; though when wet it would cling to my shoes in gobs as big as I could carry.

Mellowness in such a soil is unknown. It is either too wet or too dry for stirring, with only half an hour or so between the two conditions when it may be cultivated with impunity. Ordinary soils never get into such a condition, because usually there are some fragments of organic matter in them, and these greatly alleviate what would otherwise develop into a tight structure. This mass of clay had been excavated from levels far beneath the usual depth to which roots penetrate;

so it had no supply of organic matter. In the language of experiment station men, it was "an organic matter check plot." Its use for growing crops would show what might be expected of land in which there was no organic matter.

In the beginning I was not concerned about soil theories, but wished only to produce vegetables for home use. However, it soon became evident that I must concern myself somewhat with fundamentals of soil management or I wouldn't get anything for my work. About this time I recalled that a quarter of a century earlier, as county agent of Whitley County, Kentucky, I had tried unsuccessfully to show farmers how to improve their very poor, sandy soils by plowing down tall rye. All the early county agents probably tried this; and all of them learned, as I did, that it would not work. At that time I had decided that, if the opportunity presented itself, I would try to solve the problem.

The problem really was simple—apparently. Its essence was to find a way to put large quantities of organic matter into a very unproductive soil without ruining temporarily its ability to grow crops. It seemed that so simple a problem might be solved easily. The opportunity I was looking for (in an experiment station) never came. Instead, after having been out of professional agriculture for several years, I now had the identical problem dumped rudely into my lap —without the appropriate surroundings usually considered essential.

Such was the beginning of what proved later to be the solution of that original tantalizing problem. I tackled it without definite plan, not realizing fully for several years that I was at work on the problem first presented to me in Kentucky. It is clear, therefore, that to call this research without proper explanation and qualification would be to debase the high meaning of real research work. Such work is always preceded by carefully organized plans and pursued by accepted methods.

The elements of accident and coincidence are important in this project. It was purely accidental that of the half a dozen properties we had inspected before buying, we should have selected this one. In fact, only the night before we concluded its purchase, we had decided to buy another on the next street; but, upon notifying the owner, we found that it had been sold the previous evening to friends of ours who had suddenly made up their minds to buy. It was coincident that ours should have been the newest house on a street where none was very old. It was the merest coincidence that the site had been depressed.

More than this, the combination of circumstances in my own earlier life had favored and prepared me for just this thing. The farm on which I grew up was bottom land, almost entirely surrounded by hills. The hills were then in process of being cleared for agriculture after having been lumbered off. I had seen the same fields pass through several alternate periods of cultivation and neglect, and had noted that the mere growth of weeds and briars had renewed productivity on such land. The bottom land we owned was farthest from the stream, the highest of the entire bottom-land area; consequently the flood water that covered it once a year did not remain long, and, therefore, did not settle out very much debris to improve the soil. This fact had resulted in the abandonment of this higher ground in favor of land nearer the stream; and, since our portion had been considered worn out by the standards of 1883, my father paid little for it.

This land had declined in productivity to such an extent that its production would not exceed twenty-five bushels of corn per acre, a yield considered no longer worth the effort when there was near-by land that would grow one hundred bushels without manure, fertilizers, or any other amendment.

We owned, therefore, the poorest land in the bottoms; and my father was pitied by the neighbors when he bought it. I have since seen one-hundred-bushel crops of corn on this same land, and from its productiveness three of my brothers and sisters and I were educated through college, and two others were educated as far as they wanted to go. For many years the strip of land we owned stood out as the greenest part of all the bottoms, even though, as time passed, it no longer had the benefit of the decomposable material which the river water at one time brought. The neighbors meantime viewed with critical eyes the strange things my father was doing on that land. He hauled in manure from a near-by town, also ashes from a tannery when he could get them, and he bought a carload of fertilizers each spring, part of which he resold to any neighbors who were willing to take a chance on such stuff. And, while he was doing this, the neighbors continued to depend upon the decreasing increment of flood debris from up-river.

The sons of those neighbors now manage the land. They decided that my father's methods were worth trying. And now, after several years of the younger generation's management, that old contrast has almost disappeared, for all the bottom land has come under better management. And, incidentally, it may be said that farmers the country over now are being paid to do for their land what my father did for his throughout his lifetime. He read farm papers regularly.

He tried the methods that seemed reasonable to him. He adopted what proved to be profitable. And he had the luck to be engaged in a business which, in that location paid the highest return for liberal treatment of the land. He received good prices for staple truck crops marketed in the near-by town in the heart of what was then a coal mining area. General farming, of course, would not have repaid the costs of such treatment, either then or now; but that does not invalidate the fact that my father, starting with poor land, had made it productive. He did so at high cost. I believed it could be done at lower cost. And, the important point—by far the most important point—was my absolute confidence that the poorest of land anywhere could be made highly productive, since the undisturbed natural landscape is always highly productive in virtue of its continued year-after-year production.

With this background of home training, my general knowledge of scientific agriculture, and a decade of experience in professional agriculture in two states, it seemed to be a strange chance that I should buy the particular spot where the stage already had been set to force me into solving the old organic-matter problem.

Starting with the original spading in 1930, some organic matter was put in each season. In general, the quantity was increased as time went on. Eventually, a system of introducing leaves was developed which was very like plowing, but in quite exaggerated form. A trench was made to the full depth of the spade blade. This trench was filled with leaves, sometimes dry and bulky, sometimes wet, compact, and heavy. These were tramped in. Then the soil from the adjacent strip was thrown onto these leaves as the next trench was spaded. Repetition of this process resulted in creating virtually an organic matter subsoil beneath the surface soil. By 1937 I decided that the organic matter profile (OMP) thus created was in effect simply a magnification of the sandwich OMP produced by plowing; also, that the layer of organic matter that varied in thickness from nothing to as much as four inches became an irresistible magnet for any water in the soil, as truly as if that organic matter had been blotting paper. Once that decision was reached, it became obvious that the way to determine whether such was the situation would be to remove the leaf layer at the next spading and not establish such a layer again. So, in the fall of 1937, the area was spaded without putting in additional leaves. Care was taken to remove the entire mass of leaves from spade depth, mixing these in with the upper layers of soil.

In 1938 the soil surface was as different as possible from its condition in any previous year. Each spring before 1938 it had been necessary, in order to enable small seeds to germinate in the stiff clay, to cover them with fine sand instead of the clay. By such tactics I had been able to grow parsnips in this heavy soil. In 1938 it was so plainly evident that nothing of the kind would be necessary that parsnip seeds, carrots, lettuce, and all the small seeds were planted without any covering other than the granulated clay that was everywhere. The whole soil surface in 1938 was as granular as sugar, and it could be raked about just as easily as if it had been sand. So changed was this condition that I planted garden peas on March 11, a week earlier than the local gardeners on sandy land were able to plant them. Every crop planted in 1938 thrived, whereas, prior to 1938 no crop could be depended upon except under special conditions.

One especially fine bit of evidence was the behavior of head lettuce on this soil in 1938. A gardener friend of mine, with whom I was discussing the fine condition of the soil, challenged the possibility of growing head lettuce on it. He was so sure of it that he agreed to furnish the plants. Since the area was small I took only six plants. These were set into the soil, and once they had started nothing whatever was done for them except to keep the weeds down. No fertilizer was used, and no other treatment—not even water. Late in June this gardener came at my invitation to see how his lettuce plants were doing. They had reached almost the same size as his own, and were well headed—something he knew would not have happened in his sandy soil unless plenty of fertilizer and manure had been used. Any gardener will recognize this behavior of lettuce as unusual; indeed, most gardeners will refuse to believe it could have been true under the conditions I have described.

On July 14, 1938, by special arrangement with the Soil Conservation Service, representatives of that agency visited this project to check the soil conditions I had claimed existed. For purposes of this test, during the soil preparation in the fall a strip about six feet wide had been prepared as a check plot, as experiment station men would call it. This strip had been spaded without removing the leaves that already underlay it, and had received an additional supply, just as the entire area had been receiving for five or six years. The purpose of this strip was to illustrate the marked difference in soil texture as between the check strip and the rest of the garden.

Using a soil auger, these men followed instructions I had previously prepared, to insure that the point would be properly demonstrated. They bored into the soil in many places outside the check strip, finding that the soil was mellow to about one foot in depth, and with moisture uniformly distributed from top to bottom. There was no concentration of water at any level, and no dry, hard layer of soil anywhere. Moreover, there was no layer of leaves to be found.

In the check strip conditions were different. The initial turn of the auger flaked up the flinty hard soil from just under the surface mulch of cultivated soil. The upper eight or ten inches of soil were quite similar to this subsurface crust. It was excessively dry, whereas elsewhere in the garden there was no excessive dryness. Beneath this thick layer was the organic matter, moist, but not noticeably wet. Just under the organic matter was the moisture which should have been well distributed throughout the entire depth of soil. This check strip showed plainly one reason why crops can not grow immediately in a soil where a great deal of organic matter has recently been plowed in. There was no moisture whatever in the subsurface layer; and without moisture to dissolve plant food and carry it into the roots no growth can occur. The reason for the absence of moisture was that it had been absorbed by the underlying layer of leaves—even though the leaves did not seem moist. Their apparent innocence of moisture resulted from the fact that organic matter, as before stated, holds water within itself—just as a sponge does.

The reasoning that accounts for the flinty zone above the organic matter is so elementary that I should be embarrassed to admit that years were required for me to reach that simple conclusion. It is based upon facts so well established as to be known even to uneducated people. Yet one more illustration may help to make clearer the way this happens.

The water had been pulled downward in obedience to two forces: the blotting ability of the organic matter, and the force of gravity. Everybody knows that a bushel basket of corn cobs, if dry, could be carried by a small child, but when wet would be a load for a man. And, if they are exposed to contact with water, the wetting of cobs is automatic. To a degree, that is exactly what had happened to the water supply of the soil above the leaves. Within three or four days after the very heaviest rainfall, the excess water from the upper layers of soil would have been pulled away from the plant roots and into the underlying leaves. This produced noticeable effects. Immediately after rain, all crops were stimulated, and made rapid growth. By the end of three or four days, this stopped short, and no further growth could be observed until after the next rain.

It was with pleasure that I had set about planning the demonstration which had been inspected by Soil Conservation Service representatives. These men, not knowing the background of experience upon which I based my conclusions, could not agree with me that my check plot illustrated the normal effects of plowing—in exaggerated form. The soil dryness, recognized as common following the plowing in of great quantities of organic matter, was not caused by that plowing, they were sure. They did not agree with my conclusions. Neither did their superiors in Washington. We had correspondence following their report, as a result of which I was eventually informed that my project had "so exaggerated the effects of a bad practice" that it could scarcely be considered of value. The letter that carried this bit of unintended self-contradiction, dated November 10, 1938, was written by a man who had spent some forty years in the service of the United States Department of Agriculture and was to retire the following week. When I replied to his letter, the answer received from Washington informd me of his retirement, and gave the obvious information that he could not reply officially.

The refusal of authorities to accept and profit by the perfect demonstration I had made of the harm wrought by plowing was deeply disappointing. It had been clearly shown that the cause of the drying out of land, where considerable organic matter has been plowed in, is that organic matter. There could be no doubt of it. Stung by this flouting of an obvious point which should have been accepted gracefully, I decided that a further demonstration on field scale must be made. The story of this work appears in the following chapter. However, had I known it, this second demonstration was not needed; for, without indicating that he was interested in the matter at all, one leading agronomist of the United States Department of Agriculture had taken me seriously enough to set up a demonstration. Perhaps the intent was to disprove my theories; on the contrary, the outcome of the tests completely confirmed them. (I have been informed by this agronomist that he had nothing to do with initiating this test work. However, the fact remains that no surface-incorporation work of any kind had ever been done by any government agency prior to 1937 when I began nudging the department to do so.)

The results of this official experiment proved that, by working organic matter into the surface instead of plowing it in, the resulting grain yield could be as much as 50 per cent greater. The very first year of this trial showed such a result. So unexpected was this outcome that a report of it was published in the November, 1939, issue of *Country Gentleman,* under the title, "Right Side Up Farming."[1] Such publication was a radical departure from traditional practice. Usually a result must have been confirmed by several years of follow-up work before the public is permitted to know of it, especially in a popular magazine. This unusual advance publication of first-year results seems to indicate a conviction among officials regarding the significance of what had happened that first year.

No special acumen was required for this "research." The only "facts" uncovered were so old they had been previously overlooked as of no possible application. The direction of the pull of gravity, and the affinity of blotting paper for liquids, could scarcely be pointed out as research discoveries; and those were the only discoveries involved. Their effects were amplified by the large quantities of organic matter employed, which accounted for their discovery. Thus, the combined effects of downward capillarity and gravity are seen to be much more powerful forces than the wishful thinking, which previously has been depended upon to keep the soil moist above a heavy green manure crop that has been plowed in.

To have demonstrated the fact that such fundamental forces could be involved—which had remained undetected through a century of active scientific effort to improve soils—may be of consequence.

[1] George S. Pound, "Right Side Up Farming," *Country Gentleman,* Vol. CIX, No. 11 (November, 1939), 78.

6

PROOF ON A FIELD SCALE

THE RESEARCH that revealed the absurdity of our system of tillage was done as a hobby, at scarcely any expense other than time and the failure of the effort to produce the vegetables our family needed. The later work of demonstrating the workability of the idea on a field scale could not be done so simply or with little expense. There must be implements and power. They cost money. Time must be devoted to the project; whether it should be part time or full time had to be decided. If full time was to be given to this project, it had to be planned on a self-supporting basis. To justify full time, the area must be larger than could be found at reasonable rent near town. For such an area I had to go into the country beyond the reach of suburban cost influences.

Months were consumed in the development of a general plan. Some time was spent trying to find suitable property near the city that I could buy or trade for, develop, and later move to. None was found that could be bought on terms that would leave funds for operation. Failing in that, I decided to lease land and operate it while still living in town. The land selected was eight miles distant, but was otherwise very well suited for the work I expected to do. It was sandy loam soil, which would be more workable than the clay had been in the early stages. The owner's husband reserved for his own use the entire front of the farm along the highway. This provided a screen against too great curiosity concerning the strange methods about to be used. The portion of this land that was most promising for cropping had been used all along by a neighbor farmer-gardener to grow corn and hay. Other areas had on occasion been put to garden crops. A good deal of the area had been virtually abandoned because the owner and her husband could not manage it themselves, and none of the neighbors would rent it.

After leasing the land on February 20, 1939, I waited in vain for weather suitable for seeding rye or oats, later to be disked in as green manure. Rain fell almost incessantly. Until April 15 there was not more than half a day in any week when the land was dry enough to work. Oats bought for seeding had to be sold again. For green manure, I had to depend upon weeds the land would grow before it had to be prepared for a crop. This quirk of weather was to prove a serious handicap before the season was over. It prevented the creation of the single condition upon which success with crops is assured—an abundant supply of organic matter which may be worked into the land. (I did not realize then as I do now that it would have been possible simply to throw the seed on the land, even when it was too wet to work, and grow a green manure crop without stirring the land at all.)

Failure to establish green manure crops contributed heavily toward the financial failure of that first season's work. Had I sensed this in advance, much fruitless effort would have been saved; but, though the work was not rewarded financially, the gains in knowledge fully compensated for the monetary loss. Lessons learned through those experiences in the field made it possible thereafter to take advantage of weather rather than to be always its victim. For farmers such knowledge will be of inestimable value.

During those first rainy weeks I designed and built a crude device for locating the rows and establishing the places where seeds or plant roots were to be placed in those rows. I knew that in some circumstances green manure crops might grow so tall before the land could be worked that they could not then be completely incorporated. In such a case none of the customary planting or transplanting equipment could be used; for all machines for purposes of this kind are designed to operate by sliding through a fairly smooth soil surface. Any considerable amount of trash on the surface would make such implements useless. It was imperative, therefore, that I be prepared in advance to deal with trash on the surface, if green manure crops were so heavy they could not be put into the ground completely. The outcome of that necessity was a marker which would roll over the land, smooth or otherwise, and, without furrows, indicate the rows and the hill spaces in them. Rolling rather than sliding motion was the obvious answer. The marker was made from two discarded wagon wheels. These were fitted on their rims with lugs that would "track" the land at one-foot intervals; the axle upon which they turned was designed for row widths of three, three and a half, four, and five feet. With this implement I felt confident that any surface, however trashy, could be planted.

I was to find later that its ability to negotiate a trashy surface was not the most notable virtue of this marker. Even more important was the fact that, every time a marker lug touched the ground, it compressed with some 150 pounds of weight a vertical column of soil directly beneath the bottom of the track it made. This compression served to reconnect the soil particles which had necessarily been separated by the stirring of the surface. Pressing these particles together again restored what we may call the "wicking action" of the soil, enabling capillary water to rise without interruption to the bottom of the marker track. Anyone who has used an oil lamp will perceive the significance of this.

Compression was the principle upon which the marker worked. Where the idea originated, I do not know. Perhaps it was the result of an illustration we used to see in one of our soil texts. The illustration was intended to show the student how a well prepared seedbed should look. The light color of the surface soil indicated that this loose, "well prepared" surface soil had been dried out by wind and sunshine—as is always true—even though the area presented was supposedly ideal for seed growth. Included in the picture was a heel print. The moist condition of this compressed spot, darker in color, proved that capillary water climbed the vertical column of soil immediately under it. The comparatively dry condition of the rest of the soil surface showed that, in the loose soil, the capillary connection with the deep underground water supply had been broken. Thirty years ago, the picture meant nothing more than a clean-cut photo of an exceptionally well prepared soil in good tilth (according to established standards). Fitted into the new scheme of soil management, it becomes a significant guide to better methods of planting seeds and transplanting plants.

It is impossible now to trace the effects of the old picture on my thinking about soil conditions during a thirty-year period. But that scarcely matters. The important thing is that after thirty years the idea actually incubated. At this writing, the incubation of the idea is about as far as the process has gone. No one, either among practical farmers or among professional agriculturists, seems willing to accept an idea so different from conventional methods of planting and transplanting.

Every crop we planted in 1939 and 1940 was established by use of this compression marker. More than eighty-five thousand plants were involved, without any artificial watering whatever. Seventy-five thousand of the plants were shipped from southern Georgia in hot weather, yet no water was used in transplanting them. In some cases this may have been unwise, but this was not the chief cause of the considerable loss of plants in 1939. In 1940 there were no losses worth mentioning.

Our method involved encasing the plant roots in soil which already was being supplied with capillary water from below. Roots laid in the marker track and covered with firmed earth were considered properly set. They stood erect by next morning, always. Exceptions to this rule were sweet potatoes set in soil where the quantity of organic matter disked into the soil had been greatest. In 1939 only one field had enough organic matter, and this was the accumulation of several years of dead weed stalks. The field was on a high ridge, and was of sand so light that summer crops had died out for lack of water. The only plants that could survive the hot summers were uncultivated ones like weeds. It was impossible, therefore, for the owner to rent this land to the neighboring gardeners or to manage it successfully himself. That is how it happened to have grown up in weeds for several years. When I leased it, this field became the first area on which I tried to develop workable methods of disking organic matter into the soil. The weed debris was so heavy in places that it could not all be worked in, and some spots tracked by the marker failed to become moist with capillary water afterward, because a layer of underlying weed fragments would absorb the water and keep it from rising to the surface.

Such details had to be learned. Before we learned them in 1939, we lost a good percentage of the sweet potato plants that were set in this field, because the particular site they occupied was underlaid by absorbent organic matter that kept their roots from getting water. From this experience we learned to scan the marker tracks in transplanting; if the bottoms were not moist, even on a hot day, we searched for the underlying organic matter that prevented moisture from rising to the surface. A year later, after four-foot rye had been put into the surface of this field, sweet potatoes planted exactly the same way were ninety per cent perfect stand. This is good for sweet potatoes in any situation. Success depended upon the actual presence of capillary moisture in the marker track.

One highly amusing incident occurred in this connection. While the tomato field was being transplanted in 1939, one of the neighbors, having observed that something unusual was being done in our field, came over to inspect the technique we were following in transplanting. When he saw that we were using such "careless" methods, he shook his head sadly and cautioned us that plants handled so recklessly could not grow satisfactorily. His displeasure was evident when he left the field a little while later. He considered us a stiff-necked lot, unwilling to learn from a farmer of more experience. Later in the season, when we were picking the crop, he got as much pleasure from complimenting us on our superior stand of plants as we did from noting his changed point of view. He even enjoyed laughing at himself; but the whole situation was still mysterious to him.

The conventional method of transplanting large areas such as commercial gardens, tobacco fields, and so on, usually involves heavy machinery, made heavier by the load of water it must carry to provide a little for each plant. Our method, involving only two people, a hoe, and a basketful of plants, seems ridiculously inadequate by comparison. The results of this simple method, though, were far better both in 1939 and in 1940 than the customary method achieved locally. With the exception of sweet potatoes, we had better stands of plants than our neighbors had in 1939; and in 1940, because of the extremely wet condition of the land, we could go ahead while our neighbors had to wait for the land to dry out enough for their horses or tractors and transplanting machines to operate. (Incidentally, about five weeks elapsed before the land was dry enough.) The dry weather of 1939 and the excessively wet weather of 1940 seemed not to affect our results. The catch of tomato plants was virtually perfect each season.

It may seem that an unwarranted amount of space has been used in this discussion of the preparation of the land for transplanting and in describing the methods used. Justification for such extended elaboration of this matter is found in its illustrative value; for, if any doubt remains in the reader's mind as to the folly of plowing, comparison of the water relationships that follow plowing and disking ought quickly to dispel any such misgivings.

If rye three feet tall had been plowed in on this land, no capillary water would have been available to plant roots next day, or even next week. Scientists agree on the drying effect of great quantities of organic matter plowed in, though their reasoning on the subject is somewhat different from mine. The behavior of these plants, set in compacted, disked soil, should forever dispose of any faith in plowing. It proves perfectly the superiority of disking when great quantities of organic matter are involved.

If the purpose of breaking the land is the removal of trash so it will not interfere, then the moldboard plow is the only implement to use in starting preparation of the land for crops. It happens, however, that the crying need is for a soil surface similar to that which we find in nature—with all of the organic matter near enough to the surface that plant roots can appropriate the products of its decay. This being the object, the way to attain it is to use an implement that is incapable of burying the trash it encounters; in other words, any implement except the plow.

If space permitted, much could be said about the behavior of crops on land prepared in the unorthodox fashion that has been described. The first season's crops did not produce a satisfactory yield, because little organic matter was available to supply the needed nutriment materials. Sweet potatoes on the disked weed field were the lone exception, and, had their stand been good, they would have returned a profit that season.

The selection of sweet potatoes as a commercial crop for this latitude (only ten miles from Lake Erie) will puzzle many readers. I had observed that they grew successfully in home gardens; that they had earlier been a commercial crop locally; and that yields locally averaged much higher than the average for the United States. A successful exotic crop would enable me to succeed in a market dominated by some of the country's most capable gardeners. No novice could compete with these skilled men in the production of cauliflower, cabbage, sweet corn, or lettuce; but I hoped that, with a high yielding, non-competing crop, I might survive and make some money.

My confidence in the sweet potato arose from the fact that I had produced on very thin soil, many years earlier, a small amount of this crop, the yield of which had figured about twelve hundred bushels per acre. The fact that this amazing yield was produced by soil treatment practically identical with the new methods I intended using encouraged me to hope that I could duplicate that small-scale result on a field basis. While I failed to do this, careful appraisal of the behavior of the crop justified some important constructive conclusions.

For one thing, the sweet potato crop theoretically requires 120 days of frost-free weather to mature. Weather records show that in Ohio, where I was planting, about four months intervene between the last spring frost and the first frost of the autumn. However, in 1939 these plants produced a mature crop in just sixty days, proving that the time element is not as important as the ready availability of the wanted plant foods. Owing to the poor stand of plants, as well as to the slow start most of them got, the yield for the field was but little above the average for the country; but the speedy showing of those which did get a fair start made it impossible to overlook the implication that better mixing in of organic matter with the soil would have resulted in a tremendous crop. This one and a half acre field alone could easily have paid the entire expense of machinery and operating costs of the whole farm and produced a profit besides.

Of equal importance was the discovery that sweet potatoes produced in this relatively dry climate may not require artificial curing as do the roots produced in the much more humid climate of the Southeastern states. My crop of 1939 could have been stored successfully just as the roots came out of the ground. It is by no means certain that the crops of other seasons would be as free from moisture as those of 1939; indeed, it is known that sweet potatoes produced in my area of Ohio do rot easily; however, it may be true that sweet potatoes produced largely from organic decay are less moist than those produced in a highly mineral soil. This possibility deserves investigation.

My faith in the sweet potato as the potential mortgage lifter was high, and I had acted accordingly, by transplanting five acres of the farm to this crop. None of the land except this first field had any considerable amount of organic matter—only the self-grown weeds. The catch of plants from the other fields was excellent, but because the substance was not in the land, these fields did not produce marketable roots. In 1940 the only sweet potatoes set out were put on the field that had done best in 1939. The catch of plants was very good, at least 90 per cent; but during the entire growing season there was not enough heat and moisture (at the same time) to permit the plants to produce a satisfactory crop.

Considering all of the evidence, it seems that, for all but the occasional, exceptionally cool seasons, the sweet potato is a dependable crop for this section, provided the land is well filled with organic matter at the surface, and provided the transplanting is properly done. It should be remembered that all of these plants were from southern Georgia, and were transplanted without watering after having been two or three days on the road in hot weather. Even with these handicaps, the catch, wherever capillary water was available when the plants were set out, was exceptional. I expect, therefore, to continue to try to produce sweet potatoes on a limited scale. Whether the product could be stored without artificial drying is really unimportant in this section, for the Cleveland market would at any time absorb the production of a few hundred local acres. The first-grade potatoes I grew in 1939 brought a premium price throughout the season.

When the outcome of the 1939 season had been analyzed, it seemed fair to assume that, had the supply of organic matter been sufficient in all fields, the sweet potato crop alone would have made it a profitable season. With this view of the matter, I was not discouraged, even though considerable money had been lost in 1939. I could not foresee, of course, that the 1940 season would be so extremely wet in the months when crops usually are getting started that the plants could not even be put in. This was true throughout this entire section. None of the gardeners succeeded in planting any considerable part of their usual acreage of vegetables. Some prepared the land repeatedly, even to distribution of the fertilizers, then did not have an opportunity to plant. I was lucky enough to get tomatoes into the ground on the only day between May 25 and July 4 that the work could have been done. Many fields were set to tomatoes in mid-July with plants that were ready for setting in mid-May. It was a very unusual season in every way. Therefore, since I received income from only about two acres in 1940, quite naturally I did not make any money. The season's effort just about paid for itself.

Like 1939, 1940 taught me some important lessons, even

though it disappointed me financially. There was ample organic matter, in the form of tall rye, on every field. Seasonal conditions made it impossible to get the rye disked in at a suitable time for planting the planned crops. With the exception of a few minor crops, the entire farm income was from tomatoes, beans, and cucumbers. Each of these crops was handicapped by weather conditions, but the results in each instance were encouraging and profitable.

The tomato crop around Cleveland in 1940 was disappointing. Many growers said it was the poorest season of their experience. Extremes of wet followed by drought, and again by wet weather, produced many cracked fruits. Though there were many such in my crop, there never was a time when it was impossible to get marketable tomatoes. Most growers had to abandon their early plantings even before their later acreage began to bear. I had but a single acre in cultivation. It increased in vigor as the season advanced, and the product was in good demand at premium prices all the time. Sometimes I got as much as 25 cents a peck above the top price in the Cleveland market. One reason for this was the exceptional weight of my packed pecks. Fifteen pounds is the standard weight of a peck of tomatoes. In 1940 my crop averaged more than that. It was not unusual for a peck to weigh sixteen pounds, and many weighed seventeen. Most local tomatoes in 1940 weighed from ten to fourteen pounds to the peck. The exceptional weight of mine, and the quality it indicates, justified the premium prices I received.

The bean crop was extraordinary, too, for several reasons. At the outset, six feet of rye had to be disked down before the field could be planted to beans. And when I say *down,* the expression is accurate. In many places so thick a layer of rye covered the surface that the disks did not actually touch the ground. There was no help for it. If beans were to be planted in this land, they had to be planted in spite of this condition, and so they were. The marker was run over the field, spacing rows three feet apart. Wherever the marker had "walked" over the straw without even parting it, the straw was parted by hand and the beans were planted on the solid ground, covered with a hoeful of earth from near by, and left to their fate. The stand of beans was so perfect that it was commented upon by trained agricultural men who saw the plot during the succeeding weeks. This indicated to me, at least, that a finely worked seedbed may not be essential to success. Compare this method of planting with the one described by Ben Ames Williams, as I have quoted him on page 32 from *Come Spring*.

Since it was impossible, with the marker I had, to plant rows closer together than three feet, it seemed a waste of good space to plant this area to beans only; therefore alternate rows were planted to cucumbers. This spaced the cucumbers properly; moreover, it gave me an additional crop to grow and observe. Limitations imposed by distance made it difficult for me to get the bean crop to market, as well as to get labor out from town to pick it, so it was well that no more beans than I harvested had to be handled.

Cucumbers proved more significant as objects of observation than as a source of income. Yet, considering that this was ordinary farm land, converted to experimental garden use by the disking in of a single crop of rye, it is not surprising that beans produced better than cucumbers. Beans are better suited to hard soil conditions than are cucumbers. Indeed, cucumbers are quite insistent upon an abundance of readily available plant food—preferably decay products. In this raw soil, only partly prepared for a good cucumber crop, the quality of the fruit that actually matured was extremely high. Every cucumber was as dark green as if it had been grown under perfect growing conditions. Several grocers who took quantities said they expected to sell them as hothouse grown. There would have been no fraud, for the quality was there. From the excellent quality of this fruit, it may be determined that any land that had been prepared by a succession of disked-in crops should produce cucumbers of unsurpassed quality and in great quantity.

Beans, however, were more remarkable in their response to this supposedly crude environment. Aside from the perfect germination already described, they continued mass blooming as long as there was available water in the soil to permit it. The plants held buds for blossoms, blossoms, immature beans, and beans ready for picking all at the same time through a long period—several weeks. Naturally, the yield had to be harvested over a correspondingly long period. Five pickings—all full but the last—were required. And, even after we had quit harvesting beans for market, enough late-set beans matured to provide plenty of seed for a good-sized bean field again.

Such persistence of cropping is unusual in beans. Most bean plantings are abandoned after one picking, or at most two. One local gardener who was equipped for irrigation told me that he had used nitrogen in order to stimulate bean cropping. He seemed proud to announce that he had had to pick his plants twice—after using nitrogen and irrigation. My crop was produced without either, and under conditions that assuredly would have made irrigation profitable at certain stages. Considering the severity of the prevailing weather conditions, the fact that these beans produced two hundred bushels of marketable beans per acre seems to me quite important. It seems to indicate that, if the land were so thoroughly filled with organic matter at the surface that it would again begin to look black, it should then grow bean plants that would commence yielding in spring and not cease until frost in the fall.

In all of this, no mention has been made of the fact that in 1940 no nitrogen fertilizer was used anywhere on the farm. That fact is one of outstanding importance in summing up the significance of the project. It will be obvious to any experienced reader that such crops as I have described could not have been produced without a plentiful supply of nitrogen. It will be equally clear that land of ordinary quality could not have supplied the necessary nitrogen for good quality garden products. Only black land—black with decaying organic matter—is ever expected to produce good crops without the addition of some nitrogen in the form of fertilizers. Indeed, without applied nitrogen, such land usually produces no marketable crop at all; and the plants exhibit a yellowish, rather than a healthy, dark green, color. Usually, too, no crop at all results from such nitrogen-starved plants.

As far as I was concerned, these plants were nitrogen-starved for I had intentionally omitted the use of nitrogen. The reasons for its omission would be difficult to state, but in my home experience we often had too much, rather than too little, nitrogen, and for that reason we often suffered serious crop setbacks. Because of these unfavorable experiences with nitrogen, I have never believed very strongly in its application.

Full explanation of how my recent crops managed to get a sufficient nitrogen supply is given in a later chapter, the strangest, perhaps, of the whole book. It partakes of the mystery of Aladdin, along with the romance of smuggling, but it is a very true story withal. Reserved for another chapter, too, is the story of how these crops defeated insects and diseases. The success of the crops was in no way owing to the use of insecticides, fungicides, or other means of battling pests, for none of these aids was used.

The net result of these two years of field work was the conviction on my part that the human animal assumes in error that he can really improve on nature's well-designed arrangements for nourishing plants. Faced with the necessity of thwarting competitive growth in order to promote the plants he favors, man has rashly overstepped the bounds of biological propriety by performing operations on the soil which waste the very plant foods his own plants require. The troubles he has, then, are the consequences of this original error. My tests have proved that, to avoid trouble, man needs only to return to methods imitative of nature's own. Quite a cheerful discovery, that.

7

SOIL BY MACHINE

WITH A GOOD DEAL OF TRUTH it may be said that we have allowed our soils to degenerate chiefly because there have been too generous supplies of good soil everywhere over the face of the earth. The existence of these fertile areas, and particularly the discovery by Columbus, at an opportune time, of a few hundred million extra acres previously unheard of and unsuspected, served to make man's way easier. As long as this condition obtained, it was not imperative that man learn how to provide tillable soils where none existed.

It is now time, however, that the truth be realized. *We can recreate soil wherever good soil formerly existed, and we can do so by machinery.* Any exceptions to this categorical statement will be found to result from human mistakes, as, for example, land made untenable by the silting of the streams that naturally would drain it, or desert sands robbed of both their water-holding clay and the conveniently shallow water table. For the whole category of areas that have suffered merely water erosion, however severe, there is still the definite assurance that as good soil as ever existed upon them can be restored. Much the same can be said of areas damaged by wind erosion, or, by excessive cropping and grazing.

Nature did not put precisely the same kind of soil everywhere. There has been a great variety of difference in soils because of the complex forces by which they were created.

That we need not go into here, except to say that the one thing all soils had in common was organic matter in or on the surface. We need not be interested in the slightest as to whether the soil was what the scientist calls a podzol, a prairie, a chernozem, or just plain dirt; the significant thing about each of these, in the virgin state, was the quantity of organic matter it contained, which implies also the conditions under which the moisture supply would permit the maintenance of a certain amount of organic matter in the soil.

It is not even necessary that soil be of brunette shade in order to produce well, although soils made productive by nature always reveal their quality through the presence in them of decaying organic matter, which is necessarily dark in color. (The single exception to this statement—if indeed it can be called an exception—is the desert area to which irrigation water has to be supplied. Such soil is rich by reason of the suitable minerals which are brought up from the soil depths by water, which, on evaporation, leaves the minerals in abundance. The dependence of desert soil on irrigation really rules it out of this discussion.) Enough organic matter can be put into the surface at a single disking to make any ordinary soil productive almost immediately; yet the quantity of organic matter introduced at one time may be too little for its decay to influence the color of the soil. This was true of the soil I farmed in 1940, with rye three to six feet tall disked in to serve as the organic source of nutrients for my crops. I could never detect any of the dark tint which is associated with organic decay, yet the crops behaved as if there was plenty of fertility in the soil.

The blackness of virgin soil is the result of a cumulative process more or less complex, since it involves repeated deposits annually of plant, and possibly animal, debris upon the soil surface—to which must be added the destructive effect of an innumerable biologic population which lived and died in this environment and contributed in turn toward its enrichment. The effects of the resulting black deposit in and just under the surface—not in an impassable layer several inches under the surface—kept all the water absorbed by the soil in the same zone that plant roots would be searching for it. The supposition that for hundreds of years nothing had disturbed its surface does not satisfactorily account for the fertility of the soil. We have developed some useless theories in that field. Men have come to feel, for example, that centuries are necessary for the development of a productive soil. The satisfying truth is that a man with a team or a tractor and a good disk harrow can mix into the soil, in a matter of hours, sufficient organic material to accomplish results equal to what is accomplished by nature in decades.

In nature, long periods were occupied in developing the black OMP of the meadow or forest because the mixing in of organic matter was a task mainly for bugs and worms. The soil surface was their home environment. They worked slowly but painstakingly, and they developed that first essential of all life, the health of the land.

This has been true, necessarily, of the natural formation of soils everywhere. The grasses of the plains developed thicker, blacker layers of organic matter in the surface because they were annual plants. They died down each fall. New growth came up each spring. The dead plants accumulated, and were mulled over by the living things of the soil surface. Only a few years of this process were necessary to develop the tough sod the settlers found when first they undertook the gigantic task of plowing it. It is not surprising that in many instances ten-ox teams were necessary for the purpose.

The forest did not lay down organic layers as deep or as black. Why? Because the decay of leaves each year was more complete, and the material was re-used in tree growth. The farmer who cleared the land got merely the "crumbs" from the forest's "table." It could not be otherwise.

With the halo of mystery thus stripped from the mechanics of natural soil building, it no longer appears impossible for men to create their own soils as needed, and where needed. It has to be remembered, too, that when the soil of an old forest site has been restored to a condition as productive as the one which originally existed, there will not be the necessity of waiting for stumps and roots to rot out, as was once the case, before the land can be handled profitably. Many a farmer of another generation found that, by the time these interferences were out of the way, the soil was no longer productive. The modern farmer has a big advantage in that he can simply disk in a crop of green manure whenever he chooses and withdraw a good portion of the decay products in the first year's production. And the process lends itself to infinite repetition.

Historically, we are told, soils are very different in their origins. So different, in fact, that their adaptation to specific crops is affected. The more correct view is that these idiosyncracies of soils were developed only after the original organic profile had been destroyed and most of the organic matter used up. On good virgin land, the chief production limitations are due to climatic factors rather than to the peculiarities of soil origins. My experience in growing sweet potatoes is a case in point: the plants had completed their growth in two months, rather than four, on land near Lake Erie quite outside their normal habitat. The presence of sufficient organic matter in the soil, a plentiful supply of water in the organic matter, and the prevalence of hot, sunny weather all combined to overcome any adverse factors. I had been told by a Virginian, a local buyer for a chain-store organization, that sweet potatoes could not be grown successfully in this locality. I was disinclined to believe him. When the crop matured, he bought part of it, paying about 25 cents a bushel above the prevailing market price for the best southern-grown roots.

Personally, I doubt whether one type of soil is any better suited than another to a given crop, provided each soil is supplied with an abundance of organic matter in the surface. Note the fact that a *liberal* quantity of organic matter is stipulated, and that it must be *in the surface*. If two soils so treated are subjected to similar climatic conditions, however different they may be in origin, their respective crops will be too little different to indicate a substantial superiority for either. In other words, sweet potatoes—definitely preferring sandy soils—will produce heavily on tight clays, provided first the clays have been richly endowed with a supply of organic matter in the surface. I have already produced parsnips in heavy clay so treated; the yield figured 1,220 bushels to the acre. Parsnips ordinarily are grown in sandy loam.

I am not prepared to say that the mere disking of organic matter into the soil surface is the complete remedy for all adverse soil conditions. There are too many unusual conditions of which I have too little knowledge. My acquaintance with soils is not broad enough to justify a complete generalization for all soils. However, unless we are prepared to question the universal application of theories and principles that have been proved by generations of use in other fields, we must admit the widespread applicability of this idea of surface mixed organic matter as a remedy for many, if not all, of our soil troubles. Also, the fact that all applicable experiment station results support the idea gives additional weight to the contention I have advanced.

We do not have any implement that is well suited to the incorporation of organic matter into soil surfaces under all conditions. The disk harrow is a good one to use under a great variety of conditions, but even it has its limitations. It can not be used in soil that is very stony, even though it would successfully follow the plow in such case. It is difficult to manage on side hills. Unless special techniques in its management are used, the disk harrow does not leave a smooth surface. Some of these difficulties could be overcome by the use of power lifting devices, but such devices are of no use to farmers who have only horses. Yet, until somebody invents a better implement, the disk harrow is the one tool that can be substituted for the plow in the successful preparation of land (not in sod) for cropping. Its use for this purpose, however, is so different from its traditional role of smoothing up after the plow that a few hints should help the farmer who wants to try it. Such a routine as the following will work best:

1) Be sure the disks are sharp and free from rust. Have the entire implement in good working order, all grease cups or other oiling arrangements fully supplied with lubricant. This last is especially important, for the disk harrow was not designed for heavy work like land breaking. Work of this kind will subject it to very unusual strains, so it should be kept perfectly lubricated all of the time.

2) Use only the front section of the implement as long as you are trying to cut into the soil. Detach the rear section after reaching the field, for it will be useful in the final work of smoothing up. If it is allowed to follow along while the front section is trying for depth, its weight will tend to keep the front section from running deep enough.

3) Weight the front section heavily. Here is where some of the extra strain comes in. The plow is so designed that it naturally seeks a certain sub-surface level and therefore does not require weighting. The only force that urges the disk harrow into the ground is gravity. Weight adds to this force.

4) Set the disks to cut in—how much is difficult to say—but try adjustments at different angles to see what the effect is. Do not be surprised, though, if, on the first trip over a field, you can not see that the disks have cut in consistently. Usually they will have cut in slightly, even though the dirt is not thrown up sufficiently to be seen.

5) One important procedure to observe in putting in a tall, strawy crop, like rye, is to lay it all down in one direction, then cut across it at an angle. This serves to cut the straw into lengths that can be worked into the soil easily. For this work, of course, the disks need to be sharp. Also, there are limits to the amount of rye that can be managed by the disk harrow, however sharp the disks may be. Experience is the best guide here; no rules can be laid down.

6) It may be that a clay soil in a very dry condition will not yield at all to the disks. In that case, it probably will help to run over the field once anyway. This will ride down the green manure crop so that it will lie closer to the surface. Some improvement in moisture content of the surface soil should result. Later, say in a week, a second attempt to cut into the surface is likely to be successful. Failing this, wait for rain.

7) Farmers who have always used double-disk-harrows may need to be told that when the front section alone is used it should always be lapped half way each time in order to leave the land

smooth. This is very important if the disks are cutting in; less so, of course, when they are not.

8) Following the routine outlined below will make it possible for the operator to do a smooth job, or at least a smoother job would result than if this method were not followed. You may be able to work out a better plan for your own situation. This is offered as a suggestion, assuming a square or rectangular field:

> Decide first which way you wish to make all turns. With some outfits, left turns can be made better; with others, the turn is easier to the right. Since all turns are to be the same, it is necessary to determine this in advance.
>
> Start along one side of the field and follow the boundary to the limits of the field. Turn along the border and follow it about four or five *widths* of the harrow; then turn and follow a line parallel to the first direction to the opposite limits; return to the beginning.
>
> Repeat by lapping the harrow a half width *toward the middle of the field* as you follow the earlier track. At the ends no lapping is possible, since in going one direction the previous cut of the implement is to your right, or in going the opposite direction it is to your left. At the ends you must make this change of sides.

In the above three paragraphs you have the simple directions for what may be called a "spiral" disking routine. If you begin by crossing one end of the field, then your progress is very gradually toward the opposite end, by these crosswise trips that inch over one half the width of the implement each time.

Also, after about ten times around the "spiral," you begin to catch up with the forward side of the original first-round track. At this point you may wonder what to do. The answer is to continue just as you began, lapping one half width all the time, until you reach the opposite end of the field with the forward track. Then you will have double disked the first ten rounds and the last ten rounds, while all between will have been quadruple disked. In other words, most of the surface will have been stirred four times with the disks, but the end strips will have been stirred only twice.

It could be that, by the time you have gone over the entire field once in this fashion, it will be in proper condition for the final smoothing. However, I have usually found that, in order to prepare land sufficiently well to make the use of cultivating equipment possible, it is necessary to repeat this process exactly as indicated, except that the disk is run crosswise the direction taken by the original work. Of course, if the routine just described was preceded by the operator's going once over the area and riding down the green manure crop, the quadruple disking operation will have reduced this material to six-inch lengths. In that case, it is likely that once or twice over with the reassembled harrow may serve to complete the seedbed sufficiently to make planting possible. Do not expect it to look as smooth as it would if the land had been plowed, even after you have done all the smoothing possible. And there may be at best some trash visible here and there. Neither the lack of perfect smoothness nor an occasional bit of trash will be fatal to the use of ordinary equipment; though in planting it probably will be necessary to delay the work occasionally long enough to remove from planter shoes accumulations of the trash. A little patience in this respect will be richly rewarded later, for you will find that the crop will be much less subject to drought damage, will require absolutely no nitrogen fertilizer, and will yield out of all proportion to customary standards. This will apply, regardless of the kind of crop grown.

You may or may not have to smooth the final work of the disk with a drag. Certainly you will not have clods to contend with. Compacting is likely to be important if the weather is dry. However, the disk harrow may be used for this purpose, not as effectively as a regular roller or corrugated compacting implement, but with the disks set straight and heavily weighted it does a fair job.

One caution should be given concerning cultivation. I came near ruining one corn crop because I failed to discover that there was enough uncut straw in the surface to lift slightly almost every hill of corn as the cultivator passed. The rye on this field had been six feet tall. It had proved impossible to work it in at all, and much of it lay there, not even cut into sections. If you should have that same condition to contend with, delay the first cultivation until the straw has had time to disintegrate sufficiently that it can not interfere. This will not require long, providing a little rain falls. If the weather is dry following the planting of the corn, two or three weeks may be required. Success in this respect is wholly a matter of careful observation and management.

Of course, if you encounter such conditions as have just been described, you can not hope to plant the area by means of ordinary equipment. It was to make planting possible in such a surface that I devised the pressure marker. Planting after this rig was used had to be done by hand, but the manner in which the crops grew fully justified the hand method. It can readily be seen that, if the planter can expect several times the customary yield per acre from soil so re-created, he is justified in conceding something to painstaking care. Again, if it is possible, by renewing the soil with green manures, to cut the usual acreage to one-fifth, one-third or one-half, the concession is scarcely a concession at all.

Eventually, it is to be hoped, suitable implements will

be devised and put on the market. Meanwhile, I anticipate modifying to some extent the plans I followed in 1939 and 1940. Instead of growing green manure in quantities sufficient to make incorporation impossible with the disk harrow, I hope to spend more than one season in getting the land ready for crops; then, after working a two- to three-foot rye crop in early in spring, some summer crop will be seeded to be put in later—to be followed by rye again. This would involve two green manure crops each year. Not many such short crops would be required, it would seem, to make the soil begin to look black again. And, treasonable as it may seem, I hope that while this routine is in progress each crop will be accompanied by the germination of multitudes of weed seeds. Disking in immature weed plants with each green manure crop may be an excellent way to reduce weed growth. More is said about this in a later chapter.

It might easily be that some land would be so refractory to disking that the first crop of green manure could not be worked in at all. This event need not stop your efforts. Do not plow it in. Or, if you do plow it in, plow the land again immediately, and a little deeper. If you do plow twice, you will have created a superior soil situation by that means, for the second plowing will have returned to the root zone your mass of green manure. In this position the disk harrow will be able to reach and cut it. To your delight you will discover that no clods form in connection with the work, so the follow-up operations usually necessary can be cut quite short.

Double plowing is not a new device. Friends of mine recall that the farmers of a previous generation often plowed down clover in the fall, then plowed the land again in spring for potato growing. Apparently the method worked well.

However, much decay of the clover must have occurred during the winter, and the leaching away of much of the products would have been inevitable. Moreover, the decay of this material made it possible for the farmer to do a much neater job of plowing in spring than might have been possible had the land been plowed twice in quick succession. Many a farmer who decides to plow down a heavy green manure crop and follow up immediately with a second and slightly deeper plowing will be thoroughly disgusted with the idea before he has gone many furrows. The appearance of the resulting surface will be disheartening to farmers who have always taken pride in the neatness of their plowing.

The trouble here is not the appearance of the surface but our notion of what constitutes beauty. Few people realize how thoroughly we have become enslaved by the idea that nothing effective can be done toward preparing land to grow crops until the land has first been plowed. Plowing has been accepted as axiomatic—a necessary prelude to every other operation. Even though the work of the plow has been for many years associated with the deterioration of our land, we still have not awakened to the fact that, to solve the problem, we must cease plowing; or, if we wish to continue to use the plow, we must do the work in a different way. The methods we use, whatever they be, must produce a surface that is filled with debris that will rot. Let the surface of the soil wear a "beard" of exposed material, if need be. That condition will eventually become beauty in the soil. "Pretty is as pretty does" is not a new saying. It is particularly applicable here, for trash-filled soil alone is capable of the highest quality yields. The ancestry of a soil is a very minor matter in comparison with the present ability of that soil to supply to hungry roots a soil solution enriched by abundance of decay products.

An alternative to double plowing land that can not be managed by disking is to leave the area wholly undisturbed. This may seem an acknowledgment of failure, but the matter should not be prejudged. Much will happen to an intractable soil while the crop it has produced is decaying. The decay of a green manure crop, in place, will of itself serve to start a heavy soil surface on its way toward granulation. When granulation has proceeded sufficiently, a clay soil can be worked like sand. Moreover, if the crop in question produces seeds—which any annual crop will do—it will reseed itself naturally; and, without any work whatever, the farmer will have a second, volunteer crop of green manure to reckon with. This second crop will be very easily managed when the time comes to disk it in.

It has to be admitted frankly that the preceding paragraph is a deduction from the known effects of the practices described. For this reason, the conclusion may be considered vulnerable. My best suggestion is that anyone who is inclined to doubt the feasibility of the plan advanced should try it on an area of supposedly unmanageable clay. I have seen clay become so friable, under conditions that were comparable to those suggested here, that it could be raked about like sugar. The same clay, before treatment, was so solid that a sharp spade, with a man's weight upon it, was scarcely enough to make an impression upon the surface. I am certain, therefore, that further experimentation will sustain my contentions.

The abandonment of the first season's work in order to let nature cure the ills of the sod may seem a waste of time.

The economy of such a procedure must await confirmation until the outcome of subsequent crops can be observed. The eventual result will contain its own proof. And my guess is that those who know soils best will be the last to doubt the eventual outcome, for the renovating effect of decaying organic matter, which induces granulation of the soil, is well known and accepted. The only new thing about it is the method proposed for securing that effect.

Doubtless, the creation of soil where none now exists, through incorporation into the surface of materials grown upon the particular area, presents many difficulties not touched upon in this chapter. The idea is entirely too new to have been thoroughly investigated in all of its ramifications by a single unsponsored student in a single season of work. It is extremely doubtful, though, that the actual re-creation of soils presents any technical difficulties which can not be surmounted. The only requirement for the establishment of a new tillage system, apparently, is investigation along one or both of two lines: first, the adaptation of our customary use of existing surface-stirring implements to the job of incorporating liberal quantities of green manure; or, second, the invention of new equipment capable of disposing of all organic matter by surface mixing. No further time should be lost from the accomplishment of one or both of these objectives.

8

KING WEATHER DEPOSED

ALL PRACTICING FARMERS and students of agriculture are well aware of the controlling influence of weather in the growing of crops. To the city man a sunny day in midsummer may be a thrilling event, because it provides the ideal conditions for picnicking, hiking, and swimming. For thousands of farmers near by the same day may be an occasion of disaster involving the local food supply, in which the city dweller, as well as the husbandman, has a vital stake. Rains that arrive a day too late to save potatoes, beans, and lettuce affect both producer and consumer, but the producer more seriously.

Weather has always been considered in the category of "acts of God," and so it may very well be. Equally, however, it may be said that "God helps those who help themselves." There is nothing to be achieved here by bringing up once again the famous dispute between the Forest Service and the Weather Bureau as to whether forests actually increase the rainfall. Nor is it to the point, perhaps, to conjecture with the scientists concerning the effect of England's deforestation in the seventeenth and eighteenth centuries on present-day climate in the British Isles. But it may be useful to point out that man has it in his power to disturb some of the moisture conditions essential to plant growth, and that, by extension, he partly controls some of those conditions.

Man can conserve the moisture laid down by the heavens,

or he can waste it. The earth he took over originally was covered everywhere by a water-soaked, sometimes odorous sponge of humus. Nature maintained this water-catching cover through successive plant generations, wherever man did not disturb, and continues to maintain it down to this very hour. By imitating nature, man could have enjoyed such benefits as he has never dared hope for; by disregarding the obvious example she set for him, he has courted disaster.

Irregular moisture has been regarded as the most important weather condition controlling crop growing. With respect to moisture, the absorbent mat we find everywhere in nature serves a purpose which has not been recognized in agricultural literature. For lack of a better term, we may call this its "reservoir" purpose.

Farmers leave their hay stacked in the field exposed to all the rain that falls. They know that none of the rainfall can sink deeper than the upper few inches, because the porous tissues of the hay must first be filled. Since every inch of this top layer of hay will catch and hold nearly an inch of rainfall, the underlying hay is protected.

Knowing this, we should understand that if enough organic matter is disked into the soil surface it will constitute to its full capacity a reservoir in which a large proportion of the rainfall will be retained. If enough absorbent material has been provided to hold an inch or two of rainfall, then, when rain is falling, an inch or two of it will be retained in the surface. Naturally, this spongy mass will supply water—richly endowed with the minerals it takes from the decaying material in which it is held—to crops which otherwise would suffer seriously in the intervals between rains.

Not having this conception of the service of such a mantle

of porous material, scientists have reasoned about water chiefly in terms of capillary movement within the soil. And, strangely enough, some scientists have believed, from results of their tests, that there is little such movement in the upper layers of soil. If anybody doubts that such conclusions have been introduced into serious scientific literature, it may be interesting to relate a brief conversation I had in September, 1937, with a crop specialist I had known for nearly twenty years. It ran about like this: I had suggested doubt as to the propriety of plowing. He quickly asked, "What's wrong with plowing?" "Interferes with capillarity," I replied. He had a ready answer: "Tests show that there isn't as much capillary movement in the soil as we used to believe existed—it's relatively unimportant in many cases." "Well," I replied, "in unplowed land there must be enough upward capillary movement between rains to keep the vegetation alive." Mine was the last word.

He was correct in his statements. Such tests have been made. They were made, like all soil experiments, on plowed soil. The "reservoir" for water lies several inches deep in the plowed soil; and, since it literally robs the upper soil layers of their water as well as shutting off upward movement of capillary water rising from deeper in the soil, no other results of such tests could have been expected. If such tests were made in soil where grass is growing, the story would be entirely different.

The very nakedness of plowed land should of itself indicate a lack of capillary water in the surface. If capillary water were present, seeds would sprout and grow, for seeds are always present. Or had you noticed that the only bare soil in most landscapes is that which has recently been plowed?

I discovered that highly significant fact only a few months ago; though I had seen it daily throughout a lifetime. Since plowed land is always bare, and since practically all other land, save areas like the Sahara, is covered with greenery of some sort—which could not exist without a continual supply of water—it follows, even without tests, that there is no capillary water in the upper layers of freshly plowed soil.

It may be repeated here that, while God, not man, controls the weather, it is nevertheless given to man to control some of the fruits of weather, and of these perhaps the most important is the natural moisture of the soil surface. The first essential in this respect is to grasp the dissimilarity of water relations in plowed and unplowed lands. The next is to understand that the weather which kills vegetation on cultivated land may also cause vegetation to thrive, or at least to show no ill effects, on uncultivated land. The final phase is to connect logically the importance of the organic matter profile with both plant growth and the weather conditions under which plants may prosper.

For purposes of this discussion we may assume as normal any soil surface that has been left unplowed, or any plowed soil that has had time to recover its normal capillary water movement (because of the disappearance by decay of the organic matter plowed in). All meadow and pasture land on farms, then, as well as the land occupied by the farm fences, may be considered as part of the natural landscape, even though it is also part of the land normally subject to plowing. It is natural landscape because in its profile there is nothing to prevent water from rising to the surface. Whatever interference may have been introduced in previous times by plowing has been disposed of by decay.

By and large, the "voltage" of any soil depends upon the accumulations of decayable material available in its surface. By this standard it would be true almost always that wilderness soils, unplowed for many years if ever plowed at all, would be more productive than similar soil that had been included regularly in rotation cropping. The unplowed soil has the advantage that economical use of all decay products has been the rule for the entire period since its last plowing. The grassland in rotation, on the other hand, has periodically had a large percentage of its accumulated material removed from the surface, resulting in the wasting of the decay products. This deliberate (though unwitting) periodic waste of soil resources, after being repeated several times, finally results in a low-grade soil where formerly the productivity was high. The final result is erosion. And, when erosion has started, we may be sure there is not much absorbent material left in the surface of the soil. The remaining light-colored stuff is almost identical with that which the glaciers shunted about in their time.

An experienced farmer allows some of his land to lie in grass for a few years in order that its "voltage" may be stepped up. The longer the area is in sod the more productive it is when it is again put to corn. However, the period in which it accumulates a new supply of organic matter to be wasted again by plowing is not sufficient to enable it to make the gains that would put it in its natural condition. Indeed, the progress seems always to be slightly on the down side. No trick yet discovered has made it possible to achieve positive gains regularly on land operated in continuous three- or four-year rotation. There are probably a few exceptional cases, but this is the general rule. The wastage caused by plowing usually more than balances the accumulations made in the interim. In fine, rotation of the type described is not a cure-all for impoverished soil, and, what is more important to the thesis of this chapter, it does not get at the water relations which are ultimately desirable.

It was shown in the last chapter that a farmer may quite abruptly step up the productiveness of his soil by simply short-circuiting the wasteful practice of plowing. By mixing into the surface the decayable material which the plow would inter, the farmer sets the stage for biologically economical practices hitherto unknown to modern farming. Aside from questions of plant nutrition, there are several ways in which the surface mixing of organic matter brings to focus friendly forces of growth which are unable to operate when land is plowed.

Every ton of organic matter mixed into the surface of the soil will be able to contain much more absorbed water than it could if buried at plow depth. Why? Because, being weighted down by so much less overlying soil, its volume will be greater. And organic matter, it must be remembered, retains water volumetrically, while the minerals of the soil must hold it only upon the outer surfaces of the particles. Water runs *into* organic fragments, while it squeezes in *between* particles of sand, silt, and clay. We can rightly expect, then, that any absorbent material we work into the surface of the soil will retain rain water much more effectively than would the same material if plowed in.

Indeed, if plowed in, organic matter gets no opportunity to catch and hold rainfall until that water has first forced its way several inches down between the mineral crystals. Under most conditions it is much easier for some of the water to run off the surface than for all of it to force its way down into the soil. This means, then, that when all the organic matter is in the surface of the soil, it is able to take in water from both above and below—and in greater volume because of the greater volume of the organic matter itself.

Undoubtedly the original black soils our forefathers knew could absorb directly, and as rapidly as it fell, several inches of rainfall in a few hours. It is unlikely that very much water ever leached through the zone of surface organic matter in those highly absorbent soils. The light, fluffy leaf mold, or the springy layer of grass roots, gradually became filled with rain water as it fell. In this connection I like to remember the story told by one of the best-known agronomists in this country. He was inspecting some highly organic soil lying near the top of a mountain slope when a heavy shower developed. The slope was a little less than 45 degrees. Those familiar with geometry will recognize this as rather steep land. This agronomist remained through the storm to observe the course of the water as it fell. He said that, so far as he could determine, none ran off. If any did so, he said, it certainly did not take any soil with it.

Disking heavy green manure crops into the surface of the soil, then, is an excellent way to create, precisely in the surface of the soil, a reserve of water upon which crop roots can draw continuously until it is used up. Such an arrangement is obviously superior to the principle of permitting the water to run down through the soil and hoping it will be brought back by capillarity. Aside from holding a plentiful reserve of water in the root zone, the mass of organic matter receives capillary water continually from below, which replaces, at least in part, the reserve from which plants are drawing. This reserve supply of water serves to tide crops over extended periods of drought which otherwise would damage them seriously. From such a source water can be made available during many more days of the growing season than could possibly be the case when surface conditions are such as to let some of the rainfall run off and be wasted. Here is "conservation of natural resources."

This, however, is only part of the story. The water stored in surface organic matter is constantly being used to assist in the decomposition of the material which holds it. It not only assists in this decay, but it dissolves and in turn holds the products released. Thus, as long as water is retained in the organic tissues, it is constantly being enriched by the cast-off substances of which the organic matter was composed. And all of this enrichment is in addition to the minerals which the capillary water has picked up and dissolved in the soil depths before the water has been absorbed by the organic matter. It can readily be seen that under these conditions many influences are working together effectively which could not do so if the organic matter were located six to eight inches deep, where relatively few plant roots reach.

At this point the reader should recall that, in the plowed soil, carbon dioxide is released into the upper layer of soil; and that this gas is prevented from becoming carbonic acid because of the necessary dryness of the upper layers. In the newer situation, with all of the organic matter just in the surface, there is provided an abundance of water in the vicinity in which the carbon dioxide can be dissolved. And, since carbonic acid is one of the most efficient of known natural solvents of minerals, its work in the surrounding crystalline rock particles serves to release for plant use quantities of phosphorus, potash, and other needed plant nutrients which would not otherwise be available.

The extent to which this release of minerals from the rock itself can take the place of applications of mineral fertilizers is something I am not prepared to discuss. It is an interesting and a very important question. Every farmer will want to know, and is entitled to know, the answer. If it is possible that the carbonic acid released in the soil will supply enough fresh minerals to supplement adequately the minerals drawn from organic sources, then the purchase of mineral fertilizers would be unnecessary. Only this much can be said safely: If a farmer succeeds in working into his soil enough organic matter to equal the supply held when the land first was opened for cropping, then he might reasonably hope to grow maximum crops without fertilizers. An easy way to test this principle is to leave unfertilized strips in all such fields. When it becomes impossible to find those unfertilized strips at harvest time, because the crop is equally good everywhere, then the necessity for fertilizers has vanished. Within a few years, no doubt, we shall have official information on this point.

And how may we expect the plant itself to react to the optimum conditions described? Just as any other being reacts to a constant supply of food. Plants will establish most of their millions of roots in the organic fragments. There is not the slightest chance here for plant food to be lost. The instant it is released, the water that contains it is moved into a plant root and sent upward into the plant. The matter of deep rooting of plants, which has been widely discussed in past years, becomes a dead issue. There ceases to be any need for roots to penetrate soil depths. Their food supply is in the surface. The water in this organic matter is busily engaged in wrecking the dead tissues in order to provide materials to be built into the new growth. Bacteria, too, are involved, and without them this process could not occur. The point is that "all things work together for good" in this instance; so close knit is the process that no opportunity is left anywhere for the loss of nutrient materials. Plant roots that go deep, other than for anchorage, in such a situation are working to the disadvantage of the plant they represent.

It will now be apparent that man can control to a very considerable extent the rainfall with which his land is endowed from season to season. The reasons sustaining this conclusion may be summarized as follows:

Under proper management, the soil may be caused to hold natural precipitation at just the level where plant roots normally seek the essential nutrients. The presence of an organic mass in the surface so enriches the water by solution that, volume for volume, the water thus treated will produce more plant growth than water held in the minerals alone. Water thus held in the organic mass becomes available to plants without the opportunity for essential plant nutrients to be wasted in any way.

Considering these important factors, it is not too much to suppose that ten inches of rainfall might accomplish as much as is ordinarily expected of twenty. Again, with ample rainfall, it may easily be possible to produce several times the average production figure for the country as a whole.

The truth about the weather is that man can indeed make the best of it—if he will.

9

TILE TREACHERY

"THE DRAINAGE of imperfectly drained and saturated soils used in crop production is a well established practice." True. In fact, tile drainage probably is too well established in many places. We have installed so much tile that the community water supply has been adversely affected, to say nothing of the even more serious problem of crop yields. The wisdom that grows from experience tells us that drain tile installed where it is not imperatively needed is the surest route to low crop production.

Perhaps the most serious indictments that can be drawn against tile drainage are these: first, that the land where the rain falls is likely to need the water after it has been carried away through the tile; and, second, that innocent people downstream are apt to be disturbed by floods that are needlessly high because of water wasted through unnecessary tile installations. Tile, then, is a disturbing factor in relation to both local water resources and frequently recurring floods. It consequently becomes the obligation of everybody concerned with the elimination of an aggravating wet spot to think far beyond that immediate need before deciding to throw additional water into the streams.

That much unnecessary tile is laid with full approval of farm specialists is indicated by this further quotation taken from page 723 of the United States Department of Agriculture *Yearbook*, 1938:

For years some farmers have seen wet spots in good fields "drown out" with loss of labor, fertilizer, and seed, not to mention the seldom considered rental value of the land. Yet they made little or no attempt at drainage until they changed from horses to tractors. When the heavy machinery mired down they decided to drain. Realizing the seriousness of the situation in holding up the sale of farm machinery, and possibly wishing to improve the farmers' ability to buy new equipment, one manufacturer published a bulletin on drainage *(Drain the Wet Land,* by R. A. Hayne, Chicago, 1921), even though the company produced no drainage tools.

These quotations indicate the authentic point of view among professional agriculturists and prove that unwise tile installations may actually be put in with full approval of farm advisers. Indeed, a careful reading of the entire chapter from which these quotations are taken fails to reveal any cautions against overdoing what is considered an excellent practice. The impression one gets is that the future success of farming rests to a large extent on the completeness with which the land area is drained. The writers certainly are not nervous from dread that too much tile is being laid in on farms.

"Wet spots" present the visual evidence that tile is apparently needed. They appear on land which originally did not permit water to stand. And as the years pass, more and more of the land that formerly needed no sub-surface drainage develops these wet spots. Before we can properly diagnose this mania for excessive drainage, we should know what these wet spots really are and why they develop where they do. It will help our analysis to consider the apparently complete lack of understanding of soil facts displayed some time ago at a meeting of potato growers when this matter came up for discussion. The incident is illuminating.

A drainage problem had been found on the land of one of these farmers. He had discovered that water stood in a certain low spot in one field. He knew that there was tile not far from where this water stood. Search after the water was gone disclosed that the tile was directly under the center of the pool. Examination at the outlet while the water still stood on the land showed that the tile was running, and that it was not loaded but that it could easily have removed the standing water. Yet the water stood for days just over this active tile line.

The land in question was heavy, lake-laid clay a few miles from Lake Erie. The verdict of the farmers in conference was that this heavy clay had been worked too much, or when it was too wet, and had become puddled. Clay in such condition conducts water only by very slow capillarity; so this verdict was probably correct. At any rate, it squares well with the slow rate at which the standing water disappeared. Troweling by the moldboard plow when soil is too wet does for it just what a sow does to the bottom of her wallow when she finds a little water standing in it. She smears the mud with a sort of sliding roll which effectively smoothes and seals the surface against the passage of water. The next time it rains she will have a nice place to wallow, and the water will remain until it evaporates.

No self-respecting sow would try to make a wallow unless the site were mineral in character—entirely free from straw, corn cobs, or other organic debris. These latter materials would drain away the water, because the open, cellular structure of organic matter is conducive to moisture flow.

These farmers evidently had good hog wallow material, which was precisely what they did not want. They had it not only at the foot of the slope, but all over the surrounding watershed. Obviously, what they needed to do was the converse of the sow's problem; they must provide organic drainage for the surrounding slope so the water would not converge on the low ground. Their faith in tile, and possibly their firm, hard-headed American belief that the more a thing costs the more it is worth, kept them from thinking of this simple and inexpensive solution of their problem.

Water that falls on the upper reaches of a slope cannot possibly find its way to the lower ground if the intervening soil is absorbent. Really absorbent soil simply cannot conduct water over its surface. There are two forces operating to prevent its doing so, and the action of either is usually sufficient. The vertical pull of gravity is fully capable of pulling water into the soil, provided the surface has not been made impervious. And gravity is reinforced by the capillary pull of any absorbent surface. Let us suppose that a roof is covered with a half-inch pad of blotting paper. How soon might we expect to see water dripping off the roof? Certainly not until the blotting paper itself was completely saturated. The identical thought applies to any slope over which water is accustomed to run. If the water succeeds in reaching the lower ground, it does so only because the condition of the surface forces it to run off.

In this connection it is very interesting to recall the remarks of a prominent agriculturist with whom I was discussing this problem. I suggested that little water could get away from a "cove" soil,[1] and he agreed. He reinforced the thought with the information that he had seen cove soil on 90 per cent slopes and had been unable—though he watched during a heavy rain—to observe any runoff.

If water will refuse to run off over a 90 per cent slope covered with a layer of absorbent material, surely we have a clue that may help solve the runoff problem on the slight slopes we usually farm. If we can make the surface layers of soil absorbent to a sufficient depth, we certainly will not have to worry about runoff and erosion, just as nobody worried about these problems when the land was new. They were not problems then.

To put in a system of drain tile on land that has developed an apparent need for drainage is a matter of economic consequence. Tile costs a great deal of money. Its installation, whether properly done or not, is also expensive. And, at best, the results may be no more than the removal of symptoms of trouble which should be attacked by more appropriate means. Certainly, in view of the necessary investment involved in tile installations, some previous work designed to make the surrounding soil more porous would be advisable before the decision is made to put into the land an outlay of cash and labor which might easily equal the previous value of the land itself.

Nobody really knows whether it is possible to restore to the soil its original porosity. We do know that organic matter on the surface, as in the cove soils, does prevent practically all runoff; but we have no way of knowing whether it would be possible to work enough organic matter into a soil to make it take in all of the rainfall. We know, too, that the

[1] A cove soil is one which results from conditions that cause leaves to drift to the same spot season after season. The lee slopes of mountain tops all along the Appalachian Mountains develop cove soils, provided the windward slopes are covered with forest to produce the leaves. The annual increment of leaves keeps the soil always open, so that no water can leave the place where it falls until the entire soil mass has filled with water. The fertility of these soils is unbelievably high.

actual cost of growing a crop of rye and disking it into the ground would be a mere trifle when compared with the cost of installing tile. It is certainly true that plowing a crop of rye into the soil does not decrease runoff; in fact, runoff is at its very worst on land that has been plowed and lies bare because of having been plowed.

Knowing all of these facts about the behavior of water on the soil surface, it seems worth while as a preliminary to the major operation of tile drainage to test the possibility of curing the wet spots by preventing the runoff water from reaching them. The only way water can be prevented from finding low ground is to cause it to run into the surface where it falls. To cause an eroded soil to do this might require that several successive crops of green manure be disked in. Even that, if necessary, would be preferable economically to spending the money for tile; for if we can make all of the water that falls on the land run into it, we will have done the perfect job of conserving the water supply.

Because there is urgent need for conserving water, any suggestion of additional tile installations should be viewed with suspicion. There are important reasons for this attitude:

1) In many parts of the country there is now a serious shortage of water during most of the year. Cities are enlarging the areas from which they draw their supply, taking in whole new watersheds. The water table in most farm communities is noticeably lower, for farm wells have had to be deepened in many instances in order to catch up with a receding water table.

2) Droughts are becoming more common and more serious. Generally speaking this is true over most of the country.

Both of these conditions should be considered before one proceeds with plans to lay in new tile lines. Each indicates that the reserve water supplies in most communities are too little instead of too large. It seems foolish to consider withdrawing additional water from places where there is already a shortage indicated both by the lowering water table and by the prevalence of droughts.

It should be remembered, too, that tile is a permanent exit for water from the soil. All water that reaches it will be led away. Tile may be put in for the sole purpose of removing in springtime a few hundred gallons of water from a low spot. It remains in place 365 days a year. It has absolutely no discretion as to what water to remove. It must remove needed water as freely as it drains away that which is surplus.

What of flood effects? No single tile installation is going to influence flood height noticeably; but the combined outflow from all the tile on a given watershed does increase the freshets that follow heavy rains. Indeed, some open-textured soils, when subjected to heavy rains in spring before they have settled firmly from winter heaving, actually offer so little filtering resistance to the passage of the water that it is still muddy when it leaves the tile. This is eloquent testimony to the speed with which the rainfall—even though it enters the soil—may reach the streams to add to the destructiveness of floods. Such prompt elimination of the water which finds the tile after spring rains surely can not be in the best interest either of the farmer on whose land it falls or of those whose farms it must inundate on its way to the sea.

Tile installation is considered so virtuous an act that the only question raised in connection with it is the farmer's ability to finance the purchase and laying expenses. This uncritical approach to the problem may be traced to the fact that early drainage projects often paid for themselves by means of the crops produced the very first season. These projects were designed to lower the actual water table in swamp land. Current proposed installations are expedient in character, being designed to correct trouble obviously caused by runoff.

When we realize that gravity is constantly tugging at the runoff water to drag it into the soil, the fact that all of the water does not run in is proof that something serious has happened to the soil surface, for originally all soils were as absorbent as cove soils. The change is explainable solely by the loss of organic matter. The actual mechanics of the situation may prove more difficult to understand, because of human visual limitations.

Ants and other creeping things that belong in the soil surface recognize the changed condition. They are vitally affected by it. The disappearance of organic matter from the soil surface forces a change of habitat upon some of them. When, originally, the crystalline minerals of the soil were separated by fragments of organic matter in process of decay, these small forms of life were able to enter the surface quite readily because of its porous character. Once under the surface, they found both food and water in the organic matter itself. Many kinds of these denizens of the soil surface are now unable to penetrate the purely mineral surface because of its lack of porosity. They once aided natural drainage. Now they frequently can not. It is not in our power to remedy the defect by artificial means, such as tile drainage.

We humans detect the presence of organic matter in the soil by the smudge caused by the presence of carbonized (partly decayed) material. Though we cannot see the separate fragments, passageways afforded by its porosity permit the tiny mites of life that exist in and on the soil surface to travel about underground just as we travel by subway. Every protruding stem is to them another subway entrance to abundance of food and water. Because of the dependence of these small life forms on decaying organic matter, the disappearance of the organic matter from our soils has caused a complete change in the fauna of the soil surface. The most casual comparison of biological conditions of the forest floor with those of the eroding land of our farms will show that one is teeming with a great variety of life while the other is almost devoid of it.

With the disappearance of the organic matter from a soil previously well supplied with it, then, we arrive at surface conditions just as truly desert in all essentials as the desert itself. Only the prevalence of a higher rainfall, reasonably well distributed throughout the year, prevents the pure mineral soils of the humid East from being as barren as are the desert soils of Arizona. Some of them are almost that barren in any case. When centipedes and lizards leave farm land, they do so in response to a process in nature which might properly be called eviction. The soil may still show a little dark color when the last of such life forms disappear from it, but their departure means that the organic matter supply has been reduced to such an extent that the soil surface is no longer a suitable habitat. The eviction of minute forms of life sets the stage for those large problems of drainage with which this chapter deals. The remedy is to restore at once the organic condition of the soil and with it the teeming life which feeds upon it. This is organic balance, and it never tolerates the development of conditions which the drain tile is supposed to ameliorate.

Obviously, if the water is unable to move from where it falls, the wet spots in the low places will disappear for lack of water to make them wet. And it is equally obvious that all engineering works now proposed as means of checking the damage done to the land by rainfall will be entirely unnecessary. Except in swamp areas, tile will be superfluous. And terraces, which are often more expensive than tile, may even be dispensed with.

Preliminary to any concerted action by governmental agencies to correct the present impervious condition of the soil surface, it would probably be a fine thing if every farmer in the country would plug the outlets of most of his tile lines. This would give opportunity for a great deal of water that now floods the valleys to sink deep into the ground so it could be withdrawn again by capillarity. Such a measure carried out by all the farmers on a given watershed should prove important, too, in increasing the supply of water in the wells of the community. Many a farmer would like to be able to devote to crop growing much of the time he must spend hauling water for his livestock. If he and all of his neighbors would simply plug all the unnecessary lines of tile they have put in, they would probably discover that they no longer need to haul water.

This, however, would be only one of a number of benefits. Among these, the increased supply of water available to crops is the most important. Thus the growth of plants could be increased, and the length of time during which crops suffer between rains could be reduced. There are other less obvious, but no less important benefits that will follow the plugging of tile lines. To avoid recurrence of wet spots, however, it would be well if the farmer would work a green manure crop into the soil surrounding these spots before he closes the tile outlet.

The sooner we make ancient history of many of our present farm practices the earlier we will realize that the Garden of Eden, almost literally, lies under our feet almost anywhere on the earth we care to step. We have not begun to tap the actual potentialities of the soil for producing crops.

10

WHAT ABOUT SOIL TYPES?

When columbus and the explorers who followed him first saw our land, there was nothing about the soil to distinguish those variations in appearance and behavior now designated as soil types. Even after the European trespass had been well under way for several generations, it would have been impossible to determine whether most of the virgin soils were chiefly clay, or silt, or sand. The whole face of the earth lay under, and mingled with, a mass of organic matter so manifest as to defy the best effort of man to discover the characteristic distribution of the soil's mineral constituents. Nowhere, or almost nowhere, could soils have been classified into categories more specific than the broad general groups now known as the forest, grassland, desert, and intermediate. Soil types as we now know them have become gradually discernible as the black disguise of organic matter has disappeared. As soils have become unproductive through the uncompensated removal of organic matter, it has become possible for us to classify them into an intricate system of groups and sub-groups with quite different characteristic appearance and behavior.

No attempt will be made to clarify the highly technical matter of soil classification. For such information the reader can now be directed to an extremely readable book on the subject, written by a man whose acquaintance with the subject is probably unmatched in this country. Charles E. Kellogg, Chief of the Soil Survey, United States Department of Agriculture, published late in 1941 his *The Soils That Support Us*. In my opinion there is no easier source from which the layman can obtain correct information on the subject at hand. After reading Mr. Kellogg's book, the reader who wishes more detailed information about the characteristic soil types of a given area of the country, will find much helpful data in *Soils and Men,* the *Yearbook* of the United States Department of Agriculture for 1938. Still further detail for limited areas, such as counties, may be had by consulting the soil map, if one has been issued, of the county involved.

Our concern here is to determine how the soils we have damaged can be rehabilitated without our having to await the repetition of the natural processes by which they were originally created. Soil creation is, in nature, long drawn out. People now threatened by famine view with apprehension the supposed necessity for throwing our present depleted soils back into forest or grassland and waiting several generations for the time when a new set of soils may be cleared. Just how the intervening generations can subsist in the interim is not at all clear. There is ample justification for the gloom displayed by many of our foremost students of soils. The present chapter is intended to mitigate the fears engendered by such cheerless forebodings.

The development of pessimism among soil scientists is understandable if one studies the history of thought on the subject of fertility maintenance as it has progressed in the past thirty years. This period has witnessed the most active efforts the world has yet known, chiefly here in the United States, to restore soil to its original ability to produce. A number of ideas helped initiate this wave of national interest in soil improvement. There is the established fact that rural population had been steadily declining while urban has been increasing. The prediction has been freely made that in a few decades the world's population may be too great for the food producing capacity of our soils. There has been the increasing conviction, too, that the science of chemistry might hold the secret of permanent fertility for the soil. Such influences helped to initiate government-sponsored agencies whose purpose was to inform farmers generally of the need for definite practices looking to soil improvement. Universally, the practices recommended involved cash expenditures at one point or another. Moreover, it soon became evident that the maintenance of fertility in soils which still produced fair crops is much easier to accomplish than the restoration of productive ability in soils which have lost all of their original black smudge.

For many years there was no means by which the government could assist farmers financially. In order for a farmer to do what was recommended, he must have either cash or credit. Multitudes of farmers who were greatly in need of assistance had neither. The result was that, without so intending, we developed a more or less stratified series of agricultural classes, with distinct tendencies to specialization, thus producing several "project" classes. Some general farmers became beef-cattle feeders; some became dairymen, some poultrymen, and so on. Many in each class retained a minimum of general farming practices while fully equipping themselves with the necessary mechanical accouterments of their specialty. Because of their progress in this direction, many farmers became more and more dependent upon other farmers and the urban population for necessities they formerly had provided for themselves. Thus a commercialized, not to say industrialized, type of farming was developed by those farmers who originally were able to follow the county agent's instructions.

While this grading up of a financially fortunate group of farmers was in progress, an equally effective degeneration was taking place among those at the other end of the scale. Men whose land, prior to the launching of the government's agricultural program, had lost most of its organic matter were already so hard put financially that they could not adopt the most important recommendations of their advisers. They were willing enough, but few of them had enough cash to enable their families to live comfortably; they could spare none for soil improvement.

Belated recognition of the necessary relation of soil degeneration to lack of cash for soil improvement resulted ultimately in the establishment of legal provisions for aiding distressed farmers in the rehabilitation of their lands. A number of agencies are now in position to assist such farmers, who can obtain loans for many projects for which money was formerly not obtainable. In desperately needy situations grants in aid can be made. In fact, so liberalized are the Congressional acts and the regulations for their administration that every conceivable condition of agricultural distress can be relieved through one of several agencies, provided it can be relieved by money.

It was not, and is not now, the intention of the government to expand the present programs to include all farmers whose land requires rehabilitation. So vast an undertaking would require more cash than the richest government in the world could scrape together by taxation. The hope is that private lending agencies in the localities concerned will take over the job for their communities. In fact, in certain areas this is being done in a small way. However, in the sections of the country where the need for soil improvements is most acute, the local banks, quite naturally, are in much the same poverty-stricken condition as their farmer customers. There is not, therefore, any very obvious solution for this paramount problem of soil rehabilitation.

There are, too, other aspects of the matter that must be considered. It must be admitted that the per acre cost of production is necessarily increased by any measure which requires the establishment of terraces or other means of controlling runoff water. Terraces are engineering projects, the cost of which on poverty-stricken acres can easily amount to more than the previous value of the land per acre. The construction of them might double the farmer's investment in his land without making a real start toward increasing its productiveness. And it must be remembered that, where the need for terraces is supposedly imperative, their construction must precede other conditioning of the soil. This subsequent conditioning usually requires applications of lime, the growing of legumes, the application of basic fertilizers, the addition in some instances of the so-called "trace elements," and such other expensive operations as the rearrangement of fences, grassing or otherwise protecting the outlets for water, and so on.

The above paragraph includes much material for which footnotes might be in order. It will perhaps be more direct and helpful to refer the reader to the many government bulletins which give lucid explanations of the various steps in the conventional soil-improvement programs. A recent series carries titles which make use of the expression "Soil Defense," and a special bulletin is devoted to each important section of the country. For full information on the measures which officially are considered necessary in order to restore our badly eroded land to high production, the following bulletins, issued by the Soil Conservation Service of the United States Department of Agriculture, are recommended:

Farmers' Bulletin No. 1789, Terracing for Soil and Water Conservation;
Farmers' Bulletin No. 1813, Prevention and Control of Gullies;
Farmers' Bulletin No. 1795, Conserving Corn Belt Soil;
Farmers' Bulletin No. 1809, Soil Defense in the South;
Farmers' Bulletin No. 1810, Soil Defense in the Northeast;
Farmers' Bulletin No. 1767, Soil Defense in the Piedmont.

It is obvious that, at best, our conventional programs of soil improvement necessarily involve a cash outlay in almost all cases. The basic assumption that plant foods removed by crops must be replaced makes a virtue of the use of fertilizers and fertilizers cost money. Then there is lime, which in most situations is considered a prerequisite to the growing of legumes; and lime, too, is expensive to buy, and even more expensive to apply. Quite a list of recommendations could be compiled, one or more of which would be "must" requirements for every soil improvement project. And without exception there would be a necessary cash outlay involved.

As previously indicated, those farmers who have really received benefits from the past thirty years of intensive county agent work and the agricultural extension program in general have been helped because they were able to help themselves to some extent. They have spent a fair portion of their profits, too, in annual outlays for fertilizers, lime, legume seed, inoculating media, and so forth. As a result, the cost per acre of managing the land has increased considerably. This does not necessarily mean an increase in the cost per unit of the product. Rather, it is more likely to mean just the opposite. Hence, because of increased yields, these men have seemed to be justified in "plowing back the profits" in the manner described. The land has become more productive as a result, and is, therefore, more valuable land.

If we assume the continuance of the present agenda, it is apparent that those farmers who have been the chief beneficiaries of the extension program will continue to profit thereby, for they are best able to adopt any new recommendation requiring a cash outlay. Because this is so apparent, little thought is being given to ameliorating their situation. Under the present conventional way of doing things, these men are in the most favored position of any; so it would be considered foolish to worry about them when there are so many others in really serious economic difficulties. Nobody is worrying, therefore, about the present-day leaders among dirt farmers who seem so firmly entrenched.

It can now be said with absolute assurance that the supposedly safe position of our most progressive farmers is really destined to become the most precarious. The difficulty is the high overhead these men have developed. They have learned to make a profit on potatoes at 50 cents a bushel, for instance; they will be unable to come out whole, however, on potatoes sold at one half as much. Progressive farmers are geared to high production of a comparatively high-cost product. When their neighbors, who have formerly been too poor to comply with the ordinary requirements for soil improvement, find they can produce twice as many bushels per acre as most farmers grow—and can do it without any of the customary cash costs—the market for such crops will react downward in terms of price to the increased production. It is just this event that is going to prove the undoing of men who now are our very best farmers. In all probability the event will come almost unheralded, for the present agenda will probably continue to be taught for many years beyond the time when the first farmers begin to change over from plowing to disking. No important change in market prices will occur until there is sufficient volume of the new low-cost product to justify price reductions. The final result may be a debacle for those now in the most favored position.

Just how such men—at present the respected leaders of Farm Bureau activities, Grange work, and in many instances the chief support of agricultural "propaganda" of the government—will be able to clear their mortgages and emerge solvent from such an economic trap is not at all clear. It is difficult to understand how they will become aware of their plight until it is too late; for up to now (early 1943) no surface indications have appeared that any change in agenda is in prospect. There is evidence, however, that scientists of the government are quietly being prepared for what amounts to a plowless agriculture. The "house organ" of the Soil Conservation Service, *Soil Conservation,* has for two years been carrying articles showing the advantages of surface incorporation of organic matter. At least one committee in Congress has been made aware that a change is impending. A two-day meeting of scientific men and machinery manufacturers was held in Chicago late in 1941 at which the possibilities of designing implements for surface incorporation were discussed. The newly established soil and fertilizer investigations of the Bureau of Plant Industry presumably are to set up hurriedly the alleged experimental basis upon which the new agenda will be justified. All this is being done, presumably, without arrangements for rescuing the advance guard of the present regime when the new blitzkrieg of low-cost crops reaches the demoralized markets.

It may not be clear to the reader just how great the danger is. The average layman may not recognize the fact that there is no crying need for new machinery with which to effect the change from plowing to surface incorporation. That is just the point. Only one thing is necessary in order to prepare for immediate realization of the benefits of the new regime. That need is the education of farmers to the error of plowing, and to the fact that a properly used disk harrow can completely prepare the land for crops. When farmers have been informed that they can actually mix tremendous quantities of organic matter into the soil with a disk harrow; that they can do it safely, without the backfire that always accompanies the plowing in of such materials; that they can then produce far better and bigger crops than they have ever seen or dared to hope for—then the majority of them will begin to check the new information by private experimentation. Thereafter, it will not be long until soil types and all of the expensive treatments that go with them will cease to be of importance. If the men who now are the backbone of commercial agriculture prove to be among the tardy ones to acquire the new information, it will be at their great cost.

Much of this chapter may have seemed a digression from, rather than a discussion of, the subject of soil classification. The reason is that we are discussing practical rather than academic matters. There can not be the slightest doubt that, when soils have been robbed of their natural mantle of organic matter, they emerge as divergent and dissimilar masses of minerals. Quite naturally, these varied areas of sand, clay, silt, or what not, behave differently when planted to various crops. Possibly, too, these same soils, when re-clothed with plenty of well mixed organic matter, will yield varying amounts, because of the fact that they are of slightly different soil type. However, a difference of a few bushels per acre, when the average production is one hundred bushels per acre or more, is a less serious matter than when the differential is based on averages running between ten and twenty-five bushels per acre.

It is no credit to us, considering our mastery of machinery, that orientals produce four to ten times greater crops than we do on land which in some instances is inferior to ours. But they are doing it, and partly at least because they have grasped the true requirements of soil management. We should produce as much on lands now producing from ten to fifteen bushels of corn, for example, particularly in the humid areas of our corn belt.

With the exception of some bizarre types of soil like the ground water podzols, which carry their organic matter "concealed" by several inches of overlying sand, and perhaps other abnormal types of soil with which I am unacquainted, we ought to be able to excel any other people of the world in *production per acre* on most of the land that has been in crops in this country for generations. We have long been superior in *production per man,* because of our use of machinery. When we have begun to do by machinery what heretofore we have thought must be done by bugs and worms of the soil surface (the intimate intermixing of organic matter with the surface layers) we shall find ourselves automatically leading the world in *production per acre* as well. It is impossible now to foresee the economic changes which will necessarily follow this basic change in our relations with the soil. That they will be vast is certain.

11

COALS TO NEWCASTLE

The problems connected with soil fertility are now very grave, yet future writers may find them not serious, but perhaps even amusing. Nevertheless, our present serious attitude toward these problems is fully justified, for too many American farmers, as well as their colleagues abroad, are at death grips with the economic problems arising from the mismanagement of the soil. However, when the existing unbalance has been adjusted and we are able to look back upon the scarcely excusable follies of a pseudo-scientific agriculture, it will afford us some satisfaction that, despite man's struggle for generations against odds of his own creation, he at last discovered the truth. We have been becalmed agriculturally, like the famous shipwrecked sailors—thirsty for days as they floated in the mouth of the Amazon.

Plenty of plant food is available in our soils. There is absolutely no need for commercial fertilizers. Nature can make available annually enough new plant food to grow crops several times as large as we produce now. Our present era of decreasing crops can be explained only by the fact that by plowing we beat into unproductive submission soils which, when not disturbed by man, produce a vigorous growth continually. We have known for a long time that the "upper six inches" of soil contain enough of the least abundant plant food elements to produce maximum crops for some four hundred years. How much greater quantity must be held in the successive underlying layers between here and China! There are infinite possibilities for high production by these soils that we have worn down. Modern man has not visualized the high yields that will spring from the soil just as soon as nature receives full co-operation.

In the past, we have believed that we were co-operating with nature, but we have not made use even of well-known facts that most high-school science students grasp early in their careers. Until we begin to put these principles to work, we can scarcely be said to co-operate with nature. Instead, we have been working at cross purposes with the design for growth through which all plants exist. It is as if we tried to feed fish in an aquarium by scattering food on the plate-glass cover.

Thirty years ago students of soils at the University of Kentucky asked why it is necessary to apply fertilizers to soil richly endowed with the very elements that fertilizers contain. The answer given was that the minerals of the soil are highly insoluble; otherwise they would not be in it. This sounded logical. We could understand that, if only one-fourth of one per cent of the relatively small quantity of phosphorus in the soil could be dissolved each season, crops might easily suffer, even though ample phosphorus existed in the soil. Thus we were satisfied by explanations which seemed reasonable, but which did not take into account the inconsistent thriftiness of the natural landscape.

Everywhere about us is evidence that the undisturbed surface of the earth produces a healthier growth than that portion now being farmed. Barring setbacks such as forest fires, trees in a woodland become sturdier every year, and each tree also adds a new ring of wood beneath its bark. The minerals of the earth evidently are available in abundance to these trees—more each succeeding season, despite the heavy tax of wood growth, the foraging by wild animals, and the other tolls which, all together, must equal or surpass the drain on plant food from cultivated land.

Innumerable buffalo, wild horses, wild cattle, goats, deer, and other animals fed upon the grasses of the plains. Millions of these animals were nourished by the vegetation on the untilled prairie land. In supplying food for this multitude, the underlying soil, through the use of the "insoluble minerals," developed a growth of grass which in many places would hide a rider on horseback. All this came without the help of man. No artificial fertilizer was applied; no plowing was done; no cultivation was undertaken—there was nothing whatever of the "advantageous" contributions man makes toward plant growth; yet on these plains was found the most amazing development of nutritious grasses the world has ever seen. We may well wonder just what help man does contribute.

We can recognize the fact that man at his best contributes nothing to the growth of plants; at his worst he rapidly destroys excellent growing conditions, under the delusion that he is nurturing his crops. Millions of farmers contribute to the soil food materials in the form of fertilizers and manures; but in their handling of the land they force the loss from the plowsole of many times as much as they contribute; so that the net effect of their well-meaning work is to deprive their crops of the sustenance which nature so generously provides for all plant growth. The net effect of fertilizing the land, then, is not to increase the possible crop yield, but to decrease the devastating effects of plowing.

The manner in which plowing robs crops of their rightful decomposition products has been demonstrated in previous chapters. Now it is time to show how the land, if left to itself, is capable of far better production than farmers ever get from it. By analyzing the subsurface physical, chemical, and biological conditions created by plowing, we are able to determine definitely just why the farmer has never been equal to the natural landscape on land that had been allowed to deteriorate to any degree. This discussion is somewhat technical, but it is necessary for an understanding of the problem.

Conditions which favor decay are the same as those which favor the growth and development of those bacteria which are the agencies of decay. We know, of course, that nearly all decay bacteria are most active within a certain *temperature range,* with a certain degree of *moisture,* in the presence of a suitable *food* supply, and (depending upon the kind of bacteria) with either an *abundance of air or* a *restricted supply of air.* We know, too, that it would be difficult to imagine conditions better suited to encourage decay than are usually provided just under the surface of the soil. By plowing, the farmer places the decayable organic matter in the most favorable environment for prompt and complete decay. The organic matter itself is the *food.* The bacteria are always present in nature. During much of the year moisture and temperature conditions are within what bacteriologists call the *optimum range.* It is not surprising, then, that whatever the farmer plows into the ground cannot be recognized a few weeks or months later. It has simply vanished through decay.

All decaying matter produces carbon dioxide, a gas

which is heavier than air. The air in a well is displaced by it if something is decaying in the water. Carbon dioxide accumulates in the empty part of a half-filled silo. Many men have died in wells and silos because they did not know that this lethal gas lay below the air at the top. The smoke from a fire is chiefly carbon dioxide, but the heat of the fire provides the force necessary to lift it. In the absence of such a force, carbon dioxide *accumulates under the air, forcing the air upward.* Plowed-in organic matter, if in sufficient quantity, creates a zone of decay which is rather continuous and at approximately uniform depth. This decaying mass constantly releases carbon dioxide while decay is in progress. The carbon dioxide *must* fill the soil, gradually and completely forcing out the air which occupied the spaces between soil particles. There is no alternative, because there is no force, such as the heat of a fire, to remove the carbon dioxide generated at the plowsole.

That decaying organic matter must completely fill the soil with carbon dioxide has never been thought of as significant. Indeed, so insignificant has it seemed that the fact has never been emphasized in courses in soils. My test work in the field in 1940 showed conclusively that something important has been overlooked in this connection. There was irrefutable proof that my crops obtained their nitrogen almost solely from the atmosphere. This would not have seemed odd if the crops had all been legume crops, for the legumes have long been known to use nitrogen obtained from the air by the nitrogen gathering bacteria that become parasitic on their roots. However, the only legumes I had were green beans. My other crops were tomatoes, cucumbers, onions, potatoes, cabbage, and lettuce. All these crops, legumes or others, thrived equally well, although no nitrogen was used anywhere on the farm in that year. Moreover, the land was not capable of providing more than a small fraction of the nitrogen used, and the only organic matter supplied was the tall rye that was disked in. It is a well-known fact among scientific men that, if rye from three to six feet tall is plowed in, several weeks must elapse before it is safe to start crops in the land. Also, it is well known that, for rapid decomposition of such a mass of material plowed in, it is necessary to put in with it a generous application of nitrogen fertilizer. None of these requirements was met on my farm; yet every crop had all the nitrogen it needed throughout the growing season. Thus there was plenty of evidence that these non-leguminous crops had access to atmospheric nitrogen as completely as legumes produced under the most favorable conditions. Obviously, some unusual condition prevailed to make this true.

The only unusual condition was that all decomposition occurred in circumstances which provided an abundance of nitrogen continually to *saprophitic nitrogen-gathering bacteria* (which require no living host to provide them with the needed carbohydrates to supplement the nitrogen they get from the air). Since 1901 it has been known that such bacteria exist in the soil. Their ability to gather nitrogen under laboratory conditions has been proved conclusively in many laboratories, but these findings have gathered dust on the shelves because nobody had ever thought to force these bacteria to "eat" organic matter in the open air. When decay occurred at the plowsole, nitrogen as a component of the air was excluded; therefore, these saprophytic nitrogen gatherers were denied their atmospheric nitrogen. It appears from my field tests that if the rotting of the organic matter occurs in the open air, these bacteria are just as efficient at gathering nitrogen as are their parasitic kin. Moreover, the nitrogen gathered has no chance to be lost; for the crop roots are present to make use of it as soon as the bacteria die and become part of the decaying mass. The crop plants get their nitrogen almost directly from the air.

This discovery means that hereafter no one needs to buy nitrogen as a fertilizer. It means also that no one needs to grow legumes in order to have the benefit of the nitrogen they accumulate in the soil. Furthermore, since lime is used on the land solely because it creates better conditions for growing legumes, there will no longer be a necessity for farmers to buy and apply lime to their soil. One small discovery, then, makes possible the discontinuing of a considerable expense in farming. Nobody is going to buy lime or nitrogen fertilizer, or grow and plow down legumes, when crops can obtain their own nitrogen from the air without this bother and expense.

This, however, is not the entire story. Crops cannot live on nitrogen alone. They must have in relatively small quantities many minerals which can be obtained only from the soil. The decay of organic matter plays an important part in releasing these minerals from the relatively insoluble crystals that have resisted weather influences since time began. Organic matter itself contains some of the minerals, which, as it decays, are released for the use of neighboring plants. In the process of decay carbon dioxide gas is released; and when it dissolves in water, carbonic acid results. Thus water and carbon dioxide together are carbonic acid, the best known natural solvent for plant-food minerals. Carbonic acid readily reduces to carbonates, or other usable forms, those minerals which in the presence of water alone dissolve very slowly.

When organic materials decay at plow depth, the water below the plowsole is prevented from moving into the upper layers of the soil. (This is especially true if the quantity of organic material is so great that it separates completely the subsoil from the topsoil.) As a result, the land quickly becomes dry and remains dry throughout the period of decomposition. Because the soil into which the carbon dioxide is discharged is dry, no carbonic acid is formed, and the gas eventually escapes from the mass of minerals without having contributed to the release of mineral plant foods.

In disked soil the situation is quite different. Water from deep in the earth can rise to the soil surface, or until it is caught and absorbed into organic matter. Because the movement of water in the whole mass of soil is unrestricted, there is always water present (at any time when decay is possible) to dissolve the carbon dioxide gas given off by the decay. No carbon dioxide escapes from the soil, and most of it becomes carbonic acid. This acid releases for the use of adjacent plants the otherwise adamant minerals which are so badly needed by farm crops. By this simple and well-known chemical action in the soil, the organic matter itself goes a long way toward providing the minerals which otherwise the farmer must buy in a bag.

Can decaying organic matter in the surface of the soil release enough minerals for maximum crops? The answer seems to depend altogether upon how much organic decay is in process during the growing season. I can not state whether maximum crops can be expected from land into which great quantities of organic matter have been disked —without the application of artificial fertilizers. I feel sure, however, that very early in the process of rejuvenating soil by restoring organic matter to its surface, farmers will discover that no application of fertilizer, however great, results in an increased crop yield. This opinion is based solely upon experiences and observations during strictly unofficial tests. It seems entirely reasonable to expect that the quantity of minerals released during any growing season will be sufficient to produce maximum crops, providing the volume of carbonic acid formed by decay is adequate.

It may be suggested that—judging from experience, again—what we now think of as maximum crops will be badly dwarfed by the actual results that will follow the disking of important quantities of organic matter. I have already produced crops in excess of one thousand bushels per acre under such conditions as I am describing, without fertilizers or any soil amendment other than plenty of organic matter.

When farmers and scientific men begin to experiment with this plan for the growing of crops, they will be surprised and disappointed at the appearance of the plants during a considerable portion of the growing season. Crops that are destined to produce two or three times the customary yield will look as if they could scarcely produce an average yield. The color, during dry, windy weather especially, will not be the dark, lush green that we have been accustomed to associate with healthy crops. Even in moist, favorable periods crops grown without the use of nitrogen fertilizers will be quite ordinary in appearance. Many a farmer, when he observes this absence of dark green color, will want to crowd the crop by the use of nitrogen fertilizer. However, if he is wise, he will wait patiently to see what the outcome will be without nitrogen. That outcome will please him beyond measure, considering that all his past experience will have taught him to expect a short crop. When he discovers a big increase in yield, he will be entitled not only to wonder why, but to analyze his results.

The explanation of this strange phenomenon is simple. For as long as most men now living can remember, fertilizers have carried some nitrogen. The nitrogen in early fertilizers designed for staple crops was usually not more than 2 per cent—forty pounds to a ton. At the usual rate of application of fertilizer, at most two hundred to three hundred pounds per acre, this small application of nitrogen, four to six pounds per acre, could do nothing more than "advertise" the fertilizer by keeping the crop dark green until hot weather came. Then, the rapid loss of color would be charged against drought or some other circumstance. We may conclude, then, that our judgment of a healthy green color has been warped by our fertilizer experience.

Experienced farmers and scientists know that if a crop grows too luxuriantly in the early weeks, when there is plenty of water, it is likely before harvest time to encounter weather conditions which will make such growth difficult to maintain. Such events precede the firing of corn blades. Often, when the farmer has overdone nitrogen feeding at planting time, the rainfall will be sufficient for a few weeks to induce extraordinary growth. The almost inevitable sequel is dry weather, which suddenly stops the liberal flow of nutrients into the plant. Retrenchment in the form of dead leaves—so that the available nutrients can support the remainder of the plant—is a forced procedure. Fired corn blades, therefore, are no mystery, but should be expected as a result of certain fertilizer practices.

There is plenty of nitrogen in the air; there are practically unlimited quantities of mineral nutrients in the soil. The new practices make it possible to utilize natural forces to make these available. Therefore, we should hereafter stop carrying coals to Newcastle, by fertilizing soils that already have an abundance of plant food.

12

EXIT PESTS

THE HYPOTHESIS that environment influences plant disease and insect damage is not new. In early agricultural literature, writers generally accepted the theory that the better the growing conditions for plants, the less the risks from disease and insects. From 1910 to the present time, however, it has been difficult to find this theory expressed in writings on agricultural subjects.

It is true that the era of soil depletion has been contemporaneous with the period in which diseases and insects have become most troublesome. This could be true, of course, without being significant; but there are very good reasons for supposing a connection to exist. Many farmers can remember when there were no Colorado potato beetles, San Jose scale, and other insects and blights now common. These same men can remember also that at that time their plows separated a zone of almost black upper soil from the yellowish subsoil. This black topsoil has now disappeared; at the same time many new insects have made their appearance, and those that were present before have become much more numerous. Plant diseases have multiplied in number and increased in virulence during the same period. We may well ask, then: Is environment (meaning the soil) a factor in their control?

Certain human and animal diseases and parasites have long been thought of as environmental. Hookworms belong entirely in the South, particularly in the southeastern section of the United States. Malaria can occur only where the Anopheles mosquito is present. Pellagra and other so-called deficiency diseases have usually been thought of as belonging to certain localities. It has not been difficult to connect such troubles with the environment in which they have been found.

In recent years the control of deficiency diseases has been much improved in most areas because of the more general availability of protective foods. Coincident with this improvement, however, there seems to have been a general decline in the nutritive value of foods produced on average land. The discovery of vitamins has brought this matter into better focus. When knowledge of vitamins was new, it was thought that certain foods contained an abundance of particular vitamins. Egg yolk was said to be rich in most of them. Now it is known that the vitamin content of the egg yolk is seriously affected by the food consumed by the hen. Butterfat was considered to be uniformly potent as a source of vitamin A. More recent discoveries show that the vitamin content of butterfat or cream is largely dependent upon whether or not the cow has access to a quantity of grass, or to the richly colored foods which provide her with this essential vitamin. Neither the hen nor the cow can by herself create the various vitamins she transmits to the consumer of her products. The vitamins must be supplied to each animal through food.

These disquieting discoveries—that foods we had thought were always richly endowed with health-giving substances may themselves be deficient in certain instances—have shifted attention to the plants, which normally would be expected to supply vitamins to the animal. It becomes a complicated chain of cause and effect: milk—cow—hay, grain, or grass—soil. In other words, the blame for any deficiency goes back, in the last analysis, to the soil.

Then we discover that during the very period in which deficiency diseases are being decreased in the localities where they have been most serious, the area in which they occur seems to be widening. In the last few years certain of the deficiency diseases have been found in places where they were unknown before. And, at the very same time, we find that the soil—life's ultimate source—has declined sharply in its ability to nourish properly the plants upon which we depend.

Characteristically, Americans confronted by this dilemma of deficient foods have turned to the drug stores to buy vitamins. There is little doubt that the development of synthetic vitamins has served to postpone disaster for many people; but it seems unnecessary to pay for something whose value is not yet wholly unquestioned, when by properly modifying the environment in which our plants live, we can again build into our food plants all the vitamin richness they once had.

The logic of such a viewpoint is inescapable, yet it has not been investigated officially to determine whether it may be true in fact. We have experimental data to prove the necessary causal relationship between the completely nourished cow and the milk rich in vitamins and other nutrients. We know through experiment that only good feed in correct proportions and quantities can nourish the cow properly. We are just as sure, with ample experimental proof to sustain us, that only a soil that is capable of supplying a sufficiency of plant nutrients in suitable combinations can create foods richly endowed with the elements needed to produce human or animal health. We have, in other words, all the necessary elements of logic for reasoning from the good soil to the best of health, or from the poor soil to the direst of disease in the animals which consume the products of the soil; but we have not assembled those elements into the necessary whole to arrive at the logical conclusion. Our agricultural reasoning is in much the same condition as was the passenger transportation of the country before the existing railway lines had been grouped into great transcontinental systems. We should be able now to take the entire "trip" from starting point (good or poor soil) to terminus (good or poor health) without having to make the local stops.

In my test work and, subsequently, in field work, I discovered that soil conditions seemed to be factors in the extent to which plants were affected by diseases and insects. The evidence was so convincing that I watched carefully for verification of the idea in commercial crop growing when the tests were repeated on a field scale. The results in the field fully confirmed the earlier deductions. I am sure that the existence or nonexistence of plant diseases in certain fields is related to the condition of the soil, and that the incidence of insect damage is likewise related. No other conclusion seems possible from the amazing behavior of insects and the absence of diseases in the crops I grew on land which had been prepared by disking in (or down) great quantities of green manure crops. Yet, despite this existing chain of experimental evidence proving the truth of every element in the necessary reasoning, we can not accept such an unofficial decision as true until it has been proved so by properly supervised official tests. For such tests we shall look to the experiment stations which have been established for that purpose.

While the presence or absence of insects or diseases seems not to be necessary to this reasoning, an important purpose will be served by dependable knowledge of just how completely their behavior indicates the suitability of the soil in which the plant is growing. If insects and diseases prove to be a perfect index, as they must if they are truly environmental, then an entirely new "soil-testing" method becomes available to the farmer. Whenever his crops become infested by insects or are attacked by disease, he may know immediately that further green manure treatment will be helpful.

Since in ordinary farming and horticulture the fight against pests of all kinds has partaken of the inevitable, how, it may be asked, can a method of soil preparation possibly result in a change for the better? I had to find an answer to that question before I could accept the idea. The answer was difficult to find. No official experimentation by soils experts had been carried out on land prepared by surface incorporation of great quantities of organic matter. All experimental plots had been plowed, if there was much organic matter to be disposed of. Disking had been considered feasible only where there was little trash or crop debris involved. Experiment station results, therefore, supplied nothing directly bearing on the case.

To me it seemed necessary to assume that the soil in which organic matter in great quantities was decaying would be richer by the quantity of decay products that had been accumulated in it. As organic matter decays, soil minerals are released, as are also the additional elements which make up the organic compounds of which the living material had been composed. Depending upon the character of the organic material, decay may take place quickly or slowly. In either case, unless there are roots present at the time the decay products are set free, these used plant foods are almost certain to be flushed out of the soil by the very first rainfall. The only certain way to prevent this loss is to have roots of growing plants always present when decomposition is going on in the soil. On land that is left undisturbed, nature takes care of this. Roots are always present; therefore, no plant food is leached away.

On the farm these salvaging roots may be those of beans, cucumbers, or any other crop the farmer wants to grow. The roots of such crops will gratefully absorb all the decay products they can get. It is a reasonable assumption that the soil solution these roots pick up from decaying organic matter is different from that they would find available in pure mineral soil where nothing is rotting. Decaying material in the soil enriches the soil solution, so that each unit of liquid can supply several times as much plant food as the same quantity of water from soil not enriched by decay. That is only common sense.

It follows that the more decaying material there is in the soil, the richer the solution these roots pick up will be; the richer the soil solution carried in by roots, the richer in minerals the plant sap will be. From this point it is easy to assume that variations in the richness of the plant sap may affect the attractiveness of the plant for its customary parasites. A greater proportion of minerals in the sap may result in its carrying less sugar, and a decrease in sugar content may easily make the plant sap distasteful. Possibly cucumber beetles, for example, could be starved for lack of palatable juices, even when their host plant is enjoying the richest possible food from the decay in progress in the soil.

Such a theory is not entirely without foundation in science, even though no specific research has been devoted to it. We do know that variations in internal juices of plants are produced by variations in the fertilizer treatment and in the available moisture of the soil. This fact was established in 1918 by Dr. Kraus and Dr. Kraybill, whose report[1] has been used by a generation of students as a reference work in horticulture. There is no question that changes in plant composition are produced by changes in the nutrients available in the soil. We can not, of course, know how insects feel about having their favorite host plants overfed on minerals that originate from decay. We can only guess, from the fact that they prefer the scantily fed plants to those that are better fed, that the richer sap is less palatable to the insect.

If this theory is tenable, the human race is extremely fortunate. It becomes possible, because of this relationship between the insect and its food supply, to improve the human food supply by the very method that will starve the insects.

Apparently diseases yield even more completely to the environmental conditions which are most favorable to plant growth. I am unable to advance, as tenable, a reason for this. It appears, however, that the leaf surface of fully nourished plants is better fortified to prevent the entrance of infections. That there is a difference in texture of the leaf surface of well-nourished plants compared with those growing on thin land may easily explain their better resistance to disease.

[1] E. J. Kraus and H. R. Kraybill, *Vegetation and Reproduction, with Special Reference to the Tomato* (Oregon Bulletin 149, 1918).

In this connection, the natural resistance of healthy, well-nourished plants becomes entirely logical.

It is reasonable to believe that insects and diseases thrive only in a suitable environment, just as do other living things. Further, it appears that the environment that is best for the disease and the insect is poorest for the host plant; and the conditions that favor the host plant's development are intolerable for insects and diseases.

Scientific men with whom I have discussed this theory are not inclined to agree, because they still think the type of soil would be an important factor and doubt that the experience would be the same under other soil conditions. My contention is that the one determining condition is the surface incorporation of great quantities of organic matter, that any type of soil so treated would bring similar results—provided other conditions were no less favorable than they were for my 1940 tests. (It can be said truthfully that the seasonal conditions from July 12, 1940, to frost were such that many other plantings of beans had to be abandoned in the neighborhood where my beans thrived.)

13

WEEDLESS FARMING

I AM FULLY AWARE that it seems fantastically improbable to say that we should ever be able to farm land without trouble from weeds. Weeds have been keeping farmers busy for so many generations that they are taken for granted. In all of our farm planning, we have regarded weeds as a necessary evil; and moralists may even consider that weeds are a blessing, for the work necessary to check their growth keeps farmers out of mischief.

Thus unthinkingly we have accepted weeds as inevitable. But perhaps they are not inevitable. Perhaps they may be more vulnerable than we think. Like every other living thing, each individual weed must die at some time. None is everlasting, although there are some species which survive several years when undisturbed. In order to perpetuate itself, every species must have the opportunity to reproduce. If reproduction is prevented, the species can be eliminated.

It so happens that the majority of weeds that give trouble on farms are annuals; that is, they must originate each year from seeds produced by a previous generation. Since these annual weeds must propagate each season from seeds, it is obvious that the surest method of eliminating them from farm land is to prevent them from reaching maturity. The next season there can be no successors to those that were disposed of before they had borne mature seeds. Nobody will disagree with that statement, but everybody knows that the problem is not as simple as that, regardless of how logical it may seem. We all know how faithfully farmers work year after year to keep their land free of weeds; and yet weeds are perpetuated on the land of the most careful farmers.

Even this situation, however, is not as mysterious as it has always seemed. Without realizing what we were doing, we have buried weed seeds for future recovery every time we have plowed the land. This statement may reveal the secret of weed perpetuation. We can cultivate a corn field as long as the cultivator can pass over the corn without damage, but we must stop as soon as use of the cultivator would break off the stalks. After the cessation of cultivation, there is a period of several weeks during which any weeds that have been missed in the cultivation can mature. All such weeds bear seeds. In addition, there are apt to be seeds —brought by that final cultivation into a position suitable for germination—that will germinate, and produce more seeds in the half-light of the shaded cornfield. There should be less mystery about how weeds manage to perpetuate themselves when we realize that they do their most effective work in a field after we have stopped trying to fight them.

If the land is plowed after the corn has been harvested, millions of weed seeds per acre may be buried by the plow; but seeds that were buried by a previous plowing will be brought to the surface. Perhaps the weed seeds brought back to the surface this time will be those that were plowed under three years before after the last hay crop was cut. Although the land lay "idle" after the hay was harvested, it was producing ragweed, pigweed, smartweed, foxtail—a dozen different kinds of annual pests of cultivated fields. The seeds, after three years of burial, are now ready to germinate; and the plants they produce will create the necessity for cultivating the corn that is to be planted.

Thus, every time we plow the land, we create a new reserve of buried weed seeds which, at the next plowing, we resurrect. A vicious circle results. As long as we continue our present system of plowing the land, unless we adopt drastically different weed-control methods, we are continually undoing, at each plowing, whatever good work we started after the previous plowing. Again it may be said that we are the victims of our own system of handling the land.

Such conditions need not continue. Indeed, we can arrest rather abruptly the propagation of annual weeds in our fields if we will not alternate the base of operations every few years. By refusing to disturb the seeds which we buried at the last plowing, we will avoid creating the conditions favorable to their germination. Those seeds, on the other hand, which are placed in favorable position for germination by the act of disking in a green manure crop may be controlled with reasonable ease.

It must not be assumed, however, that a single field, properly handled with reference to weed control, will eliminate the possibility of weed growth, for seeds and fruits are wind borne in many instances. Success thus presupposes the application of controls by farmers generally over a considerable area. For the same reason, school lots, public lands, and all other similar holdings must not be left out of account. Weed control on a single plot will show very positive results, but as long as surrounding plots are contaminated to any considerable extent the labor of eradication must be continuous.

Here are my suggestions for eliminating weeds:

Seed the land to a green manure crop: rye in the fall, or a suitable summer crop in the spring. Let the green manure crop grow until it has reached the proper height to be worked into the soil with the available equipment. If weeds growing in the green manure crop begin to bloom, it is important that the crop be put into the land immediately. However, few weeds mature quickly enough to rush the incorporation of the green manure. Under almost all ordinary farm conditions in the humid section of the country, it will be possible to grow a winter crop and a summer crop, put each into the soil with its accompanying immature weeds, and in a short time bring about fertility of the soil and at the same time help rid the land of the weeds that create the necessity for cultivating farm crops.

In this discussion rye has been mentioned prominently and often—not because rye is the only crop for green manure, but because it is more suitable for a larger area of the country than any other winter-growing crop. Many other crops may be used with equal success. In sections where other crops are as good as, or better than, rye, such crops should be used. Summer crops, too, can be varied to suit the climate or the farmer's pocketbook. If a farmer has millet seed, it would be poor policy for him to trade it for soy beans for use as a summer green manure crop. It should be remembered that when these green manure crops are disked into the land instead of being plowed in, they are able to use air nitrogen just as well as the legumes do; therefore, there is no reason to prefer a legume for green manure. If the farmer has no seeds of any kind and the land is covered with weeds he can disk them in before they are mature and thus have adequate organic material. Anything that will rot will be advantageous when disked in and will improve the soil for the production of the next green manure crop.

It is impossible to determine in advance how many crops will have to be put into the soil before the land will begin to look black again; but disking ought to be continued until that point is reached. A rapid succession of summer and winter green manure crops should be used until the soil becomes highly granular and absorbent. It is difficult, also, to predict how many crops of immature weeds will have to be put into the land before the green manure crops will be free of weed growth, but the desired condition will be realized eventually. Inasmuch as the same few inches of soil are affected by each successive disking, every weed seed native to the soil zone chosen will finally have sprouted. Thereafter weeds will be produced only by those seeds which are wind borne or transported by other means to the area under treatment.

The eventual elimination of much farm work can be predicted on the assumption that weeds can be controlled. If weeds can be so controlled that the farmer's crops are not forced to compete with them for the plant food in the soil, then it goes without saying that no cultivation should be undertaken. There are important reasons for this, the most obvious one being that, since plant roots tend always to develop very near the surface of the soil, cultivation can not be accomplished without cutting these roots. Destruction of plant roots is definitely not beneficial to the plant itself; therefore, if the plants are free from weed competition, to stop cultivating farm crops will be mandatory.

Crop rows are customarily spaced three to six feet apart, partly to permit the destruction of weeds that spring up between the rows. If few weeds are going to spring up, then it is obvious that the rows in which crops are planted may be spaced as close together as the supply of available food in the soil will permit. Ordinarily plants are placed closer together in the row than the rows are placed to each other. Potato plants are usually placed twelve to eighteen inches apart in the row, but the rows themselves are three to four feet apart. Without weeds to interfere, potatoes may just as sensibly be spaced eighteen inches apart each way. The ideal arrangement would be to space the plants close enough to each other that their roots would completely occupy the intervals. This would prevent the loss of nutrients which otherwise would be released by decay into soil unoccupied by roots.

One important fact deserves consideration at this point. Living plants require in their growth, and their dead bodies contain in their substance, only about one-tenth as much material by weight from the soil as they do from air and water. The contribution of the soil, then, to 100 bushels of corn weighing 560 pounds would be only about 56 pounds. Even if the entire 100 bushels were produced on one acre, the grain itself would take from that acre only 56 pounds of material. If 100 bushels of corn should be burned, the resulting ashes would weigh about 56 pounds. Therefore, it is evident that the growing of crops can not be unduly wearing on the land. If, as indicated in Chapter 11, we can use soil acids formed in the decomposition of organic matter to obtain minerals, and the native bacteria of the soil to pull in nitrogen from the air, the production of crops several times as abundant as we have grown is just a matter of sensible technique. Properly handled, farm land can be just as self-sufficient as the soil of the natural landscape has always been, because, when properly handled, farm land will be maintained in approximately the same physical condition as soil always is in nature.

The theories presented in this chapter have not been fully demonstrated, but experiments are under way at the present time to test the truth of the statements. No prediction can be made now as to when the experiments will be completed, since there is no basis for knowing positively just how long a time it will take to empty the upper few inches of soil of its stock of weed seeds, or when the soil will begin to look black again. My guess is that two to five years will be necessary. In the meantime, the succession of green manure crops will be planted twice a year and disked in before the weed seeds have matured. Then we shall be in a position to speak of the "when" as well as the "how" of weed control.

14

MOTHER EARTH CAN SMILE AGAIN

IN THE PRECEDING CHAPTERS the moldboard plow has been shown to be the villain of the world's agricultural drama. Here in the United States it is suspected of wasting from the plowsole enough plant food to sustain crops with which to feed half the other peoples of the world—a suspicion based upon official reports. Elsewhere the record is less clearly defined; for nowhere else are moldboards of the sizes common in the United States in general use. The "bigger and better" the plow, the more devastating its effect.

When this appraisal of the plow has become official, as eventually it must, American agriculture will undergo drastic revision. It is hardly possible to make a blueprint, or even to hint at one, in terms more trustworthy than the usual perspective of greener pastures elsewhere. In this spirit, therefore, I undertake now to forecast some of the changes that are likely to result from the new agricultural scheme.

The pastures of the land will be greener, literally; crops will grow in better fashion, with immeasurably less attention than they have customarily been given in the past; the vitamins and minerals our foods used to contain in abundance will again be present in similar measure; and in consequence we shall undoubtedly be healthier, some of the tensions of civilization will be relaxed, and our lives should be more comfortable.

This is the favorable aspect of the picture. That the benefits will not be the same for all people, especially in the initial phases of change, is a perfectly admissible deduction from history. Technological change always brings temporary maladjustments; from the individual standpoint, they may even be considered disasters. Thus, when we begin to apply our new agricultural principles, which acknowledge the co-operation of the eternal forces of growth against which we have hitherto been working, many people will be adversely affected. The position of some of them will be made almost completely untenable, until the wisdom of government has found a satisfactory solution.

The swiftest and most perceptible disturbance will occur in the economic field—specifically, the price structure of unprocessed farm commodities. As soon as crop yields several times as great per acre as our customary averages begin to come into the world's markets, prices will decline. This does not mean necessarily that those who practice the new agronomy will be the losers; their cost of production will be so low that their position will be greatly improved. It does mean, however, that those who do not take advantage of the new methods will suffer, and those who are now considered marginal producers will lose out entirely.

Moreover, renewed thought will have to be given to the so-called economy of abundance. There is such a thing as an upper limit to the amount of food that can be consumed by the population of the United States and by the now undernourished populations elsewhere in the world. For this reason, as the new methods of agriculture are applied generally, it may be found necessary to reduce the acreages devoted to staple food crops. It is not at all unlikely that the farmer whose land produced five times as much the first year, under the new methods, may realize a tenfold increase the second on the same land. Such possibilities preclude any prompt and completely effective economic curbs by acreage reduction. What would the farmer do with the acres withdrawn from the production of the given crop? Up to this time he has been told to devote the surplus acres to land-improving crops. If the basic principle of the new agricultural method proposed in this book is recalled, it will be clearly seen that the older methods of land improvement do not apply. Hence the impasse that appears when we resort to traditional methods of meeting the threat of crop surpluses.

Part of the result will be that the chemurgists are given an opportunity to take over and find economic uses for large areas of land that will not be needed for the production of food crops. Since, under the methods proposed in this book, the land so utilized will produce raw materials for the chemurgist at a mere fraction of the previous cost, vast opportunities are open to those who perfect and bring into production the countless products and commodities for which there will be a ready market among producers and consumers of fabricated goods.

In this connection, it must be remembered that we have literally been living on borrowed time. Consider the rate of the use of forests. If we have used far more timber than nature can allow us for such traditional things as we know, it is likely that the new uses which have been developed in the last ten years will exhaust our available timber at an even greater rate. The outlook for wood plastics is very intimately connected with the prospect that, under newer agricultural practice releasing land from food crops, we shall have areas which can profitably be returned to woodland.

Petroleum reserves, too, have been distributed with a lavish hand. That our large coal reserves might supplement our dwindling oil reservoirs is scarcely as happy a thought as possibility that surplus lands may be used for the production of materials easily distilled into fuels. And from this comes the easy corollary that the waste products from the refiner's retorts might be restored to the land as fertilizer. We should then experience a condition which the world has never before known in connection with the land—soil cropped annually without loss of virtue. For it should be clear by now, from the contents of this book, that cropping can build soil instead of destroying it.

Other influences will operate to modify the American landscape. With the invention of suitable mechanical equipment for use by the suburbanite in coaxing from his home site the foods his family needs, a gentle transformation of urbanities into suburbanites may be expected. There is nothing new about this, of course, except that what has heretofore been a fancy which could be indulged only by the well-placed may be open to the many. Thus, the decentralization of populations, urged for reasons of individual health and efficiency by industrialists and for reasons of defense by military authorities, may well become a reality. The beneficial effects on American civilization are sufficiently apparent to obviate discussion of them.

It is not enough that we should have in prospect supplies of food which would eliminate man's historic worry about shortages. With cheap production of foodstuffs, we should be able to look forward to the lowest-cost standard of living of the world. We have hitherto boasted of the "high standard of living" in America, but we have neglected to interpret that claim in the light of what our achievement has cost us. Food and other products of agriculture have figured prominently in the high costs of our present living standard. There is an intimate connection, moreover, between the cost of man's bread and the cost of everything else he produces. Despite the rejection by economists and humanitarians (and justly so) of the so-called subsistence theory of wages, perhaps insufficient thought has been devoted to the disproportionate expenditures for the products of the soil and the relation of these to costs of operation in every other field of human activity.

If all the other benefits to be derived from a revitalized agricultural method could be dismissed, the one which would attract us still is the physical well-being of man himself. Foods are the sources of the vitamins, proteins, carbohydrates, and minerals by which man lives. He thrives or he fares ill in proportion to the availability of these essentials in the foods which are supplied him from farms and gardens of the land. Agronomists as well as nutritionists are aware that lands which have been exhausted of their essentials produce foodstuffs which are deficient in the end-products required by human beings. It is not too much to expect that, by the restoration of the vital ingredients needed by our lands for the production of lush, vigorous, healthy crops, the vitality of man himself may be enormously enhanced, his deficiency diseases greatly reduced or eliminated, and his life expectancy increased. This result, if no other were envisaged, would be adequate justification for a "new" agriculture which is in reality very old.

A Second Look

A Second Look

To THE AMERICAN FARMER

whose princely income (by non-American standards) is woefully inadequate to support him and the rest of us who, on one pretext or another, claim a vested share of it. May his income decrease, to the ultimate profit of the whole American people, including, first of all, the American farmer

Preface

For more than two years it has been evident that sooner or later some of the information which was presented in *Plowman's Folly* must be placed in better perspective. The questions left dangling by that book have kept me busy much of the intervening period, trying to answer the queries of several thousand correspondents who had been troubled by ideas they picked up in reading the book. Only recently has it become possible to spare the necessary time for writing what may be taken as a sequel. My purpose in this book has been to point up the whole theme of redeveloping soils for better living.

Since agronomists throughout the country had also been deluged by inquiries from a disturbed public, it seemed to me necessary, before planning such a book, to learn all I could of official reaction to *Plowman's Folly*, as well as to refresh my own point of view—on the scientific information in the field of soils and their management. Research information might be obtained by correspondence, of course; but I knew that the more incandescent scientific sentiments about *Plowman's Folly* itself would never be entrusted to paper, but must be learned, if at all, by personal contact.

This meant that, if adequate preparation for this new

undertaking was to be made, considerable traveling must be done. With Mrs. Faulkner to help me keep to a minimum schedule, I set out and covered some seventy-five hundred miles, mostly by automobile, visiting twenty-four states. The unavoidable hazards of highway travel, including weather, made it inadvisable to schedule in advance our arrival at any point; so, arriving unannounced, we missed some of the most important men; but we did talk with more than one hundred agronomists, and discussed as fully as possible the purely scientific aspects of soils and their management.

Of the states east of Montana which separate Canada from our deep South, only five were omitted from our schedule: South Dakota, Kentucky, Virginia, Vermont, and Maine. We visited the agricultural college or experiment station in each of the other states. At each institution we spent from one to five or six hours. Interviews, or conferences, often extended through lunch; and there were many delightful occasions when a half dozen or more of us sat down together and continued the discussion through the meal. As a rule, the end came only when my schedule permitted no further time.

The benefits for me were all that could have been expected. I checked as completely as possible the basic information upon which disagreement seemed possible or likely. I hope there were mutual gains. If any agronomist had misgivings, I hope he found me less of the thoughtless radical than he had been led to believe. At no time was there display of temperament; and friendly smiles were the rule throughout. They always help.

One red-letter day was the time spent at the Washington offices of Soil Conservation Service. In one of the several offices I visited, the director called in his staff of a dozen or more men, each of whom was in charge of operations for the entire country in his own field—engineering, trash mulch culture, and so on. The spontaneous round table that developed in this group was one of the most interesting experiences of the entire series of visits. Additional time was spent during the tour of the states at Soil Conservation Service operations in Ohio, Nebraska, and Oklahoma; and much was learned through study of these operations. Much credit must go to this agency of government for its work in helping farmers bring their farms back into profitable production after they have been badly misused. A great deal of improvement has already resulted. I believe, too, that this agency's work may in future be even more significant. For the sake of the record it should be said that Soil Conservation Service has spent more than a decade working in the field of soil improvement. Its work in some areas has always been in line with the surface treatment of soil suggested in *Plowman's Folly*—even years before that book appeared.

When our stimulating travels were over, I still had obtained no tangible clues to errors in *Plowman's Folly*. Possibly our method of personal interviews was at fault. Perhaps some other approach would have revealed faults the gentlemen I had interviewed hesitated to tell me. Early in 1946 came two occasions for testing other methods.

During the first week in February, Farm and Home Week was held at Ohio State University. This is a post-war revival of Farmers' Week which is intended to give farmers a chance to obtain the latest information for immediate use. In three days at these meetings I learned little that could be called new. It became obvious, moreover, that the urgency of supplying farmers with information they can apply immediately must, in the very nature of the case, provide small incentive for developing long-range thinking about soils.

Three days of the last week in February were devoted to attending the combined sessions of the American Society of Agronomy and the Soil Science Society of America, also in Columbus. These meetings, designed for mutual sharing of information among agronomists, were open to anyone who was interested. This was a fortunate chance, I thought, to hear all phases of soil management discussed without the handicap of courtesy that could prevent frankness in an interview. Little was said even here that implied necessity for soil development, and that little was overwhelmingly in the conventional vein. Only one speaker of all those I heard seemed to sense that the key to future success in farming lies in the development of soils of livelier internal biologic conditions.

While the addresses at this meeting were much more technical than those at the Farm and Home Week meetings, I was surprised to note that they revolved largely around ways of relieving the immediate needs of farmers. There was little evidence that the speakers were seriously concerned with the development of long-range self-sufficiency in the soil. Indeed, it seems certain that none of these men believes the soil can be self-sufficient. Each speaker assumed just the opposite, in fact. To this extent, therefore, the thesis of *Plowman's Folly* has no standing in this group.

Yet there is no answer, so far as I have been able to learn, to my argument, as developed in that book, that the earth is completely self-sufficient for nourishing the life it develops. Much of the detail omitted from the first book will be included here, and I am sure there is no refutation possible.

While all the preparation I have made for refreshing my thinking has revealed no basic errors in the first book, the experience demonstrates that science really supports the self-sufficiency idea. Otherwise somebody would have neatly refuted that thought. Scores have been given the chance.

The need for action looking to permanence in soil productive power has never been greater. We can ill afford to trifle longer with expedients in soil matters. The fact that converted war plants can now supply the farmer with cheap nitrogen is no argument for him to desert earth's special ways of supplying his nitrogen without cost. Certainly not, when it is so obvious that because of past reliance upon chemicals our farm land is tightening up in structure. As it happens, natural ways of obtaining nitrogen provide at the same time the remedy for our soil structure problems; which bolsters the idea of relying upon natural forms of nitrogen instead of buying it.

Unconsciously, our conventional soil theories stem from economics—not from science. The economic approach, in keeping with perfectly correct economic theory, demands restoration item by item of all plant nutrient elements taken from the soil (thus making the soil no longer a resource). True science, on the other hand, recognizes within the unweathered rock crystals of the soil ample nutriment for crops. The eternal forces that have wrested from the earth enough nourishment for all life that has preceded us on the earth have but scratched the surface and taken only a pittance of the total held in trust for living things. That pittance is represented in our coal, oil, gas, rock phosphate, limestone, etc. We still have left an earthful—the whole planet, eight thousand miles in diameter—which, as far as anybody knows, consists of plant-food minerals mixed in with many other substances.

Moreover, Nature hands to man the key to this limitless store of plant food—the many acids that develop in the soil as organic matter decays. Including carbonic acid, we have more than a dozen organic acids that attack the mineral crystals, etching away in solution sustenance for plants. Soil yields nutriment in proportion to the quantity of these acids. Further, the amount of these acids depends in turn upon the quantity of decay that occurs in the presence of plenty of nitrogen and oxygen in the soil. In other words, the more organic matter that has been mixed into the surface of a soil to generate these acids by decay, the more plant nutrient elements the soil will "manufacture" precisely where the plant roots will be hunting for them. In this way the microscopic crystals, containing phosphate along with every other needed element, release that phosphate to be acidified on the spot—at no cost to anybody. And nothing could conceivably reduce the supply enough to be detected by any known means.

This information, in skeletal form, came to me from an authority than whom there is none greater in this country. He has been quoted as an authority since I was teaching agriculture in a high school twenty years ago. The presentation I have given above will be elaborated in the book that follows.

Edward H. Faulkner

Elyria, Ohio
March 8, 1947

A Second Look

A Second Look at I : Plowman's Folly

LIKE MOST BOOKS, *Plowman's Folly*[1] was not perfect. It said too much to suit some readers and too little to suit others. It delighted some and displeased others. It seemed strangely to align people either for or against it; and thousands who read it wrote to the publishers or to the author to express their pleasure or to condemn it. In the main, it seems, they approved. And hundreds asked for more. Almost every letter to the author contained questions, frequently requiring from one to three pages to answer adequately, and the handling of that correspondence was at times a full-time job.

Reviewers were, for the most part, unexpectedly generous in their appraisal. Many were quick to sense the mood in which the book was written. When Philip M. Wagner called it "an angry, optimistic little book" in his *Herald Tribune* review on August 15, 1943, he revealed a canny ability to read between the lines and grasp unexpressed meanings. And he was not alone. Hundreds of others in as many varying attitudes have had their say about the merits or shortcomings of the book. Dozens of writers actually promoted sales as actively as if they had themselves written the book. And not a few readers volun-

[1] Norman, University of Oklahoma Press, 1943.

teered to assist in any way they could to further the cause for which the book stands, by helping to organize nationally a campaign for putting into effect the ideas expressed in it.

I certainly could not have asked for more complete co-operation than was forthcoming voluntarily from practically everybody who was impressed by what the book had to say. Such spontaneous generosity puts me under obligation most difficult to meet, considering that no amount of money could have bought what these people so freely gave.

Such loyalty is certainly no light matter. It requires as recompense something more than mere mumbled thanks. The most appropriate thing I can think of is to do what so many have suggested: set up in more complete form some of the ideas that were passed over too lightly in *Plowman's Folly,* and contrive a clearer presentation of the scientific aspects involved. It is desirable also to suggest applications, to a limited extent, for different crops and regions. This last, however, must be restricted, since there are so many different crops, climates, and other variable factors. He would be foolish, indeed, who would attempt seriously to provide anything approaching a manual for universal application of these ideas in this country.

I dislike to seem to withhold what will seem to some readers the information to which they are entitled. Many reviews of the book assumed that the book itself was a sort of universally applicable manual. My intention in writing it was far less ambitious. It was my thought that our whole scheme of managing our land was misdirected, and that the blame for this lay in the first operation of plowing. The book tried to make this clear, and to prove by actual test work on both a small and a large scale that plowless routines could be adapted to the growing of crops. Since this had been my intention, the wholesale acceptance of the book as a guide to methods indicated to me that it had not been written with enough attention to the known limitations.

Lest the reader imagine that the reception of the book was entirely favorable, I may tell him that in college circles in one state it is referred to as "Faulkner's Folly." Several colleges of agriculture have had to publish statements about the book. Most of these have agreed in part while regretting that there could not be complete agreement. At least one college sent out such a statement without identification or signature to indicate its origin. On the other hand, the University of Idaho, while making no pretense to complete accord with the views I had expressed, wrote a statement that was completely fair in every respect.

Critical as have been some of the professional reviews of the book, none has actually touched upon what seem to me to be its outstanding limitations. There are a number of points upon which it may be fairly criticized, none of which seems to have been discovered by any reviewer. If I may be permitted, I should like to discuss frankly some of the points in *Plowman's Folly* which, in my opinion, need re-evaluation:

(1) The purpose of the book was incompletely stated

in the opening sentence of the first chapter. While the book was intended to draw an indictment of the plow, the far more important purpose was to show the reader the need for highly developed biological activity in the soil. If biological activity were not the fundamental consideration, the discussion of the plow's faults would be pointless. In other words: if the soil in question has no organic matter to be disposed of, then there can be no essential difference between the effects of disking and the effects of plowing. Many people have missed the real mission of the book because they saw in it only a fight *for* the disk harrow as *against* the plow. The fact that I did not make it clear from the beginning that soil development and conditioning were the prime issues lays the book open to the criticism of ambiguous intent.

(2) Nowhere in the book did I say explicitly that the discussion was directed almost wholly toward a single class of farmers: those whose land already had become so unproductive that it could no longer finance, in the conventional way, its own rejuvenation. Failure to indicate this "slant" in the text caused many people to encounter difficulty when they tried to apply the ideas of the book to land that already was in highly productive condition. The principles that apply are uniform everywhere, of course, but the method by which those principles may be successfully applied varies with circumstances. Too little attention was devoted to clarification of this point.

(3) This next point borders on deception, and is therefore very important. I failed to make it clear that differences in the texture of soils will necessarily make

for differences in the speed with which soils can be transformed from an unproductive to a productive condition. As a result of this failure on my part, hundreds of people have assumed that they could transform tough, plastic clays in a single season, as I succeeded in doing with the sandy loam on which my field work was done. The truth is that, in selecting the soil for my field work, I had little choice but to accept whatever land was available. Luckily this land was of a texture which responds quickly to treatment, so that a single season produced remarkable results. Because I was not fully aware of the importance of this factor, the book was written without sufficient caution to the reader about allowing time for his soil to become granular under treatment. A number of agricultural commentators have come near discovering this soft spot in my argument. They have said that the ideas of *Plowman's Folly* are applicable to some land but not to all. It is more nearly correct to say that benefits may be obtained much more quickly in some soils than in others.

My own failure to recognize this point and to warn readers against expecting too great an effect immediately constitute regrettable faults in the book. They reveal something about my own thinking. Without realizing the fact, I tend to think in terms of the possible accomplishment, unconsciously minimizing the tough going that may be met on the way. I failed, therefore, to warn every would-be experimenter that one essential ingredient for success is the determination to succeed despite early disappointments.

(4) Unfortunately, much of the text of *Plowman's*

Folly sounds like a manual of procedure that should be applicable everywhere. This is particularly true of that portion of Chapter 7 which is devoted to an explanation of how I used the disk harrow. To the extent to which this is true, it belies the intent in its writing. The field work I was doing was designed solely to prove that plowless methods could be developed, not to establish methods others should use. The truth is that each farmer will have to develop methods that are workable under his conditions.

(5) Inadvertently, I failed to mention my use of fertilizers in connection with the field work of 1939 and 1940. This omission caused some misapprehension on the part of the public, as well as on the part of my publishers, who assumed, not without justification, that no fertilizers had been used. The truth is that I used no fertilizers whatever in the "research" work that preceded the field work; but in 1939 and 1940 I did use a phosphate-potash mixture in liberal amounts. *No nitrogen was used, and I would not expect to use any commercial nitrogen under any conditions.* I used the phosphate-potash mixture because most of this land was of low productivity naturally, and my situation (operating the land upon borrowed capital solely) made it necessary that I succeed promptly. More complete discussion of the whole fertilizer situation will be given in a later chapter.

Briefly, these are a few of the points upon which the book may properly be criticized, and I am glad to be the first to mention them. The amazing way in which the book has been received despite these shortcomings indicates how generous well-disposed readers can be. Fan mail is always heart warming to a writer, I am told, but in my own case I have had to evaluate it in somewhat different fashion than a novelist might, let us say. In *Plowman's Folly* I was dealing with a severely practical problem, and all of my correspondents were practical people. The great majority of them wrote enthusiastically of the central ideas I had expressed; many were even concerned that I should become the target for attack by a more conservative school of opinion.

A few hundred correspondents have marveled at my "courage" in going against the currents of conventional thought, but opposition has been the least of my worries. It required no more courage to say what I thought about soil facts than is required to say that two times two are four. There is equally valid proof in either case, and there need be no fear of expressing such a conviction. It is notable that, in the adverse criticism that has been leveled at the book, nothing has been said against the basic idea it contains—the necessity for plenty of decaying material in the soil surface. Nobody even hinted that the argument *for* soils high in active decomposition was faulty; and that idea was the heart of the book. Everything else was subordinate—even the quarrel with the moldboard plow. I am not allergic to the plow, save in the aspect that it cannot do for poverty-stricken soils what must be done to make them productive again.

Here is a good letter from a plowman, H. E. Wimer, of Blencoe, Iowa:

I am convinced that the idea of incorporating large quantities of vegetable matter in the topsoil is correct, but our farm is heavy Missouri-bottom gumbo, and disking when it is wet—as it has been the last two springs—caused it to become so hard that planting and cultivating with the implements I have was not very successful. This trouble will doubtless decrease as more humus is incorporated in the soil.

In this locality nearly all plowing is done in the fall. I removed the moldboards from my plow, leaving the shares on, and this implement did a satisfactory job of mixing in the trash when followed by a disk; and if done promptly after harvest there is usually enough wheat or oats on the ground to start a cover crop. The "one-way" disk, as it is locally called, may be a good tillage implement to replace the plow.

And note what this farmer sees ahead for health and happiness:

This year I am inaugurating a change in crop rotation that seems better fitted to right-side-up farming. To date, with what I have been able to do, my crops have averaged about normal in yield. The exception was the 1945 garden and wheat. The wheat, I think, was the best around here. The straw was rank and the kernels plump. I grind our own whole-wheat flour, and bread made from the 1945 crop has a better flavor than that from former crops.

We have always had a good vegetable garden. In the fall I spread manure on the garden plot and, together with vegetable residue, plowed it under. In the fall of 1944 I used the moldboardless plow and in 1945 the ground seemed in better physical condition and the vegetables were of better quality.

My wife and I are alone on 120 acres. She does much of the garden and poultry work, but the rest is up to me, including chores, dairy, and haying. To look for someone to help has been a waste of time, so I have been able to do but little experimental work. I feel certain that the idea of an abundance of organic matter in the topsoil is right and will solve some of our most vital problems.

Because this comment is so down to earth in its seriousness I have used almost the whole letter.

This man uses good English, but is certainly no professor. He is doubtless one of Iowa's intelligent, unpretentious farmers, a man who thinks deeply and acts upon his own judgment after due consideration of all the facts. His letter came in response to a form card I sent out to some two hundred and fifty farmers and gardeners who had previously indicated they intended trying out plowless methods. For strict sanity of viewpoint, no reply received excels this one. He was under no illusions as to my intent in writing *Plowman's Folly,* even if many learned men did trip up in getting at the inner meaning of the book. His care to mention his discovery that the more granular soil produces crops of better flavor shows that he observes closely what happens in response to proper ways of handling the land.

G. Elwood Bonine, of Vandalia, Mich., farming fifteen hundred acres, has decided after years of experimenting to farm without either plows or animals, selling everything off the land, and using a minimum of fertilizer. Since he changed methods, he has multiplied his yields several times over what they used to be under tenants. Knowing of this farmer and a dozen or more others who have carried on the business of farming without plows, I cannot be impressed very much by diatribes against the book by those who write but do not cultivate the land.

Recently, when the director of an experiment station asked whether I had not decided to tone down some of the more strikingly unorthodox statements in *Plowman's Folly*, I regretted having to disappoint him. The fact is, however, that nothing dogmatic went into the text unless it was warranted by ample evidence. I accepted evidence that experiment stations would have rejected, true enough; but, even so, the experiment station authorities continue to say farming cannot be done on a large scale without plows, even when some of them know of my friend of the fifteen hundred acres.

Scientific men have thought my book was based solely upon evidence furnished by a few years of private test work. That is only partially true. It is true that the story stems from the experience of those few years, but it is also true that several decades of careful observation as a county agent, a Smith-Hughes teacher of agriculture, and a special investigator in soil problems, as well as experience on the home farm, had furnished strange bits of evidence which my special work corroborated. No statement went into the book that did not fit into the thought frame that had evolved during nearly half a century of living and working with growing things. Admittedly, the evidence I had was not "official," but it was no less valid.

Objection was made, too, to the fact that my work had been done on a small scale. It may be as well now as at any other time to dispose of the idea that small-scale tests are insignificant.

The truth is that the whole fabric of industrial progress in this country has been woven from a multitude of small-scale tests. The validity of small-scale testing is axiomatic throughout industry, because it has been the foundation upon which industrial prosperity has been built. It is no uncommon thing for fortunes to be spent on the development of gadgets that can later be bought at the dime store. In practice and in science there is nothing wrong with the principle of the small-scale test. Consider the pilot plant.

Agricultural investigators have been embarrassed, however, by the persistent tendency of supposedly basic findings in the field of soil science to become obsolete with time. It has been impossible to depend upon practices that were valid a decade ago. Why? One reason, I believe, is that, throughout the period when we have been most active in trying to develop higher and higher production per acre, we have been actually degrading our land. The soil itself offers a different set of working conditions today from those prevailing at the time the now invalidated findings were first approved. It is much the same as if the telegraph engineers, having found that bare wires carry current well enough on glass-insulated crossarms, should expect the same quality of service if they put their wires on the bare pins, without the glass insulators.

American farmers plowed with impunity (or perhaps without knowledge of penalty) as long as their land was black, for such land absorbs and holds much moisture—at least until it is about to lose its last vestiges of organic matter and color. When the land had finally faded to the color of the native stone, the pernicious effect of putting all the fresh organic matter at the plow sole could become obvious, and not before. When rainfall could no longer be held in the upper inches by the black, partially decayed organic matter of those upper inches, it readily yielded to gravity and the absorbent effect of the layer of organic matter beneath, and soon descended to the plow sole or below. Because of this change in character of their land as it lost what remained of its effective organic matter, farmers became conscious rather suddenly that "the rains don't last these days like they used to." The truth was that the rain which fell either ran off or, if it ran in, was not held near the surface by a good quantity of spongy organic matter in the upper inches. Hence it was quite natural that the benefits of rain should not continue through as long a period as they had formerly.

This characteristic of the soil that has no organic matter was easily demonstrated on my small test plots in my back yard. The cellar dirt, with a leaf layer at plow depth (spaded in to form a continuous layer), apparently held the water for three or four days after a rain. At least, following a rain the vegetables grew very nicely for less than a week; then they stood still, without any growth whatever, until the next rain. This sort of behavior, repeated season after season, finally impressed me as signifying that the leaf layer beneath was stealing away the water that ought to be available for my crops. I maintain that the fact that this test was on a few hundred square feet instead of a hundred-acre field has nothing to do with its validity.

None of the experiment station people, apparently, had awakened to the fact that a complete layer of organic matter at the plow sole effectively prevents the rise of capillary water until I pointed it out in *Plowman's Folly*. Yet, as early as 1915 that possibility was discussed theoretically by the agricultural colleges. Why nobody tried to find out the facts is not entirely clear.

You would not expect to find entertainment in the criticisms so seriously leveled at my book, but one argument, at least, always provokes a smile. I feel almost obliged to say, "Sorry, lady, but your slip is showing." Then think better of it, knowing that a man wrote the argument. Set off by itself, it sounds plausible enough, but it is in curious disagreement with the objector's own beliefs as expressed at other times. That is what makes it amusing to me. Here it is, as presented in a four-page statement on the book by one of the colleges:

> In the first place, the author of *Plowman's Folly* would have us believe that, in plowing, the residues turned under always lie as a mat at the bottom of the furrow, thus definitely and effectively insulating the furrow slice from its subsoil. Any good plowman would, of course, object most strenuously to such a premise. At the very least such an assumption is unfair to the plow. As to the average layman, he is likely to be misled by the assurance with which this oft repeated presumption is maintained.

In his enthusiasm to defend his loyal friend, the plow, the writer forgets that only by incorporating great quantities of organic matter into the soil can we recreate the granulation that he approves elsewhere in this article. And he knows as well as I do that, when there is any great amount of organic matter to be disposed of, "any good plowman," in order to do a clean job of plowing, will burn or otherwise remove enough of the material so that the remaining "residues" can be plowed in. (Incidentally, this statement says nothing about green manures, which are essential for the rejuvenation of soils that have already reached a state of unprofitable productivity.) By omitting to mention anything about burning, or the necessity for incorporating much greater quantities of organic matter than residues usually furnish, the writer makes his argument sound plausible without actual distortion. The "slip" that shows is the axiomatic necessity for greater amounts of organic matter.

He could not face the issue of green manures, for when such crops become tall—as they frequently will when wet weather prevents plowing them in at low heights—they refuse to permit the edging of furrow slices. The stem pressures of tall rye, for example, between adjacent edged slices push the last slice back into the furrow from which it has just been edged up by the plow. Only by inverting the slices, thus weighting down the green manure and interposing it as a barrier to the rise of water, can a tall crop be successfully plowed in. This is the situation *Plowman's Folly* argued against. The professor doesn't even mention it. Has he answered my argument? The failure to do so should be obvious.

Perhaps one reason that agriculture "limps" when it should "leap" is that at no time in agricultural history has the plow (which does the initial tillage upon which all later work must be based) been subjected to validating tests. If this seems unthinkable, in view of the fact that every other known factor in the field of agricultural practice appears to have been thoroughly tested, note the following statement by an authority in agricultural engineering:

> I wish to advise that, as far as I know, without exception the moldboard plow for this purpose (the job of land-breaking) has been generally recognized without experimental data. This is true not only in this country but also in other countries where the agricultural history predates ours.
>
> . . . With such a background of general acceptance it hardly seems necessary that tests be made to validate this type of implement.

There you have it. I believe this statement, taken from correspondence of several years ago, shows that the "major premise" of farming—upon which all subsequent practices are necessarily based—has not been subjected to such systematic tests as are considered necessary for every other factor that enters into farm operations.

Despite this obvious flouting of natural principles in our farming, American farmers have managed, by dint of great expense and effort, to postpone actual starvation; though no one denies that our soils are in a bad way, nor that our foods are deficient in elements they should have in order to promote vigorous health. We now pay dearly for the inadvertent crimes we have committed against that God-given medium in which plant roots are supposed to gather for us the elements of health. If Roger Bacon were alive today, he could capitalize and underscore his thirteenth century adage that so aptly fits our twentieth century situation: "The one rules nature who follows its rules." *Plowman's Folly* tried, awkwardly for all its earnestness, to say the same thing.

A Second Look at II : Real Soil

THE MANTLE of real soil which originally covered our hills and plains has all but disappeared, yet we have scarcely rationalized what has happened to us. Few who live today can remember the black, friable earth in which the pioneer planted his seeds and from which he took a bumper crop with no effort other than the planting and the harvesting. Some three to ten generations have lived on the land in various parts of the country since the regions were first opened up. Today's farmers, therefore, cannot imagine the soft snap their ancestors had growing the first crops. Not that previous generations had it easy: few tasks were harder than tearing up the sod on the Great Plains; and the clearing of the hardwood forests of the eastern half of the country would have grown blisters on Paul Bunyan's hands. However, once the land had been made ready, it did its job with an exuberance which no one who has not seen it in action can understand.

In our stupefaction today at having lost that original cornucopian zest from our soil, we reason wildly in the course of our lamentations about our plight. We weep over the doings of the water which, excluded from entering the land, can but run off over it. We castigate the farmer, charging that he takes but does not give, meanwhile forgetting that it is *for earth to give* and *for man to take.* Maudlin phrases about "our dying soil" are heard. Wise in money matters, we invent the worthless "bank account theory" to justify our traditional disregard of the natural provisions for having each crop take its sustenance completely from the powdered rock right in the soil. Whereupon, we bring to the "defense" of the soil tons of unnecessary and expensive "aid." Helpless soil! Nothing was ever less true; and it is, besides, an affront to Creative Design to assume that man must restore item for item what he removes by his cropping. The human race would be in a serious plight, indeed, if existence depended upon the "defense" man can bring to the soil.

Ignorantly we say such things, because we have never known the qualities of real soil. Indeed, when later on the characteristics of real soil are enumerated, few who read will be able to believe such a medium for growing crops could exist. However, there are some people who can verify the existence of such soil. It is entirely different in almost every way from any of our present-day field soils. It is more like the soil we like to imagine we have in our gardens. It is black, crumbly, loose enough to be springy when walked over, free from crusts under all circumstances, and may be worked almost at once after rainfall when once it has warmed up in spring.

At about this point you may decide I am referring to muck soil, since the description fits muck soil perfectly; but the fact is that any soil, properly managed, can be just like that. Soil just as black as muck, and just as friable, can be restored on much, if not most, of our uplands if we but take the trouble to refill the surface with repeated annual batches of green manure or other organic matter.

To put this description of real soil into other terms, we may say: (1) If you can't walk comfortably over it barefoot, even though you never went barefoot in your life, it isn't real soil. (2) If you can't pick it up in handfuls without effort, it isn't real soil. (3) If you have to dig to loosen it, it isn't real soil. (4) If in handling it you can be sure whether its mineral particles are sand, silt, or clay, it isn't real soil. These admittedly are stringent requirements for a real soil, but if you have an acre that meets these requirements, you can be independent of the rest of the world insofar as food is concerned. You probably can sell your neighbor part of his food. Any doubt that there is such soil, or that it can be as productive as indicated, may be allayed by recalling what the British did during the war years. England and Wales together have less than one acre per person. For the preceding one hundred years or more, Britons had not tried to produce their own food, since it was easy to buy food from the proceeds of their exported manufactured goods. The war stopped all commercial exports. Consequently the English and Welsh learned to grow two-thirds of their food, instead of the one-third they had been growing before the blockade began.

The alternative of starvation or soil improvement has never been imposed upon us here. We have thoughtlessly allowed our land to deteriorate with each succeeding generation, until we now keep it producing only by strenuous effort and at considerable expense. We need to consider most seriously the possibility of restoring our land to its former condition of real soil. Until we do, we shall continue to doubt that any soil can grow large annual crops continuously for years without the importation of outside aids of any kind. The fact that the peoples of other countries have kept their land in a high state of productiveness since the time of Moses, under the land's own natural, unaided power, has never impressed us. But unless we also learn to do this, we are destined to be plagued always by the inevitable problems of farming poor land.

It may be well to tell of my own experience in developing a plastic, yellowish clay into a real soil. This incident, I should add, is not something that lends itself to regular farm or garden practice. Few people could do what was done in this instance, for it involved a great deal of unnecessary work. It is chiefly of theoretical interest, but the end results will interest both farmers and gardeners.

Late in 1943 my wife and I asked the city street department to deliver five truckloads of leaves to our back lawn. These leaves were soaked, since it had been raining for several days just before they were gathered. The mountainous mass they made in the back yard was enough to cover the entire lawn area to three or four inches in depth. In the spring of 1944 I spread them over the lawn with the idea of killing off the grass, so that in the following war years we could grow a garden there. It was the easiest way I could think of to destroy the grass; and during 1944 we grew a few vegetables in the mulch formed by this leaf mass. The most significant thing that happened, though, was something I had not expected.

By late fall it became evident that the land would be bare the following spring, for before winter had set in much of the soil had already become entirely bare. The leaf layer had simply decayed and its substance had become intermixed with the upper few inches of clay. And the clay seemed to have disappeared. In reality, what had been clay was now the soft, granular sort of material I have described earlier as real soil. It was so easily handled that, when Mrs. Faulkner asked to have some flower pots filled, I scooped up a couple of handfuls of this formerly stiff clay and filled the pots with it. It was exactly what your great grandmother wanted when she asked her farmer-husband to bring in some "woods dirt" from the back field. Thus we now had on our back lawn a real layer of forest soil—thin, but real, and very fertile.

The best possible proof that this really was a forest environment is the fact that a pair of woodcocks made it their feeding ground throughout the summer and fall. Woodcocks are almost extinct in some parts of Ohio now, and neither of us had previously seen one; but these were on hand every day for their diet of earthworms, not the least disturbed by the fact that there were no trees to hide them. In fact, woodcocks need no cover, for they are as nearly invisible among forest leaves as anything possibly could be. When we wondered whether they were around, we would walk out into the garden, wander around until they suddenly zoomed up from almost underfoot to a height of about five feet, and away.

As has been said, this "soil-making" procedure is not to be generally copied. It proved very clearly a few facts, the most important being that tilth is created by decay, not by implements, as we have often thought. Also, a mulch of decayable material, if deep enough to be continuously moist at the ground level, will actually create topsoil conditions if allowed to lie undisturbed on the surface all season. Many people whose garden space is too small for the use of farm machinery would do well to create such a friable soil surface by use of a mulch for a year or two. This would spare the necessity for spading—a special advantage since it now is practically impossible to hire such work done. Once the surface has been mellowed by such a mulch, planting can be done without any preliminary stirring of the soil. The perfect seedbed is already prepared, by natural processes.

This discovery that raw clay soil can be transformed into unrecognizably new condition points up emphatically the principle involved in renovating our field soils. Not that we must use mulches. There may be advantages from mixing into the farm soil the equivalent of the mulch the gardener may use. Mulch makes soil, all right, but the same material, when mixed into the surface, does precisely the same thing, and perhaps with increased efficiency. While it would seldom be possible for the average farmer to put into his land at one time as great a quantity of organic matter as was contained in my layer of leaves, he could each year introduce smaller quantities, thus building up the quality of the soil while harvesting annually bigger and better crops as compensation for his effort. By intelligent use of machinery, the farmer can create in a few years the equivalent in productiveness and quality of what Nature would require centuries to develop in the land.

Most other countries lack the machinery to do this. Even their plows are incapable of introducing very much organic matter or of putting it very deep into the ground. Because of these limitations, and for other reasons, such as topography unfavorable to machinery, abundance of cheap labor, and the general use of hand methods for every kind of work, the necessary additional organic matter is often supplied in a predigested form known as compost. Because of the prevalence of conditions quite opposite in this country, the making and use of compost has never developed as an art in large-scale farming. Nevertheless, there is good reason why people with very small areas for gardening should look into the possibilities of compost for their use. Much may be learned about the general idea from books you might like to read. Here are a few of the most informative:

Farmers of Forty Centuries, by F. H. King, published by Rodale Press, Emmaus, Pennsylvania. First published 1910.

Artificial Manures, by Dr. A. B. Beaumont, published by Orange Judd Co., New York, 1943.

Pay Dirt, by J. I. Rodale, published by The Devin-Adair Co., New York, 1945.

For periodical information about compost farming and gardening, *Organic Gardening*, published at Emmaus, Pennsylvania, is especially good, since this magazine keeps its readers up to date on foreign developments in this field. Inasmuch as there is almost no general practice of composting in this country, the best information in this field comes from abroad.

Zealous advocates of composting will have their honest doubts about the possibility of duplicating on a field scale (by machinery and green manure crops) the efficiency of compost. Lacking experience with the making or use of compost, I am unable to give comparative results; but the most enthusiastic reports of compost yields read very much like my own experience with the incorporation of green manures. It seems to me, therefore, that there can be no advantage in composting over surface incorporation of the equivalent organic matter, wherever areas are large enough to permit the use of farm or heavy garden equipment. In some ways, it seems to me, there may be advantages in the machine process.

Proper moisture and temperature conditions for composting are not easily maintained, but in the soil these conditions are automatic, which means that, through a wide range of air conditions, decay proceeds continuously—not intermittently, as must sometimes be true when compost becomes too hot, too cold, too wet, or too dry. Losses of carbon dioxide, moreover, are at a minimum within the soil, thus assuring a maximum of carbonic acid for releasing minerals from the mineral portion of the soil. After a few years (I can't say how many) the machine-managed soil approaches, in texture, the condition of compost itself. That is what had happened in our back yard while the soil was covered by its coating of leaves.

Most advocates of composting believe that some animal products must be used in the compost heap, and assume, therefore, that field methods of "sheet composting" would be inferior unless animal manures were incorporated along with the green manure or other vegetable material. It strikes me that if this were really true I could not have experienced results similar in all respects to those claimed by compost advocates. The farmer referred to earlier, who has fifteen hundred acres, no livestock, and no plows, surely could not have developed in the last few years the great yield increases he has experienced. Too, we must remember that in the beginning plant life preceded animal life, for the reason that animals must subsist directly or indirectly upon plants. Yet this is not to say that compost heaps should be attempted without the use of the recommended proportion of acceptable animal products. You will do well to follow the practices suggested in the books cited if you plan a compost heap. The success of field work that uses no animal manures may result from unrecognized compensating factors in the soil.

In short, "schools of thought" in the field of agricultural propaganda may be completely ignored by Nature herself as she issues the rewards for effort earned by any and all methods. Farmers who use compost succeed. Farmers who use equivalent methods without compost succeed. Even farmers who plow—but are careful to "toe the mark" in adhering to natural law—also succeed. There are no hard and fast rules. This makes it all very disconcerting to those of us who think our own special method is an open sesame to success. The key to the whole complex maze of successful practices, each violating somebody's pet rules, is the compensating adherence to natural law.

Because of natural conditions in this country which encouraged us to step off on the wrong foot in developing our agriculture, we have been wringing success from our soils the hardest way. We have succeeded in keeping crop yields high enough to withhold our population from the grave, but the quality of our farm products has not been high enough to keep most of our people out of dentists' and doctors' offices.

The maintenance of real soil has been especially difficult for American farmers because of the great expanse of land each farmer has chosen to till. The necessity for having everything convenient, so that every operation can be done quickly, has resulted in standardizing farm practices to such routines as could be accomplished by machines. And this standardization has resulted in our growing far too many acres of the crops that lend themselves best to machine culture, and too few of equally good, or superior, crops that cannot be grown without some hand work. The fact that we in this country must "do something" with more than seventeen times as much land per person as is available to each person in England and Wales may account in part, at least, for the better care the English land gets. The English have sometimes told us that the trouble with our management of our land is that we have too much of it. I'm inclined to agree.

We can't shrink the area of our country, but we can do a better job of managing fewer acres, allowing some of the remaining land to return to natural conditions of grassland or forest. Certainly, we can't afford longer to continue practices known to predispose our people to illness (from lack of essential vitamins and minerals), and the comparative ease with which surface incorporation methods may be adapted for use on many of our lighter soils suggests that authorities ought even now to be teaching their clientele how to make the change from present practices to such new methods as can be made workable. Disking is not always the answer, certainly, but in the majority of areas it probably can be adapted. In any case, the ideal of real soil as the ultimate goal of permissible farm practices ought to be kept prominently before farmers as they struggle with their problems.

A Second Look at III : Substandard Soils

IT HAS BECOME FASHIONABLE to lavish harsh adjectives on the plight of our country's soils. So much talk has been devoted to that subject that it sometimes seems pertinent to remark that "soil conservation" easily degenerates into "soil conversation." The adjectives really make little difference. The fact still remains that most of our land—even the very best of it—is distinctly substandard by comparison with its original condition. The degradation our land has undergone is deplorable. It is only of late that the general public has become aware of this serious threat to the welfare of the country. Newspapers now give editorial space to discussions of the "huge losses of topsoil" that have long been publicized by Soil Conservation Service, Friends of the Land, and other groups.

This sudden interest in dust—that which the circumspect Israelite used to shake from his feet in disgust—is significant. It means that self-preservation, the most basically selfish and most powerful of human motives, still rules. Many of our people are frankly frightened. Hearing how many millions of acres of topsoil have been lost down our various watersheds, they sense the implication of hunger in any long continuation of such losses. Newspaper and magazine articles that play up the generally accepted estimates of government agencies are disturbing to everyone who has lost his connection with the land. Frightened people, staring at the prospect of hunger, will not rest easy until something has been done about it.

The most ominous aspect of the matter, however, is the probability that something will be done about it; and that such action as is taken will be a continuation of traditional symptom-treating practices. Instead, major effort should be directed toward establishing real soils. Otherwise we shall be troubled forever by the same symptoms of substandard soils.

These symptoms? The most obvious is, of course, *erosion.* Another related symptom is *firmness* of the land as you walk over it. Less obvious, but no less certain is the destructiveness of insects or diseases, or both, to growing crops. Freedom, or near freedom, from pests proves that a crop is growing under good conditions, the most important of which is the character of the soil.

Experimenters are not likely to agree with this point of view—which isn't strange, since experimental work has usually been done on land in much the same condition as the near-by farm land, both substandard to some extent. Substandard conditions have prevented entomologists and pathologists from having real soil on which they could conduct the necessary "check plots" to provide the contrasting effects that real soil develops.

Such observations as I have made have been chiefly on the same soil before and after treatment. I have seen crops literally devoured by insects on clay that had no organic matter, and have later seen that same clay, when well supplied with organic matter, grow the same crops with negligible injury or none. Also, I have seen the same soil in near-by fields growing the same crops, the plowed soil growing insect-ridden crops, the soil into which organic matter had been mixed supporting insect-free crops only a stone's throw away. The evidence just cannot be ignored in such cases.

Knowing, then, that pests index the substandard soil, the farmer who must use such land at least temporarily must be prepared to fight the customary pests. Not only should he be realistic about pests but he probably will find it best to follow the advice of his county agent, Soil Conservation technicians, or others authorized to instruct local farmers in the use of fertilizers, lime, etc. In other words, substandard land, as long as it must be used as such, requires the treatment that will give the best results "under the circumstances."

Many readers will wonder how the author of *Plowman's Folly* can give, or even justify, such advice. The explanation is fairly simple. *Plowman's Folly* was designed to show farmers how to manage land by *improving the "circumstances."* Theoretically, and for the long pull, that is exactly what every farmer should plan to do. But many men are actually unable to make major changes in their practices now, and may not find it possible to do so for some time. For them, it is only sound to advise that they follow the conventional pattern in their land management.

The fact that experimental work has always leaned

heavily toward helping the farmer with his immediate problems means that the results obtained are designed for land management "under the circumstances." Moreover, the fact that both the experimental land and the surrounding farm land are substandard increases the chances that the experimental results will apply to the land of local farmers.

All of which is quite different from giving blanket approval, for the long pull, to conventional recommendations. Indeed, a poll of opinion taken among agricultural technicians engaged in activities that bring them into regular association with farmers and their land operations probably would show that these men recognize an urgent need for improvement in soil-management methods. The Soil Conservation Service quite frankly urges, in much of its territory, methods of tillage that do not include use of the moldboard plow. Officials were doing this, incidentally, before *Plowman's Folly* was issued. In some places county agricultural agents are making recommendations substantially in line with the suggestions of that book. Many others no doubt have the feeling that one man expressed to me: "You can say those things, Mr. Faulkner, we can't." I know that many of the serious-minded fellows who work with and for farmers day by day are honestly thinking their way through to new practices that will be better adapted locally for the immediate needs, and will be better for the long pull as well.

A multitude of men are now coming into farming with little or no experience. Many of them have written me for advice about procedures. In most cases I have referred them to their county agents or other technical men who serve the communities in which the farms are located. Their first work will necessarily be with substandard soil in almost all cases. They should accordingly be advised by men who know local conditions. As these new farmers get experience, they will be able gradually to develop their land to real soil. Were they to try to do this in the beginning, they might be foredoomed to failure because of lack of know-how.

When he is planning his first farming operations, the new farmer should ask advice about what his land will require for the prevention of erosion while he is working it the first season or two. This is a problem for somebody who is familiar with the local soil conditions. Technicians of Soil Conservation Service specialize in measures that will work best for the kind of land to be served. It may be necessary, however, for the inquirer to become a member of the local Soil Conservation District in order to qualify for this service.

Not all substandard soils are alike, naturally. Almost everyone who has tried to grow flowers or a vegetable garden has found that some soils are easier to work than others, and often the results are better in one soil than in another. This is putting it very simply. Scientists have separated the various kinds of soils into hundreds of types, as they are called, and as late as a decade ago were urging the necessity for mapping all these types, county by county, all over the United States. This would have been a tremendous job, appropriately expensive, and of doubtful significance when it had been completed. At that time some agronomists believed that the particular "type" of land a farmer was working might prove to be the determining factor in his success or failure in the operation of a given farm. Within broad limits this probably is true, but events during the intervening years have put the emphasis elsewhere. It has been found, for instance, that regardless of soil type, "soil conservation practices" judiciously applied effect marked improvement in the performance of all kinds of soils that are suited to farming.

No extensive study of the many kinds of soils to be found in the several parts of the United States can be undertaken in this brief chapter, of course, but it may be helpful to discuss briefly a few of the general aspects of our soils that demand special treatment. Fifty years ago some of these special soils could not be identified because they were still enveloped in the mask of coal-black humus that characterizes real soil. As this color has faded, it has become possible to distinguish in the different kinds of soil, features which are of fundamental importance in properly managing them.

West of the Mississippi, great expanses of soil are found to be seriously lacking in the extremely fine material necessary to "cement" the mass together in the presence of moisture. Lacking this sticky quality when wet, these soils are completely at the mercy of running water and erode badly. They did not erode at all when the land was first plowed. Why? Probably because the whole mineral mass at that time was imbedded in the partially decayed remains of vegetation and was held together by the grass roots that interlaced the mass. As continued cropping removed this organic matter, the grass roots gradually decreased until they, too, were gone; finally the residual fine sands and silts could no longer resist the pull of water that ran through or over the soil. Such soils as these are known as *loess* soils, and offer no resistance whatever to moving water; when dry and bare, they are also easily carried away by wind. The famous dust storms of a decade ago were playing with this loessal type of soil.

If you wonder why such a transitory sort of soil material should exist so generally west of the Mississippi River and almost nowhere else on the continent, that, too, may not be difficult to answer. To begin with, loess is material that was brought to its present location by the wind and laid down in a layer covering the original soil surface to depths sometimes as great as one hundred feet. As is well known, wind carries the finest particles farthest; the coarsest are dropped first, and the medium sized in between. In general, then, the sands are west of the silts and the silts west of the clays all through much of the West. This pattern has infinite modifying factors, but applies in general. The result is that along the Mississippi much of the land is fine silt or clay of the intensely sticky sort known as gumbo. In short, if the wind had not meddled, this sticky gumbo would have been mixed in with the coarser material from which the wind separated it, and the mixture would have been better able to resist the urge to move with the water.

It seems evident, then, that the dust storms of a decade

ago, which muddied freshly washed windows from Oklahoma to the Atlantic coast, were but a faint imitation of similar but more pretentious exhibitions of prehistoric time. In the days before grass had taken over, before roots of vegetation had "nailed down" this vagrant rock dust, the constant winds must have kept the air always murky with dust they had picked up as they tore through the Garden of the Gods and other soft sandstone areas like the famous "bad lands country." The clay, silt, and sand originally cemented together in the stone were divorced by the wind as they were laid down in the valleys to the east. Thus, erosive quality literally has been built into the coarser of these loess deposits.

The muddy character of the Missouri River, "native" to the very regions from which the wind brought much of this material, can be blamed on those rock-carrying winds. Continuously swept by gusts that blew the soil away before the grass could get started, the "bad lands" that gave birth to the Missouri were forever loading it with debris the wind no longer could carry. (Which may or may not justify the M.V.A. now being urged.) This restlessness of loess deposits definitely pegs the need for terraces to hold them in place against water erosion until binding grass roots can be renewed. My first close contact with loess soil was at the Red Plains Conservation Experiment Station at Guthrie, Oklahoma, where technicians in charge took in hand my education in the lore of this free-moving soil. They showed how badly it is disturbed by water when bare, and how losses are slowed down by a minimum of cover, that a decent protection (with sod) results in losses so slight as to be scarcely measurable. Which means that, as the doctor would say, a grass agriculture is "indicated" for these lands, with only brief periods of row culture in the future, so that organic binders will not again be lost.

Most of the land north of the Ohio and Missouri rivers was overrun by ice in prehistoric time. The scouring produced a land surface as irregular as a strip-mining operation, leaving shallow depressions in which the water became filled with lush vegetation. Each year's growth developed, died, decayed, and fed that of the next season. To this circumstance we owe the existence of vast areas of easily worked, but minerally substandard, soils known as "muck lands." Because of the completeness with which some minerals leach out of organic matter when constantly exposed to water, muck soils require mineral fertilizers within a few years after they are opened for cultivation.

The novice at handling muck soils should not be misled by the vigorous weed growth frequently found on them, for this vagrant fertility is quickly used up by the first few crops the land produces. He should consult competent authorities and follow their advice in the fertilization of such land. He might experiment a little, though, with two short cuts I have heard rumored: road dust is said to provide the necessary minerals quite as effectively as fertilizers on some muck land; and I once heard the president of a muck-farming corporation say his organization had discovered that soybeans disked into the surface proved better for the following crop yield than when plowed in. Remember: these are but rumors, to be tried warily if at all.

So much for two of the numerous special kinds of soil. Popular legend has it that our future life on this planet hangs by a tenuous nine inches of topsoil. Personally, I would not know where to look to find that much real soil in our cultivated fields. Moreover, the world's population has but two acres per person as source of subsistence. Thus draping the picture in mourning, popular writers and speakers proceed (quite sincerely in most cases, I am sure) to throw a scare into a population already made susceptible by newspaper and magazine publicity.

Neither the nine-inches-of-topsoil idea nor the two-acres-per-person figure fairly represents the situation, it seems to me. Aside from the impossibility of locating many acres of farm land with nine inches of topsoil, there is the certainty that, regardless of how many acres per person there may be in this country, half or more of our people are completely isolated from any chance to use more than the fraction of an acre contained in the back yard of a city lot. If there were tragedy in the faded condition of our soil—I mean, if that condition were not quickly curable—there would be reason indeed to worry. But we have only to proceed with sane remedial measures in order to start such soil on its way to recovery within a season or two. The most eroded of our land, once it has been made over into real soil, will readily support one or more persons per acre. I see no need for tears.

Knowing the full self-sufficiency of the soil when properly handled, I cannot conscientiously join the current campaign to induce every farmer to spend his last dollar —and borrow more if necessary—in order to restore "item for item the plant food his crops and animals have removed." Bankers, honestly frightened by the general tone of current propaganda, are offering 4 per cent loans to farmers who will use the money for "conservation" purposes. Substandard land already carries too much of a financial load in many cases. It is high time we made up our minds to adopt natural, economical ways of remaking soil. Such methods, appropriately applied, will make profitable soils out of our poverty-stricken lands—and make them yield a profit while the renovation process is going on. All current efforts to spend the farmer's income for him (albeit, they are wholly sincere) may quite properly be spurned by the farmer and his family, since, after his debts are paid, no one except the farmer and his family has the right to suggest how or whether the farmer should spend it.

The renovation of substandard land is a subject for action, not for words, nor even for financing. It cannot be done all at once, or in big batches. The work will be hard in many instances, but it can produce results if determination backs the effort, and the rewards for so doing are rich indeed.

A Second Look at IV : Sources of Life

SCIENTIFIC INVESTIGATION into soil problems got off to so late a start—so long after the establishment of the Gobi, Sahara, and other desert wastes—that the specter of previous failures beclouded man's vision of the possibilities of soil maintenance. This partly explains why we accept as axioms ideas that cannot possibly be true.

One such idea is the almost universal belief that minerals could become scarce on this earth of ours, which obviously is made up of many cubic miles of "nothing else but." Even while we are saying that there is a shortage of phosphorus or potash, or lime, or any of a dozen others, we know that within every single grain of rock crystal (impenetrable as these crystals are to water) is held precisely the same constituents that were there when the earth finally cooled sufficiently for life to begin. If it were otherwise, the first few rains would have begun to dissolve away the rock and would not have ceased this action as long as a single crystal remained. Our soil is so far from being deficient in minerals that even the sea, which finally gets whatever mineral solution our farms lose, is only salt. If any great amount of earth substance had leached away, sea water would be so salt that no fish could live in it. Instead, the original chemical substance of the earth remains today substantially what it was in the beginning.

No, soils may be *delinquent* in the fulfillment of their duty to supply minerals to the plants which cover the nation's farms, but they cannot be *deficient* in the possession of these minerals. Any thought to the contrary is preposterous, and the sooner we forget it the better off we shall be. Our problem, then, is to determine how the heavy, lifeless stone upon which we construct our skyscrapers and golf courses becomes translated miraculously into living trees, flowers, birds, bees, and even humans. For it does make that transformation in a perfectly normal way and by processes which were in full operation millions of years before the first animal life appeared on the earth as single-celled forerunners of the living occupants of the earth today. Those same processes continue to work now wherever they are not interfered with. Unfortunately, much of our work with the soil tends to make impossible the normal processes which, unmolested, would enable our soil to feed us much more completely and efficiently.

We neglect to recall that in those earliest days, while our earth was cooling to temperatures which would make life possible, these same forces were in existence. As soon as there was a suitable degree of both moisture and warmth, the mystery of life began to stir. From that day to this it has not ceased. If soils were ever deficient, they should have been so in that period when there was not even organic matter to help provide the minerals that would be needed by the emerging life. But even then natural forces easily solved the problems that confront us today. We in this age, with our test tubes and soil augers, are far less adept at handling the current, less serious problems.

But how does rock come alive? That question, with its host of corollaries, forms the basis upon which we have built the United States Department of Agriculture, one or more experiment stations and agricultural colleges in each of the states, and many other special institutions that attempt to find the answer to some phase of this big question. It isn't a $64 question. If Ferdie Deering's calculations are correct, it is a billion dollar question (annually) for the U. S. Department of Agriculture. In his book, *USDA*, he says: "The American public, through the United States Department of Agriculture, is spending upwards of $160 per year for the benefit of each of the six million farms in the nation. This does not mean that each farm receives that much from the government (although many farms receive many times that amount), because most of the direct appropriations go for the salaries, operating expenses, buildings, research, and literature of the many branches that reach out from Washington to touch the farmers in countless ways."[1] Thus you, as a citizen who must help pay the costs of finding the answers, have a right to inquire *whether the nation must support its agriculture,* or *whether,* on the other hand, *properly managed soils can be made to support the nation,* including its farmers.

Believing, as they have been taught, that they must

[1] *USDA,* by Ferdie Deering (Norman, University of Oklahoma Press, 1945), 12.

"feed" the land if they expect it to feed the nation, farmers are easily persuaded to invest an increasing amount year by year in fertilizers, lime, and other "aids" to higher production. (And it should be repeated that so long as the soils they are working are so managed that natural forces cannot operate freely, this necessity for outside "aids" to agriculture is very real. Hence we must not criticize either the farmer or his advisers for doing what in the circumstances is necessary. But we can properly urge that the circumstances be changed.) Millions of tons annually of both lime and the various kinds of fertilizers are applied to the land in the hope that the harvest will be sufficiently larger to pay the extra cost. Usually, though not always, this hope is realized; but in few cases does the land today respond with yields as big or of as fine quality as those it produced when it was first farmed. Currently, farmers are being urged to use still greater quantities of these materials as a means of repairing the "damage" alleged to have been done on their soils by the extra production made necessary by the war emergency.

No permanent good can come of this campaign, and much real harm may result. In the first place, what the soil needs is not another pittance of lime or fertilizers. The earth already provides, in minerals within root reach or in transportable liquid form, enormous tonnages per acre (of more than a few inches depth, to be sure) of everything plants require. What is really needed is the essential activity within the soil of beneficent organic decay. Nothing less will release in the soil the "good fairies" that can again start the wheels of normal productivity. All other treatments or manipulations of the soil for increasing yields are but temporizing with the situation. We may forget with impunity all that science has taught us about soil, if only we give full play to the natural forces which wait merely upon the proper signal. The response to enough properly distributed organic matter in decay will be as normal as the response of a baby to its mother's breast.

If lime and fertilizer campaigns were not of themselves enough to sicken us of such bungling of so vital a matter, we must consider other serious facts. Though at the moment farmers generally can buy more lime and fertilizers, within a few months or years they may need the money they now hold for other and more critical purposes. The age-old problem of crop surpluses definitely lies ahead, and other problems threaten to join in. This prospect is freely admitted even by the men who now are advising greater expenditures for lime and fertilizers. Surplus crops traditionally mean but one thing to farmers: lower prices for the fraction they are able to sell, and loss in many cases of all the rest. Government action has minimized somewhat the economic effects of surpluses, but agencies of government have tried only such remedies as may ease the pain—they have not tried to remove its cause. Indeed, the lime and fertilizer campaign can but help build up even bigger surpluses, thus increasing the very trouble that seems imminent as soon as war dislocations have been relieved.

Perhaps it is not clear just how plants are enabled to "feed at the breast of Nature," since the minerals that constitute an essential part of the diet of plants are securely locked inside crystalline bits of rock that are soluble in water only at rates that chemists express in p.p.m. figures (parts per million). It would seem under such circumstances that plants would be doomed to death if they must wait until rock fragments released enough for their nourishment. So we must proceed to "change the circumstances," and loose within the soil natural forces which greatly speed up the release of plant nutrient elements. The result is that those crystals that yield only a few parts per million of phosphorus, potash, and other minerals to the ordinary water of the soil soon begin to release several times as much. (Ordinary drinking water, it may be recalled, will support plant life. In fact, in an unfertilized soil that has little organic matter in it, the liquid which plant roots deliver to plants is just that, the very dilute mineral solution we drink at faucet, well, or spring.)

Water that contains acids picks up more minerals than can dissolve in pure water. This is especially true when the acid is the simple one formed by the union of water and carbon dioxide—carbonic acid. (H_2O plus CO_2, or H_2CO_3 when the liquid water and the gaseous carbon dioxide have joined.) There are other important acids, *also generated during the process of organic decay,* that are efficient in extracting minerals from rock. These are called *amino acids,* and are different from carbonic acid in that they contain some nitrogen as well as carbon, hydrogen, and oxygen. It may be well to note that protein, with which we are a little more familiar, also contains all four elements. In fact, amino acids are said to be near relatives, chemically, of the proteins. If the exact genealogy were known we might be able to say either that the amino acids derive from proteins as organic matter decays, or that when amino acids are carried up into a plant in water solution they are easily made over into proteins. These are aspects of the problem which we might investigate if more were really known about all this. Scientists do not yet know all of the ways in which amino acids may be important in the soil, in the crops that grow from the soil, and even in the animal body.

If you are disappointed that the scientist really is not better informed about things as important as amino acids, proteins, and so on, consider just one protein of which the exact composition is known, and then recall that nobody knows how many different proteins there are. This one protein is called legumin and is found in the seed of certain kinds of peas. Look what is in it:

Carbon, 118 parts
Hydrogen, 1158 parts
Oxygen, 238 parts
Nitrogen, 214 parts
Sulfur, 2 parts

The complicated work and the expense of analyzing this one protein could hardly be justified for the uncounted number of proteins known to exist. Fortunately, to know the analysis of a protein isn't half so interesting as to know its taste, if it happens to be the principal protein in your favorite food. We may readily exchange our right to know such facts for the pleasure we get from rich flavors.

Mention of flavors in connection with the enrichment of soil by the evolution of multiplied quantities of all the organic acids easily suggests that there may be a direct connection between crop growth (which is promoted by these natural agencies) and those flavors which are remarkably richer and more tasty than any that can be achieved merely by the addition to the soil of fertilizers, lime, etc. Consider some of the differences:

Turnips grown in a heavy clay soil with little organic matter are apt to develop the "hot" characteristic so frequently found in this vegetable. In my experience, I have seen ordinary soil produce some of the hottest of turnips year after year; then have seen that same soil—with no difference, other than that plenty of organic matter had been well mixed into its surface—grow the sweetest, tenderest of turnips.

In the early days of the "research" work in our back yard, we tried to grow turnips, but were able to harvest only hot, wormy roots. Once we foolishly included some of them in a batch of soup, assuming that they would be neutralized by the many times greater volume of other vegetables. The result was soup we could scarcely eat because of the bitterness generated by the turnips. Turnips grown in this same spot since the layer of leaves "melted" into it by decay have been as nearly perfect as any we have ever seen.

At our farm in July, 1945, I hacked down the tall weeds that surrounded an old stump, threw on the soil surface some turnip seeds that were seven or eight years old, and left them without further attention. The catch was not heavy, but we enjoyed all the fresh turnips we could eat for several weeks in the fall. We dug and trenched in about three pecks for winter use, and in January, after the ground had been covered by snow for several weeks, we found that enough turnips had reached edible size that we could have another meal or two from that carelessly planted crop.

The sketchy manner in which these turnips were planted was merely a way of improving what had previously been an eyesore. The weed patch surrounding the stump was a source of annoyance, and its removal was very much to the point as a matter of pride. The turnips that rewarded the effort had the advantage—a real advantage, it seems to me—that they grew under perfectly normal conditions. No hoeing or other cultivation to disturb their roots in their search for food among the decaying mulch of leaves that covered the soil surface. Plenty of natural acids probably helped to make them exceptionally sweet and well flavored. Other turnips, grown in rows near by in the same kind of soil and cultivated along with the other row crops, were coarse, rough, excessively wormy, and of indifferent flavor. Also, the land had been plowed; its weed crop, similar to the weeds around the stump, having been turned under.

But turnips are only one item. One of the most responsive of all vegetable crops is the tomato. Growers of this crop know only too well how it is influenced by growing conditions. Extremes of quality from flabby, thin-walled, watery blobs of imitation tomato to thick-walled, crowded, granular-celled fruits that lose almost no juice upon opening may be found. The differences reflect the great variety of conditions under which the respective crops have grown. Real soil, or a near approach to it, bequeaths to the crops growing on it qualities I have never observed in the same crops growing in substandard soil. Lively and effective organic acids surely have something important to do with the development of high flavors and other excellent qualities.

Vegetables grown in soil that has been restored to naturalness can be eaten daily without the risk that the consumer will grow tired of them. This is true of turnips, tomatoes, potatoes, beans, and all the others that we have grown. Even cucumbers, which we have found difficult to grow without any insect or disease trouble, were as excellent in quality as any of the others in 1945. Often the cucumbers we have grown have developed a slight bitter tang, even though they were otherwise perfect. The 1945 crop was free of this fault, as well as completely free of either insects or diseases. The reason, we think, is that the soil was filled with organic matter, as well as covered with mulch. Also, rains that came too late to do the earlier vegetables very much good were better suited to the cucumbers. I believe, of course, the most important factor in this, as in the case of other vegetables, was the presence in the soil of natural agencies which served up the exact diet the cucumber needs.

Parsnips are another case in point. Many people dislike this vegetable. We grow parsnips, however, with mulch, applying enough to keep the ground surface cool and moist as soon as the plants have grown tall enough.

All the rest of the summer they grow in this mulch-covered soil. Only after they have been frozen do we begin to use them. Occasionally we offer some to the neighbors. In one such case the neighbor's husband had previously refused parsnips, but he ate some of these. Later he called to say that they were the best parsnips he had ever eaten. That had been our verdict, too, but we enjoyed hearing the sentiment from a man who had been prejudiced against this vegetable. Flavor again—lots of it—and of a character to win friends and influence people. Who can doubt the role of the natural organic acids in contriving these flavors under such conditions? How else?

At least one of the war stories out of Europe depicted the Greek people as spurning American white flour when it was offered them by the American Red Cross. The Russians, too, asked our government to adulterate our flour with soy flour so that Russian soldiers would use it for bread making. Color and taste in bread are what the European wants. He has never been able to afford to have his wheat robbed of its best nutriment before he made bread of it, as we have done. We could submit to that emasculation of our wheat because we had plenty of land; and, fortunately, losses from the wheat could be made up from our vegetables and fruit. This was possible years ago. Today it is a different story. Even the vegetables and fruits "ain't what they used to be." We have reached a time when none of our foods can be depended upon under all conditions to be fully nourishing, and most of them are known to be definitely deficient in certain vital substances. Butter, for instance, may or may not have plenty of vitamin A, but we are sure that most of our other foods do not contribute enough of this vitamin to enable us to dispense safely with butter. Many similar examples could be cited. Yet, when our soils were new, people could live comfortably and well on a diet that never varied from week to week. Their foods were satisfactorily nourishing.

Why were the foods of the pioneers superior to ours? Any reply to that question must involve some speculation, of course, for we have no experimental data upon which to base an opinion. We do know that the soils worked by the pioneers were deep and black—deeper in some places than in others, but universally black. These black soils teemed with organic activity; all kinds of destructive organisms lived off the decaying material so abundant everywhere, and contributed their dead bodies in turn to be wrecked and "fed," as decay products, to the hungry rootlets of near-by plants.

Plants growing in such soil surely participated in a far richer diet than is available to plants growing in our faded, solidified, substandard soils of today. Who knows whether, in their race to get as many as possible of the cast-off decay products, plant roots may have found in those black soils amino acids, many kinds of proteins, and miscellaneous organic combinations already partially finished for use in new plants? It is certain that the underprivileged plants we now grow in our pavement-like soils are extremely lucky when they get even a few fragments of ideal building material. Remember, though, that this reasoning is chiefly speculation. We can only guess at the full truth involved here. Yet, if he has the courage to adventure, nothing can hinder a farmer from trying to develop real soil on a small part of his present substandard land. It is a great thrill to watch the generous manner in which an artificially-developed real soil (or even one that is approaching that state) feeds the plants growing upon it.

Earlier I objected gently to the term "deficient" when it is used to define the delinquency of our soils in furnishing everything needed by growing plants. "Deficient" is not the correct word, unless it is understood to mean *a lack of ability to extract minerals from the rock particles of the soil.* Minerals are present in superfluous quantities in almost every mineral soil now being farmed, but the organic activity necessary for liberating them from the crystalline form is lacking. Soils cannot be deficient in minerals; they can only be delinquent in giving them up. And this delinquency will begin to diminish immediately the necessary well-distributed organic matter has been supplied in quantity.

This is not to say that the very first time a large quantity of organic matter is worked into a heavy soil it becomes a real soil over night. Prompt reformation comes about only in the lighter sands and sandy loams, in which manuring makes an otherwise worthless soil produce unbelievably large yields—if there is enough water at the right time. In soil of this kind throughout the South, crop yields as low as ten bushels of corn per acre are not uncommon; yet the judicious use of green manure or any other kind of organic matter may result in yields of fifty to one hundred bushels of corn, or appropriately high yields of other crops. The explanation for this free and easy disposition of the lighter soils must lie in the fact that air can penetrate freely and participate in the development of the right kind of environment. Both the oxygen and the nitrogen of the air take part in the decomposition of organic matter, and when admitted freely—without consequent drying out of the soil—they hasten both the decay of the organic matter and the re-use of the decay products in the growth of new plants.

Heavy soils lack this ability to admit air. Before they can let air in freely they must develop deep and thorough granulation. Until this granulation has been accomplished, it is difficult to incorporate the needed organic matter, and several successive attempts must be made in some cases to complete the mixing of green manure crops with the soil. Once the decay of these crops has established granular structure in the soil, air passes in and out about as freely as in the lighter soils. Then, and not until then, the ability of the soil to produce begins to hit its maximum stride. The happy aspect of heavy soils, though, is that this open structure can be maintained after it has been established. Thus heavy soils, when productive, do not quickly lose this ability to produce.

The melodramatic character of what we might call the chemical "sources of life" is something to marvel at. The chemist is familiar with what he calls the "properties" of oxygen, hydrogen, carbon, phosphorus, and all the other chemical units that become part of living things. Most of these "elements" detest being alone. Oxygen, for example, is most difficult to keep in a state of "single blessedness." Only by confinement in "solitary" can it be restrained from joining up with one or more of dozens of neighboring elements, especially if they too are "on the loose." The enthusiasm with which oxygen forms these unions is usually quite evident from the heat that is generated in the process. You need but raise the temperature of wood or coal to a few hundred degrees Fahrenheit, and oxygen freely parts company with the other elements it is associated with in the air, and unites vigorously with the carbon of the wood or coal, with ever increasing heat. And, if oxygen is being held in the pure form (incommunicado, so to speak), a few iron filings thrown into its cell will become a sparkling, hot shower as they are seized by the oxygen. Whole books could be written about the antics of oxygen alone. Other elements that are part of all living tissues are equally spectacular.

Carbon, for example, is one of the busiest, measured by our usual commercial standards. The lead of your pencil is the most familiar example of carbon on the job. Unlike some of the others, carbon is able to go it alone; and does so in several other forms besides pencil leads. Diamonds are pure carbon. Coal and charcoal are impure forms. Combined with oxygen, carbon exists as a gas, a liquid, or a solid. The solid form is popularly known as "dry ice." The liquid is the intermediate stage between the solid and the gas, and is produced by compressing the gas. Gaseous carbon dioxide is the chief constituent of smoke, and for that matter, of your breath. Plants take in carbon dioxide and release oxygen, just the reverse of the breathing of animals. The truth is that carbon is a part of every organic compound. It may be said that living things owe everything they have, and are, to this midnight black element carbon and a few of its cronies. Every substance ordinarily used as fuel, from natural gas through alcohol, the gasoline family, kerosene, and coal—all are fuels solely because they contain carbon so held that it can still combine with oxygen. The enthusiasm with which these two elements meet creates the heat.

Hydrogen also tags along, chiefly associated with oxygen, as a component of organic compounds. Hydrogen is very elevating. It lifts airships and toy balloons. Its chief claim to fame is the fact that but for it there would be no water to drink. Combined with oxygen, hydrogen holds together that liquid on which we float all our battleships. If the two are separated, as they may be in the laboratory, we have nothing left but a couple of rowdy gases.

Unions, in various proportions, of the three elements we have discussed, account for all our sugars, starches, alcohols, and the whole list of related substances known as carbohydrates. No other elements enter into the composition of the carbohydrates. The same is true of the fats and oils. So these three in an all but infinite variety of combinations make up the greater part of all organic compounds. They may not sound like sources of life, but we couldn't live without them.

But we have only started. While the "big three" we have named make up by far the bulk of all living organic matter, and its dead remains—90 to 95 per cent as a rule —there are a score or more of elements plants obtain from the earth (the above are contributed by air and water) that are just as vital to the existence of every plant and animal.

One of these, the gas, nitrogen, prevents violent clashes between oxygen and many other substances. If nitrogen were not constantly present in the air as a dilutant of oxygen, few things would be safe from what the chemist calls oxidation. Iron, for instance, rusts (oxidizes) at relatively slow speed—solely because nitrogen, the chaperon, we might say, cools the ardor of the oxygen, which otherwise would destroy iron (as such) in very short order. Railroad rails in the presence of pure oxygen would fall into rust in a matter of days or weeks.

Air fills every empty space, in soil as anywhere else, of course; and nitrogen enters the soil with oxygen (as part of the air), the two of them literally feeding the fires of decay, and generally speeding up these processes. The nitrogen, in this instance, is consumed as food by bacteria which are busy wrecking organic matter in the soil. Later this same nitrogen assumes its role as a key part of proteins being built into the tissues of new plants. Thus this "good fairy" of both plant and animal nutrition leaves its natural state in the atmosphere and co-operates with other chemical elements in the making of plant (and later animal) tissues (proteins).

Of the elements plants must use, some found in minerals are surprisingly dramatic when alone. Phosphorus is so "in love" with oxygen that the two literally fly together on contact. Because of this unusual trait of phosphorus, chemists who make use of free phosphorus keep this bad actor under water all the time, thus preventing contact with the oxygen of the air. But only an instant of exposure to air is needed to cause it to take fire, because of violent "oxidation." Yet, in company with other elements in the rocks of the soil, phosphorus is quite decorus. When it is diluted by many hundred times its weight of other elements in living tissues, we don't even suspect its presence; but it is essential in every single cell of our bodies. Without it the cells soon cease their work and are useless.

Potash, or potassium, as the chemist calls it, is almost as unruly as phosphorus, save that its behavior is somewhat different. In the laboratory potassium must be kept submerged in oil—to protect it from oxygen. If a bit of potassium is dropped into water, it divorces the two elements that make up the water (hydrogen and oxygen) and combines with the oxygen at so great a heat that a flame actually rests upon the water until the action is complete. (Note that potassium must be kept in oil, while phosphorus must be kept in water. Reversing them would be disastrous, as the above indicates.)

Calcium behaves very much like potassium when it is in pure form, so little need be said about it in that respect. Its most common combined form is limestone—in which calcium is combined with carbon and oxygen, the two elements first mentioned. Limestone is much more easily dissolved by water than are any of the other stones. Throughout the world there is usually a high proportion of calcium carbonate (as compared with the other earth minerals) in the water. For all plant-food purposes, the soil water of most localities has plenty of "lime."

Iron and sulphur are the only two elements with which most people are familiar that are taken by plants in their inorganic forms from the earth. Pure iron and pure sulphur are not unusual, and they do not exhibit the nervousness for "company" that characterizes most of the others mentioned.

Besides those mentioned, there is a long list of elements whose habits are not so well known, and whose function in plant life is equally vague. Little can or need be said about them, even though they are just as vital, in some situations, as are any of these others. A list of those known to be present in the tissues of some plants is as follows: Aluminum, arsenic, barium, beryllium, boron, bromine, chlorine, chromium, cobalt, copper, fluorine, germanium, gold, iodine, lead, lithium, magnesium, manganese, molybdenum, nickel, rubidium, selenium, silicon, silver, sodium, strontium, titanium, vanadium, and zinc. Thus nearly forty of the known chemical elements have been found normally in plant tissues. Some of those named have seemed to be present in the soil in too small quantities, and in some instances additions of these to soil have resulted in increased crop yields. However, it seems reasonable to assume that any adaptation of farm practices that brings enough of the major elements into active condition in the soil will also restore these lesser elements in the same way.

If you are looking for the material sources of life, then, these are a few of them.

A Second Look at V : Rewards for Your Work

MOST OF US accept without question the thought that we benefit from any given activity only in proportion to what we have put into it. Yet if we examine the facts we soon find that in many things this adage is not true. Many an unsuccessful purchaser of a home or a farm can testify that he failed to realize a profit, and lost the property besides. But perhaps that isn't the kind of thing that is intended by this proverb. Regardless of just what kind of venture is supposed to yield according to what one puts into it, the idea has been applied to farm work without protest for many years. The farmer who uses much fertilizer, does a "good" plow job, and cultivates often is thought to be more certain of a deserved reward than is the fellow who gives his work "a lick and a promise" and lets it go at that. Nevertheless, it doesn't always work out that way.

I can never forget the amusement my father's hired men got out of the well-known fact that some of the hill farmers in our area cleared a piece of land during the winter, planted it to corn in the spring, using a mattock or a pointed stick to make the "hills," then worked away from home all summer without even seeing their field of corn, and came home in the fall to harvest more corn per acre than father could expect from his bottom land richly fertilized and well cared for all summer. Father knew this was true, but never suspected why. He was good natured about an occasional jibe, for he knew the hired men didn't know why either. Both he and they realized from experience that the hill farmer could do this only the first two or three years. After that the land either produced little or was allowed to "lie idle" for a few years until it grew up again to trees; then it would be cleared once more for another period of good crops.

The second period of culture did not produce the lush kind of crops that had developed in the original clearing though, for weeds had become established during that early cropping period when cultivation was impossible because of the tree roots that still remained in the soil. Thereafter it was necessary to fight weeds in the clearings just as in our bottom land. And the corn yields never again reached the high standard, either in quantity or in quality, of those first few years. This seemed, of course, to vindicate as long-time practice our ways of handling the land.

At that point we apparently stopped reasoning about the problem. Our land was growing several times as heavy yields as it had grown before father bought it. It even grew better crops for one or more decades than the adjoining land, which had been better than ours at the time father bought our farm. All these facts suggested that we were probably producing as large yields as we had a right to expect.

In all those years, though, corn roots would gather on

the cultivator shanks as they passed through the soil. Since we used walking cultivators, we continued working the corn until it tasseled, which was several days, or even weeks, after the neighbors had quit. Even so, our fields in the fall bore no happy comparison with those of our neighbors. Our fields contained more weeds than theirs because we used large quantities of manure hauled from Jellico, Tennessee, a few miles away. Our neighbors used none at all, so far as I ever noticed. Inasmuch as we spread and disked in this manure after the plowing, the upper few inches of the soil were full of it, encouraging the corn roots to develop there, and furnishing an ideal environment in which weeds could develop after cultivation was over.

This weed problem always worried father, for he prided himself on having the cleanest fields in the neighborhood. As a matter of fact, the promise was greater than the fufillment when corn-cutting time came round in the late fall and our weed crop was exposed to full view, like dirt swept under a rug. Father tried to remedy the situation by having us go through the standing corn with hoes in September. This was done for two seasons, and we cut out every weed. Those two seasons proved, however, that the desired results could not be achieved by this method. There were just as many weeds to fight next season as before. Father didn't realize, as most farmers do not, that the plowing which effectively buries this season's weed seed, just as effectively brings within germination range the seed from previous seasons' weed crops. Hence he was never able to solve the problem presented to him.

All of which emphasizes the confusion that has resulted in our surrender to weeds on American farms. And "surrender" is, in my opinion, the correct word. We do not realize that weeds were not present until the land had once been cleared of trees and brought into cultivation, or that our manner of handling the land has fostered weed development. If only for the sake of avoiding some of the labor we now have to devote to our crops, we owe it to ourselves to get rid of weeds. Yet freedom from weeds is but *one* of the probable benefits of weedless farming. We have a right to expect that decidedly higher crop yields will result, and that the crops themselves might actually be higher in nutritive value.

We have lived with weeds for so long, fought them consciously, and unwittingly planted a new crop each time we plowed our land that we consider anyone stupid who suggests we could be rid of them. Even though in *Plowman's Folly* I titled a chapter "Weedless Farming," caution prompted the statement that "the theories presented in this chapter have not been fully demonstrated." Unfortunately, circumstances did not permit the completion of tests I then had started for the purpose of proving the possibility of weed elimination. Subsequently Mrs. Faulkner and I visited a farm in New York where for more than a decade the land had been farmed without plowing; there the possibility of banishing weeds had been proved. George H. Beach, the proprietor, had grown vetch and wheat in winter to be cut in early summer for hay or silage, and had followed with soybeans and Sudan grass for late-summer hay or silage. The semiannual mowing of the land, plus close-growing crops exclusively in his rotation, had made it impossible for weeds to mature seeds. The land, save for one field, was completely free of weeds. Yet Mr. Beach had not been fighting weeds consciously. He had merely been keeping the land busy so continuously, leaving no time for weed-seed development, that weeds had simply been ruled out by circumstances.

The one exceptional field mentioned above was excessively weedy. On inquiry we learned that this field had been started into this rotation only the preceding spring. Taken over from other uses, it had been seeded to soybeans and Sudan grass in the early summer. At the time we were there these had been only partially harvested. The extremely weedy condition of the unharvested crop highlighted the effectiveness of Mr. Beach's rotation in conquering weeds, originally just as bad in all the fields.

We may believe with reason that the pattern of our farming may have developed around attempts at weed control—chiefly so that crops would not be shaded by weeds. There is no positive proof to the contrary.

We can only speculate as to why we plow the land in preparation for growing a crop, and later cultivate that crop by stirring the soil surface; but we know that the farmers of antiquity followed methods that differ from those of today's farmers chiefly in matters of detail. They had no moldboard plow, but they did try to kill off the vegetation already on the land before they planted their crops. This they did by using plows of the crudest sort, but quite similar to implements being used today in some backward areas of the world. If destruction of volunteer growth was, and is, the significant advantage to be attained from plowing and cultivation, perhaps crops would thrive in soil that had not been stirred, if weeds were kept in check. There is evidence that this is really true.

I have grown crops in soil which had not been worked down to a seed bed before they were planted, and which, in some cases, was not stirred afterward. The results usually were good, and correspondents often report growing crops under similar circumstances. A victory gardener of Dayton, Ohio, writes:

> In 1944 the garden which had grown a dense crop of weeds was plowed and gardened that year. It lay next to a wood, and I gathered leaves, decayed bark, and twigs, and scattered them under the tomato vines in 1944. In the spring of 1945 I cut everything on the ground in March with a hoe, only striking hard enough to cut the trash to small bits and mix it with the topsoil. No plowing was done.
>
> In the tomato patch the soil was loose enough to press the hand several inches into the ground without difficulty. I set the plants and had an abundant crop.
>
> None of the other patches was plowed, but the soil was not so loose, because there was very little cover on it the year before. The entire garden made a better yield, and this was especially true of pop corn and sweet corn. The garden was planted after only the topsoil was stirred. I used level cultivation and never plowed with a cultivator. My garden plow was fitted with an inverted tool (similar to a hoe) about twelve inches wide. This enabled me to skim the topsoil and cut the weeds. I raised more corn than ever before.
>
> Watermelons did fine though they were started late.

Another correspondent in Yonkers, New York, says:

I was attracted to your book because of certain practices which I had followed for several years to restore humus to our local heavy-clay soils. Last year, using your suggested methods, I grew the best tomatoes in the neighborhood, picked fruit a month earlier, and had it while prices were still prohibitive in the stores. Two neighbors using the same field never did get a crop.

Similar quotations from victory gardeners and amateurs all over the country could be given. Most of these people were delighted with the discovery that better crops can be grown with less work. An occasional report, of course, doesn't glow. Usually people who did not succeed report that they intend trying again, indicating that they believe the trouble may have consisted in the methods they used. Though not all succeed, we can be sure that if plowing or other breaking of the land were essential, *none* would succeed without it. Yet the overwhelming majority of people who have reported did succeed.

The letters quoted came from men who can resort to mulches or other dodges to avoid work. Not all reports are from amateurs. This letter from George H. Beach, owner of the weedless farm discussed earlier, shows that men who are deep in commercial farming may adopt methods that do not require as much work as those generally prevailing:

I bought 800 acres back in 1920-21 at Chatham, New York, all abandoned hill farms—110 acres crop land, the rest woods, brush, and rock pasture.

[It is] a clay soil with hardpan—rock clay—six to ten inches down. We plowed and spent many thousands of dollars for fertilizers [doing] the conventional type of farming. I was making money [elsewhere] and the farming was play. Then in the 1930's the plan had to be on a practical basis—and right there, from our experiments, we ceased to plow except the gardens, and after reading *Plowman's Folly* we quit even that.

We began to have better hay crops than anyone around; every three or four years top dressed with fertilizer or manure; broadcast legume seeds on the stubble; and on 110 acres [grew] 250 to 300 tons of hay for 150 to 200 head of stock plus grass ensilage for 80 milk cows.

For some years we disk-harrowed clay for soybeans and Sudan grass ensilage—the clay so hard that the disk made only little dents, but the broadcast seed returned a bumper crop. Then the topsoil got mellow and now we broadcast seed on stubble and then disk it in.

Plowing is a terrific expense, and when we quit we began to get somewhere.

Two years ago we disked our garden, and had a wonderful garden—everything in it. Last year we could disk long before plowing was possible, so I got our garden in early. We had a fair result, but no one else had any garden to speak of in our clay country. I planted ten one-hundred-foot rows of corn in the hard clay, pulled topsoil over it, and [had] a beautiful corn yield both years in spite of terrible weather last year.

Mr. Beach was the first of several men who wrote, after reading my book, to tell me they were farming and had not plowed for years. Mr. Beach's first letter was so interesting that in September, 1944, Mrs. Faulkner and I made a trip to his place, and there spent a delightful day with him and Mrs. Beach walking over and studying his mellow, weed-free soil.

The work of two other farmers, Arnold G. Ingham, of

Virginia, and Mack Gowder, of Georgia, has been given wide publicity by *Soil Conservation,* a little magazine issued monthly by Soil Conservation Service. In recent months I have had some interesting correspondence with Mr. Ingham, who hasn't plowed for more than fifteen years. Mr. Gowder has not used the moldboard plow for breaking his land in the thirty odd years he has farmed it. It is richer now, he thinks, than it was when he cleared it of trees.

The experiences of such men are highly significant. None is trying to show how farming ought to be done. Each is interested only in the superior results to be had by the use of unusual methods. Their land must pay the bills, and their long-continued loyalty to plowless methods proves definitely that, under their conditions at least, plowless methods are profitable. No state-supported experiments, it seems to me, could be more significant, for they would necessarily lack the financial authenticity that goes with the practices being used by regular farmers who must get the cost of their operations from the land.

But we started out to discuss the benefits the farmer gets from his work. The benefits of actual weedless farming would scarcely be disputed by anyone. Once farm land has really been made free of weeds, the necessity for cultivating crops would cease, for years ago it was decided that the only real benefit achieved by the cultivation of a crop was the control of weeds. The absence of weeds to be controlled would save the farmer a large part of the cost of growing his crops, to say nothing of the time saved for other purposes. For instance, late planting of corn in recent years has pushed the cultivation period of the corn crop deeper and deeper into the first days when hay should be cut. And at every meeting he attends the farmer is urged to cut his hay earlier in order to get it into the mow at its richest condition. He can't be in the hay field and in the corn field at the same time—though some farmers compromise by trying to cultivate corn early and make hay late in the day. They usually wind up by not getting the cultivation done, nor the hay in without damage by rain. Freedom to make hay early, without bothering with the corn, would make for better farming, to the extent that the hay would be of better quality.

But this might turn out to be a minor advantage. Had it ever occurred to you that in cultivating your crops—thereby keeping the upper two or three inches of the soil continuously dry—you rob the crop of the chance to gather plant food from those upper inches? That is most certainly true. And that is not all. There is a good chance that the plant food materials to be found in the upper inch or two of the soil might be even of better quality than those that are gathered at greater depths. There is reason to think so:

We are thinking, of course, of conditions in a real soil—one in which great quantities of organic matter are continuously decaying. In such a soil plant roots would find decay products at all levels. Carbon dioxide would be released at all levels as a product of the decay. It is certain that the amount of air present would be higher in the upper inches than at greater depths. It is also true that, in a granulated soil which admits air freely, capillary water also finds its way upward very nearly to the surface. Thus, every necessity of the growing plant is brought into the most vital zone of the soil—the upper inch, or the upper few inches. The more liberal supply of nitrogen that can enter these upper inches suggests the possibility that the carbon dioxide given off by decay may be quickly made over into an amino acid of some character; or that proteins of a sort may result from the intimate association of water, air, both carbonic and amino acids, and other decay products. All this, of course, is but an exercise of the imagination; but the performance of growing plants under such conditions makes this seem plausible. Also, the taste of foods grown under such conditions makes it necessary to assume that something out of the ordinary does happen in this zone, otherwise there is no way to account for the greatly improved palatability of crops so grown.

If the actual goings-on in the soil bear any relation to what has been imagined here, would it not be a crime against Nature to force our food-crop plants to forage for their food at depths to which nitrogen and oxygen could not penetrate freely? Would it be too much to assume that crops might have a higher protein content, if their roots could invade every cubic inch of the soil, than they could have if the roots were excluded from the upper two or three inches by the loosening and drying effects of cultivation? There are reasons for thinking this might actually be true. However, no official tests have ever been made, so far as I know, to determine what differences, if any, would exist in two such situations. All I know is that the crops I have grown under such conditions as permitted their roots to feed freely upon organic decay have uniformly been of better taste than I have ever experienced in any such food grown in the usual way.

This, then, is the many-sided result that seems possible—even probable—from our making substandard soils over into real, honest-to-goodness soils. We have no way of knowing how inferior in quality almost all of our food may now be, because of the fact that nearly all of our land is managed with a view to covering the largest possible area with our operations, rather than with the determination to grow the best possible quality of product. No one who has not experienced the difference in taste between one of our machine-grown carrots from the grocer's shelf and one grown under mulching in his own garden can imagine the extent of that difference. Some writers have said that carrots may vary so much that one may have sixty times as much of a given human food requirement as another. I am in no position to know whether this is true; but I do know that vegetables you can grow in your own garden with abundance of organic matter have a flavor *not* to be matched in the market. And I don't believe the result can be traced solely to the freshness of the home-grown product.

Indeed, there are rewards for your work worth insisting upon.

A Second Look at VI : Soil "Needs"

NO THESIS in the whole field of soil management theories is more implicitly accepted than the counting-house notion that, in order to continue growing profitable crops indefinitely, the soil must be reimbursed for its past outlay of chemical elements. This must be accomplished, of course, by the liberal use of lime and fertilizers. The agronomist who recently told me he could give complete approval to *Plowman's Folly*, except for its assumption that fertilizers are not needed, may have expressed a view held rather widely among soil scientists today. He assumed, correctly, that green manures cannot restore to the land anything save the elements they take from that soil and from the air and water. Yet, in order to assume that earth does not (and cannot) provide plants with every required mineral, scientists must forego consideration of much contradictory evidence from both laboratory and field.

Before we make further examination of this idea it may be well to note the implication of the necessity for reimbursement. Such a theory can be based only upon the assumption that the soil in which a plant anchors its roots is little, if anything, more than anchorage and (to a certain extent) water supply. If that were true, then it would be necessary to provide in some chemical form every ounce of each essential food material. Then, having provided for the plant's need, we should be able later to analyze both plant and soil and recover from the soil the exact amount of excess plant food we had provided. Also, analysis of the plant would show just how much plant food it had used. From this data we could easily set up a complete balance sheet showing all these details. Every agronomist knows that no such accurate plant-mineral inventory is possible.

Instead, if a real attempt is to be made to approximate the amount of minerals a plant uses, greenhouse "pot" experiments are made in which pure white silica sand is used in lieu of soil, and all the needed minerals are supplied. Since the silica sand crystals furnish none of the essential plant-food elements, suitable technique does make it possible to arrive at a general notion of the amount used by the plant, and the amount remaining in the sand. The results of field tests with fertilizers, however, are never expected to approach bookkeeping accuracy, and are expressed usually in terms which state whether the fertilizer applied was "paid for" by the increase in yield. "Check" plots, unfertilized, show what the untreated land would have grown. In such work, just as in the farmer's fields, no one can be sure how much of a given crop was an effect of the fertilizers used. There is always a free donation from the soil, the amount of which cannot be tabulated.

If nothing were contributed to a crop by the soil in which it grows, it would be perfectly feasible to produce a balance sheet showing the amount of fertilizers used and the quantity of these same chemicals that could be recovered by analysis from the ash of the burned crop. Since it is demonstrably possible to produce good crop yields continuously year after year from the same land—as many world peoples have done for untold centuries—it is pertinent to try to establish the reason for this paradox. We may be sure that *unless soil really is self-sufficient, its future complete exhaustion is predictable, regardless of future farm practice in the use of fertilizers.*

In other words, the future of the human race depends upon the self-sufficiency of the soil that grows our crops. This unusual view must, of course, be supported by incontestible evidence if it is to stand. I have no hesitancy in attempting to give it the support it requires.

Our civilization would flicker out quickly indeed if the supply of plant-food minerals should become exhausted. Food is the fuel of life—from plant to animal—and man is dependent directly or indirectly upon plants that must find in the earth the minerals they need. The failure of plants to find sustenance in the earth would be our failure as well. Hence, unless the soil contains an absolutely inexhaustible supply of minerals upon which plant roots can draw at will, we may as well drape our shrouds about us. I call attention to this theoretic dilemma of our civilization so that you may realize how tenuous is our life tenure, if food production depends really upon regular applications to the land of lime, phosphates, and potash salts.

We face several facts in this connection: 1. The supply

of fertilizer raw materials is limited. Known deposits probably will supply the needs of American farmers for a few more generations, but there is of necessity an end to the supply. 2. If American soils, despoiled by less than four centuries of use, require replacement item by item of all the used minerals, what of the soils elsewhere in the world where dense populations have been supported for uncounted centuries on land that still shames the American farmer by its outstandingly high production? Is it not logical that Chinese, Burmese, Indian, Japanese, African, and other world farmers must also "reimburse" their soil for its outlay of minerals in growing these big crops for so long? If so, each oriental acre would require many times as much replacement as most American acres. What would that do to the supply of fertilizers? Obviously, every known source of phosphate would soon be exhausted, and other materials would eventually disappear.

This clear limitation to the earth's ability to supply world agriculture indefinitely with supplementary plant food means one of two things: (1) Civilization, even life on the earth, is doomed to cease shortly; or (2) our theories of soil fertility are incorrect in some respect. I prefer to believe we have made some mistakes in our thinking about the soil.

Theories aside for the moment, we know that the earth did support for millions of years before man arrived on the scene both vegetation and animal life on so stupendous a scale as to dwarf the present known total of living creatures. This knowledge supports the idea that our soil-fertility theories must have become snarled. Basically, life evolves from earth minerals somewhat in this fashion, to put the matter in its most elementary terms:

Plants take minerals from two general sources within the soil, *primary* and *secondary* ones. Primary sources are solid rock, finely powdered, and varying in size from a fineness that few microscopes can detect to the coarse sands and fine gravels. Most soils contain the whole range of sizes of rock particles (*primary* source material for plant-food minerals), and the bulk of most soils is made up of just plain powdered rock—90 to nearly 100 per cent, in fact, are of this *primary* source material. It is this preponderance of *primary* source material in a soil that makes it so light in color. If there is any appreciable amount of *secondary* source material in a given soil, it appears usually as a smudge of black, indicating the presence of partially decayed organic matter.

Indeed organic matter is, or should be, the chief *secondary* source of plant-food minerals in a soil. However, all the other forms in which these minerals can be held in the soil are included in the term *secondary*. At any rate, secondary sources include *organic matter in decay*, *water* carrying dissolved minerals, *colloidal* forms of both mineral and organic substance, and even *crystalline* forms of mineral that was left in the soil by the evaporation of soil water which had dissolved this mineral from *primary* sources, or from other secondary sources, and had held it in solution in the soil. Many soils in regions of low rainfall carry much of their *secondary* plant-food minerals in this quickly available, crystalline form. And as compensation (in order to be equally fertile), soils in areas where rainfall is high must have correspondingly greater quantities of their *secondary* sources of plant-food minerals in the less leachable, organic form.

Since the *secondary* forms of plant-food minerals have derived in one way or another from the rock itself as the *primary* source, it should be obvious that high productivity can be expected from a soil only when it holds an abundance of mineral plant foods in these readily available sources. It should be clear, too, that the wise farmer must look well to maintaining the supply of *secondary* plant mineral sources in his soil if he wishes it to keep up high production. Indeed, if any single difference distinguishes the American farmer from his colleagues in other parts of the world, it is the careless attitude he takes toward his soil. Dissipation of *secondary* plant-food sources has meant little to him. He could always make up for the lower yields per acre by using more land, or cheap commercial fertilizers, or both. Farmers of other parts of the world have been forced by limitations of both finance and land area to follow practices which, while unmechanized, have maintained at a high level the rate at which *secondary* sources of plant-food minerals have been evolved from the rock itself. On this account, it is still true that farmers of many foreign countries do—and always have done—a much better job of crop production per acre than our own farmers.

The progressive bleaching that has occurred in American soils during the past several decades reflects the reduction in their stores of available minerals—which are, of course, plant nutrient elements in *secondary* forms. Within the last ten to twenty years, this depletion has become so serious that farmers no longer dare plant their chief crops until they have had their soils tested. The tests used are designed to inventory roughly the amount of minerals the proposed crop can be expected to get from the soil in question during a normal season. The results correspond rather closely to the *secondary* minerals present in the soil at the time, and have little or no relation to the infinite quantity of *primary* source material from which, by proper management, an abundance of *secondary* minerals is derived.

During the past thirty years these "quick" tests have been brought to a high degree of efficiency. Some specialists in soil testing are now able to predict rather accurately the yields that may be expected when the farmer follows the recommendations which officials base upon their tests. Accuracy of this kind makes the tests of great value to farmers in planning for the current season's crops, and it is natural that they should place great reliance upon test findings. Unfortunately, however, farmers get the idea that their soil contains only the amounts of plant-food minerals shown by tests. They fail to distinguish between the incalculable stores of *primary* source material and the *secondary* materials usable during the current season. This failure makes it difficult to convince farmers that their soil is potentially very rich, despite its present quite low capacity for crop production.

There is a consequent tendency on the part of farmers to become ready customers for fertilizers and lime. Without thinking, they follow the recommendations that grow out of these quick tests, little realizing that such practice makes permanent a type of farming which inevitably must continue holding the land on a low plane of productiveness. Farming of this type is virtually "hand to mouth" feeding of crops, yet farmers think of it as scientific. Nothing could be further from the truth.

It is proper, certainly, for a farmer to gauge his applications of fertilizers and lime by some accurate indicator of the amounts needed for the current crop. Measured applications often produce the expected yield at smaller cost than might be achieved otherwise. But it is not a good thing for the farmer to accept the dependence upon lime and fertilizers that this practice plainly encourages. Expenditures for these items must be returned to the farmer in the selling price of his products, if he is to continue in business. The cost of the lime and fertilizers must come out of the pockets of consumers of crops, eggs, pork, milk, beef, and other food items produced by farmers who employ these "aids" to production. Food costs for everybody in the United States, then, are higher by that much, because farmers thoughtlessly accept the "bank-account theory" that minerals removed from the soil by crops must be replaced. This theory is perfect economics, but rotten science.

For proof that there is no scientific justification for "feeding" fertilizers to crops, we need only recall how our deposits of fertilizer raw materials came into existence. The story is so well known that most high-school freshmen in general science can repeat it without difficulty.

In the beginning, the whole mass of the earth, as it cooled to temperatures that made life possible, was rock. The effects of weathering through millions of years broke up this rock and fined the fragments to the particle sizes we find in today's soils. This was all *primary* source material for plants, which, incidentally, could not exist until after some breaking up or dissolution of the rock had occurred. And the very earliest land plants—the lichens, mosses, etc.—had to start from this pure rock. This means that they had to get their phosphorus, potash, lime, iron, sulphur, magnesium, and all the rest directly from rock. And the rock from which these earliest plants obtained their sustenance was just like the rock particles of our soils today. No change in rock substance could have taken place, for the crystals of which all rock is made are impervious to water. Water can dissolve away slight amounts of mineral from the surfaces of rock particles, but it cannot invade the crystal itself. Therefore, plant food that was held originally in the earth's rock is still so held, waiting for organic decay to release it for use.

To continue the story of the earliest plant life:

As the first plants died their remains became *secondary* sources from which later plants could obtain minerals much more easily than by the slower method of absorbing minerals dissolved from rock. After thousands of years, the gradual accumulation of previously used plant-food materials built up in favored areas masses of real soil which contained a high proportion of *secondary* sources of plant-food minerals. In these fertile areas grew literal "forests" of the simple plants of the period—ferns and other intermediate plants preceding those that later produced true seeds. With the satisfactory establishment of these plants, it became possible for animals to exist by grazing.

The plants used minerals, including phosphorus, from both *primary* and *secondary* sources. The animals, in turn, built these same materials into their tissues, retaining large portions of phosphorus in their bones, just as all animals do today. Apparently death came to multitudes of these animals as they sought water at the muck-filled ponds and lakes. Hordes of them were trampled into the mire by others in search of water. The accumulated bones of these animals eventually became solidified with other materials into rock, and our present source of phosphorus for fertilizers lies in the beds of this rock found in Tennessee, South Carolina, Florida, and elsewhere.

It should be clear that there could be no "deposits" of phosphate rock from which to make fertilizers unless the soils of millions of years ago (like soils today) were made up of rock particles which could:

1. supply phosphorus to plants, which in turn could
2. supply phosphorus to animals, which died and accumulated the beds of phosphate rock which can now
3. supply phosphorus to fertilizer manufacturers to be made into fertilizers for American farmers.

Therefore, unquestionably, the mass of powdered rock making up today's soils—unchanged from its chemical condition as of the Year 1, geologically—still holds all the phosphorus needed by today's plants.

While the above analysis applies to phosphorus only, an equally simple story explains the potash beds from which essential salts are now being mined for the fertilizer and other industries. Limestone, too, had to be precipitated from sea water (which accumulated it from the land through the water which had dissolved it from earth rock). Crustaceans used it for their shells, as may be seen by examining the shell imprints in many ledges of today's limestone. All of which shows that the rock originally had—and must still have—the minerals of life. Knowing that all soil contains *in its original chemical form* every substance that ever existed in the soil rock, our task is to learn to reduce this *primary* plant food to the *secondary* forms which crops can readily use. Discussion of how this may be done is reserved for the next chapter, but we may say here that throughout most of the world impecunious farmers who couldn't buy a bag of fertilizer if their lives depended upon it are producing *secondary* forms—and their ancestors were doing the same thing for uncounted generations before them.

Despite the known fact that most of the world gets along nicely without using commercial fertilizers, to suggest that American farmers could feed our population without their use will cause grave misgivings. Scientists will be inclined to remark that there are no supporting experimental data. That statement will be perfectly true, but it will not be significant, for, while experimental data are lacking, the premises upon which this point of view is based are far older than the oldest of the world's agricultural experimentation—just as the law of gravitation was working millions of years before that apple bumped the scientist's head.

With all the earnestness in the world, we have been studying abnormalities of crop growing, when we should have been trying to find how crops normally do their best. The substandard soils we have dealt with did respond to applications of fertilizers, because their natural means of preparing *secondary* forms of plant food from the *primary* sources had been taken away by past cropping without replacement. Once we have developed real soils from those that are now badly substandard, the use of fertilizers will cease to produce an increase in crop yield. That is the goal toward which our soil science should be working.

By eliminating the expense of lime and fertilizers, our farmers will contribute importantly toward lower living costs for all of us. The resulting cheaper farm products will move more freely in trade, both here and abroad. Surpluses, so-called, will become more manageable. By taking full advantage of the productive capacity of real soil, at the same time retaining their mechanical lead over other farmers the world over, American farmers can again undersell the rest of the world on many farm products that move in world trade. Lowered living costs within industry will similarly ease world competition for manufactured goods. The whole world will benefit from a reduction of per-unit costs for both raw materials and manufactured goods; and trade will flourish without the recoil that accompanies subsidies and other subterfuges.

All this, without even considering the improved quality that always accompanies higher yields so obtained. Plenty of *secondary* food material in easy root reach means complete health for crop plants: richer flavor as well as the higher yields attest this fact. Perhaps it sounds paradoxical to suggest that unfertilized crops will actually contain more minerals and a greater variety of them than would be found in well-fertilized crops, but there is considerable body of evidence indicating that this is true. Moreover logic may be on the side of the unfertilized crop.

Nobody as yet even pretends to know all about the complexity of nutrition of either plants or animals. We can learn something by analysis of plant and animal products for the detectable elements they contain; but even then we have no way of knowing what undetectable elements, vital to health, may be present, or worse, may be absent. In a fragmentary way we know a little in the field of vitamins, minor minerals, and other critical items; but we have no more than a faint conception of what constitutes complete, natural health—the kind that results from a plentiful supply of naturally grown food. Our thinking in this field has been devoted chiefly toward *correcting a faulty situation* rather than toward *developing the faultless environment* in which health—for the plant first, then the animal—is a necessary outgrowth.

Even our research in the field of nutrition has a sinister way of thinking in terms of what the laboratory can do for us (to prevent what seems inevitable, note) instead of helping us to develop sites for living—homes with gardens of real soil—which will make the laboratory unnecessary. I was amazed when discussing this point with a man in charge of work at a national nutrition laboratory to have him stare at me blankly when I suggested that proper research work in his institution might eliminate the need for the synthetic vitamins, hormones, and other substances, with which his mind seemed cluttered. That a nickel's worth of seeds planted in the right kind of soil might obviate the necessity for ailing people to call in the physician or to swallow a vitamin pill was an idea he was unable to comprehend. He was too close to the laboratory to visualize health as a natural product of the soil.

Similarly, though soil students have known for years about the many benefits organic matter confers upon the soil environment, it seems not to have occurred to them to organize their forces to help farmers take full advantage of these benefits. Instead of filling the soil with organic matter so that its decay will make the soil porous, farmers (as they are taught to do) buy lime to do the same thing. Instead of making their soil spongy with organic matter so the rainfall will be unable to run off over its surface, farmers (as they are taught to do) seek to divert around the slope water which otherwise would run directly down the hill via the nearest gully. Instead of using organic matter—decaying and releasing a variety of acids—for acidifying the infinite tonnage of low-grade phosphate ore, *which all soils are,* farmers (as they are taught to do) buy relatively minute quantities of acidified phosphate rock to induce higher productivity from soils they have robbed of their life-giving organic matter.

These concepts are merely illustrative of the ways in which "scientific thought" has shied away from well-known and proven information of a generation ago in order to keep faith with the test-tube and experimental-plot "discoveries" of later vintage. There can be no question about the validity of these later discoveries, especially for soil that has lost its organic matter; but why should farmers continue fighting a losing battle with substandard soil instead of working gradually toward restoring to their soil its organic matter (the loss of which made the soil substandard in the first place)? My view is that truths of a generation ago are truths today. We knew then that organic matter decaying within the soil opens it to a highly granular condition; that this porosity made runoff (and therefore erosion) impossible; and that acids were released by this decay. No scientist denies these facts even today; but neither does he suggest making use of these ideas as an adequate approach to completely fertile soil.

The truth is, the soil needs little except a chance to develop within itself the character that Nature intended should be in every good soil. It does not even "need" earthworms. Not that earthworms are not all they are said to be by their enthusiastic promoters, but wherever decaying organic matter is, there gather the earthworms—naturally, automatically, whether you want them or not. Without the organic matter, earthworms simply cannot thrive; with it, the scrawny, pallid, shrinking-violet type of earthworm quickly becomes fat and robust, a wriggler nearly a foot long, as thick as your finger, and a saucy fellow to meet. When you are tempted to invest in earthworms for the good of your soil, try first the effect of introducing into (or spreading as a mulch upon) your soil the amount of organic matter you would need to provide, in any case, to "feed" the colonies of earthworms you would buy. A few weeks later, examination of your soil will make you wonder whether some friendly magician hasn't kindly supplied the earthworms you intended to buy. In other words, earthworms quickly take advantage of any supply of organic matter that lies on or has been mixed into the soil. Whether they benefit the soil (independently of any and all other agencies), I have no way of knowing. The evidence regarding earthworm benefits is by no means complete; and, since you may have them at will there is no urgent need for further investigations into the subject.

The most urgent "need" of every soil is the intelligent application to it of the homely information we have had for many years but have not used.

A Second Look at VII : Nature's Soil Makers

THE IMPRESSION that Nature requires centuries to create enough topsoil to justify cultivation seems still to prevail in some quarters. But it isn't necessarily true. Much depends upon the kinds of plants that are doing the work of producing the new soil; for, after all, *soil is created by the growth of plants,* despite the idea that has gone abroad that cropping wears out the soil. Many people who evidently have not thought the problem through praise trees as soil builders. While it is true that where trees have grown for long periods good soil is usually found upon their removal, trees are not efficient soil builders, and for very good reasons.

At least one fact should be obvious in this connection: trees are perennial plants, i.e., they continue to live and grow year after year. The fact that a tree trunk becomes larger as the years pass means that the tree is taking substance from soil, air, and water, and is converting it into wood. Enlargement of its trunk can be accomplished in no other way. Hence, regardless of our eventual verdict as to the importance of forests in the formation of soils, we must not forget that trees exact an annual "harvest" of board feet from the land. And this means necessarily that trees do not develop soils at maximum speed.

Indeed it may be said that the development of soil under forest is quite incidental to the growth of the trees. Trees develop soils because they cannot avoid that outcome. An excellent discussion of the fundamental work of the forest in creating soils is given on pages 738-39 of *Soils and Men,* Yearbook of the U. S. Department of Agriculture for 1938, as follows:

> Each year from one and one-half to three tons per acre of dead leaves, twigs, branches, and tree trunks, collectively known as litter, are deposited on the forest floor by a dense stand of trees, and a large number of roots in the soil die. This material is rapidly consumed and converted to colloidal forms, and, except in the colder parts of the country, the total accumulation of such litter on the forest floor is seldom more than three or four times as much as the annual deposition.

The text continues with a graphic description of how this mass of organic material is chewed up by an estimated ten thousand insects and other destructive organisms *per square foot.*

Vital to the tree's life and vigor is the eventual complete reduction of this material to liquid decay products. The latter are picked up greedily by the roots and are carried away to be used in developing leaves, roots, and wood. Annually this cycle is repeated. Each autumn the tree drops its leaves, thickening the mass already on the ground and in process of decay. Throughout the fall and winter the destructive processes are going on at ground level, except when freezing temperatures make them impossible. With the first impulses of returning spring, sap begins to flow in the tree, carrying decay material upward to assist in the elaboration of leaves from the tree's buds. Once the leaves have expanded fully, the grand-scale movement of rising sap begins; and in the leaves the mineral solution from the soil is artfully blended with incoming gases (water vapor and carbon dioxide) into whatever compounds the tree needs in its structure. In all of this, you see, there is no provision for soil development. That is incidental.

In its growth a tree works solely to its own advantage. Yet it cannot avoid dropping each year another installment of leaves. Luckily these leaves form the bill of fare of a host of ground-line wreckers of organic matter. Bugs and worms, like trees, are interested solely in their own health and vitality. They do not consciously create soil. They merely live by digesting masses of leaves and other organic matter to the "colloidal forms" mentioned in the quotation. (Colloids are extremely fine bits of matter, so small as to be barely visible in the microscope; indeed, some colloidal material is much too small to be seen under the high-power lens.) Thus these living hordes of insect and fungus life serve the grand design of soil-making by being concerned solely with their own affairs, for it is but a step from colloidal forms to the liquid products of decay, at which point the tree again claims the materials.

As long as there is no major change in the near-by environment, this continuous process of gradual decay and subsequent growth proceeds at an even pace year after year. And, as indicated in the quotation, given earlier, the total recognizable organic matter on the forest floor may be as much as three or four times the annual leaf drop. However, let us suppose that a forest area of one hundred acres is cleared—all but from one to five acres left as a wood lot. The environmental conditions have definitely been changed for this wood lot by the removal of the trees from the surrounding acres. Wind movements which formerly stirred scarcely a leaf at ground level in the forest will now dry out the litter more rapidly. If, before clearing takes place, decay in the leaf mold and the upper soil layers is slowed down by the extra water present throughout this region, under the changed conditions decay in both soil and overlying material may be speeded up. The net result of such change may be a degrading of the forest-floor soil. Instead of steadily accumulating colloidal organic matter (dead roots, leaf and twig fragments, etc.) in the upper layers of soil, the new conditions may actually encourage decomposition at a more rapid rate than before. Soil degradation can happen, then, even in what we think of as virgin soils—so defined because they have borne no farm crops.

An even more important cause of deterioration of adjacent "virgin" soils is the usually inept management of the cleared land near by. Because the original supply of organic matter is gradually lost from the cultivated acreage, rainfall begins to run off instead of sinking where it falls. This loss of water over the surface gradually lowers the water table. When the level of water beneath the surface drops, the effect is felt in the adjacent forest as well as the crop land. In extreme instances the soil of open wood lots may, from a combination of causes, become but a hard-bitten imitation of its original condition. Quick tests have shown that soil of this kind, though it has never produced a farm crop, has lost in both phosphorus and potash content. Mysterious as such results may seem, they merely confirm the reduction in organic matter caused by the more complete removal of it through decay under the changed conditions.

As long as the level of water below the wood-lot soil remains approximately where it was before the trees were removed from the adjacent land, the accelerated rate of leaf decay may provide a stimulus to the growth of the wood-lot trees. But when erosion has cleaned the last vestiges of topsoil from the cleared land, the subsoil water level may sink to a point at which trees of some kinds cannot get enough moisture. This state of affairs has apparently made life impossible for the birches of much of our northern woodland areas. Such is one important register of retrogression in the soil.

If we consider the intimately related environmental conditions of an area, we can often explain progressive deterioration of both the forest land and the cropped areas as the result of a common cause—land management that has permitted the lowering of subsoil water levels. In regions where the lowered water table results in a ground surface considerably drier than that which existed when all the land was covered by trees, forests are more ready prey to fire. And when fire strikes under these conditions it takes a heavy toll of the surface organic matter.

It is difficult to say whether reforestation can again build soil where mismanagement has destroyed what the forest built before. Environmental conditions have been seriously altered, otherwise the lamented soil losses would not have occurred. If forest is to succeed on a depleted site, the environmental conditions must be restored to at least some approximation of what they were originally. But, if we restore environmental conditions as a preliminary to reforestation, we shall thereby have removed the need for reforestation as a means of restoring soil.

I hope this discussion does not mark me as a tree hater, for I am not that. My concern is that we rightly understand the part trees play in soil creation. By all means let us grow trees for their own sake, and so that our needs for wood products will be supplied. But we need not become hysterical about forests in relation to the restoration of our soil. If soil could not be restored more quickly than by growing trees on the site for a generation or two, then we should have to reforest as a matter of course. But trees as soil builders are not in the same class with the best and quickest creator of real soil—grass.

The most notable difference between the soils of forest areas and those of our grasslands is in their depth. From one to three feet of black soil existed in the rich spots of the hardwood forests covering the eastern part of the United States, whereas the black soils of the western prairies were often several times as deep. There is an excellent reason, which has little or no relation to the mineral parentage of the soil as determined by soil surveys.

For the most part the grasses are annuals. Their remains go back to the soil at the end of the season. If perennial, the top growth of each season equally is contributed in toto to the fund of organic matter available for development of the next season's growth. In other words, while trees are by nature soil robbers—to the extent that they develop new wood each year—the grasses are not. They go wholeheartedly about the business of soil development. But here again the development of soil is merely a by-product of the principal end of "making a living." Grass rises each year "on stepping stones" of its dead self to bigger and better growth. This difference in character between the soil-building effects of grasses and of trees accounts for the fact that the Great Plains area was populated by millions of animals while the woodlands of the East supported a far smaller number.

We do not know the whole truth about the grassland country, especially for the period when it first was broken, but my surmise is that there were many places where the actual mineral soil lay several feet beneath the surface in which the farmer planted his crops. There would have been no neat dividing line, of course. More or less rock dust (some brought by winds from areas hundreds of miles farther west) would have been mixed in with each year's growth of grass. Rodents, earthworms, and animals of the varied life of the prairies would have accomplished much mixing of minerals with the soil's organic matter. But it is certain that the spongy soil into which the pioneer farmers of the prairies first planted their crops was wholly unlike the substandard, pavement-like, erosive land in which their descendants plant crops today.

We have done much woolgathering in our thinking about how soils are developed and how they are destroyed. Grass, growing without hindrance, builds soil. Trees also build soil. But the soil-building enterprise gets only the crumbs from the forest's table, whereas grass gives its *all* without reservation. And when soils are "worn out" they have but lost their organic matter—the substance which, as it decays, releases the acids needed to dissolve minerals from the richest known source of minerals, the rock powder of which soils are composed. Free-growing grass, then, is the best possible builder of soil. But little of today's grass is allowed to develop freely. For the most part, the grass on farms is grazed heavily, or it is cut for hay; in consequence, it contributes little toward real soil building. And the most underprivileged of all grasses is that growing on most American lawns. Why?

With thoughtless fastidiousness, we insist that our lawns be as smooth as velvet, short trimmed, and green. Grass must be maintained in this highly unnatural state regardless of what tragedy is thus wrought upon it. To allow it a sabbatical year of untrimmed growth would be a social error of the first magnitude. The knowledge that such a change would transform a weedy, thinning stand of grass into a fur-like coat the next season gains no supporters. Because we are so fearful of what the neighbors would say, we are forced to fertilize a lawn which, properly managed, would grow perfectly without outside help.

No tidy person is going to let his lawn grow wild, of course—not if he values his place in society—but I can't forego relating our own experience in learning the facts of grass life in our back yard. The "research" work discussed in *Plowman's Folly* had been done there, but in 1939, the field work having been undertaken on a leased farm, it was decided that the back yard should be brought back into grass again. Since we had added leaves to this soil for several years, we thought it would grow grass again easily. Consequently the only preparation it got was a once-over with a rototiller, intended to dispose of any chunks of leaves that might lie just under the surface. This work was done in the spring, and from then until late August nothing was done except to rake off stones twice, killing at these times all weeds that were starting. The surface became extremely hard, and it was cracked by seeding time, but since there would not be opportunity later, we seeded it in that condition.

Without so much as scratching the surface, I carefully scattered Kentucky bluegrass seed over the entire area. Immediately this was covered by what was calculated to be an eighth of an inch of sand—to prevent birds from picking up the seed. This done, the lawn was in fact seeded. No water was applied then or afterward. Nothing happened until rain came in September. Then the ground began to look green in places and with the passing days the green patches began to merge. In another month we had a complete stand of thrifty grass. It was so thrifty that it was mowed several times that fall. The well-mixed supply of leaves kept this grass so well fed that it either had to be mowed regularly or it would have been a wilderness to mow next season.

In 1940 mowing was done every week throughout most of the year. All this time I thought the grass was being exceptionally well cared for, because the mower was adjusted to cut *as high as the manufacturer had provided.*

We were cutting this grass each time as tall as possible. Nevertheless, when the next spring came, it was evident that we had a very sick stand of grass. I was quite naturally puzzled. Weeds were gaining on the grass everywhere, in spite of the fact that during the past season I had carefully rogued them out several times. This was the spring of 1941.

Mrs. Faulkner stood for my inaction as long as she could, then one spring day she walked me over the lawn, kicking up the brown patches of grass to show me that there were no roots. "You've got to bring somebody here who knows how to grow grass so he can show you how." That was putting it to me quite frankly. By this time I had found an explanation for this poor condition: I told her it seemed to me the grass was dying because its roots were starved. The leaves, I explained, had been kept so short they could not manufacture enough food material to keep the roots supplied with nourishment. I believed that the grass needed nothing else than more leaf surface. It was a quick come-back, but she was not convinced. She admitted, however, that the idea sounded as if it could be true, and wanted to know what I was going to do about it.

I telephoned a woodworking shop to turn out a roller about four inches in diameter. This roller was substituted for the 1½-inch roller that came with the machine. (Any other means of raising the cutter bar would have been just as effective.) The only treatment the dying grass got was regular mowing with this big roller holding the cutter bar high. The result was convincing. Though it took two seasons for complete recovery of the grass stand (because I used no fertilizers or lime), when the full effect of the higher cutting had been realized the grass was as thick as the bristles in a brush, even where the ground had been bare before.

The use of fertilizers and/or lime would have speeded up this recovery, even with the larger roller. I used neither, because that much extra stimulation of the grass would have kept me from learning what I needed to know. I already knew that fertilizers would speed the growth of grass. I did not know how quickly the grass could recover without such stimulation. People who wish the quickest possible development of good grass should combine the two treatments: fertilize and cut the grass high.

One unsightly feature is apt to mar the recovery. The thin stand at the beginning proves to be a handicap. The mower wheel levels the grass it runs over, and without the support of near-by shoots this depressed grass does not rise again in time to be cut at the next round. The lawn consequently has an unattractive, striped appearance after mowing, unless one takes the trouble to go over it again next day to clip this uncut grass. Even if fertilizer is used, this may happen for a few weeks. By the second season our grass had completely recovered. This method certainly deserves trial.

Soil improves or deteriorates in proportion to the activity of the plants growing in it. This story of the lawn experience shows how the close cutting actually made extension of roots impossible. Unless roots can be extended plants cannot reach more distant sources of decay products. Failure to extend roots as necessary means death to the plant; unless, as is usually recommended, fertilizers or lime, or both, are used. These materials judiciously applied enable the grass to "feed" without root extensions. Moreover, the improved condition resulting from the fertilizers would make possible additional root extensions. A number of lessons may be learned from a study of this grass experience, it seems to me. Particularly, I believe it has a bearing upon the proper management of grass, for its own improvement, on farms. Of all the crops the farmer grows, the most automatic is grass; yet few farmers do a good job—even in their own estimation—of growing meadows or pastures. Application of the same principles to pastures or meadows will in many instances be the best possible treatment. It should often save plowing up and starting all over again.

Whether soil is made by the time-consuming forest, by the much more rapid grassland, or by the artificial mixing in of great quantities of organic matter of some kind, the essential processes are the same. Decayable material is subjected to such conditions of moisture and warmth that decomposition is encouraged; plant roots in the vicinity rush to the feast, appropriating the products as fast as they are released; and these same plant roots die as soon as their mission is ended, becoming additional organic matter to be salvaged in the same way.

Soil creation is automatic if plants are allowed to grow without hindrance. Farmers can create their own soils by simulating the conditions under which natural soils are created. Such are the soil makers as they exist in Nature.

A Second Look at VIII : Soil Machinery

THE MOLDBOARD PLOW, as villain, occupied front-and-center position on the stage of *Plowman's Folly,* not because of what it can and does do, but because of what, by the nature of its design, it cannot do. Designed at a time in agricultural development when man's most effective enemies in his eternal fight for food were the encroaching forest and grassland, the plow's ability neatly to squelch those threats was its chief virtue.

Before the days of the moldboard plow, the best way to clear off the dead leavings of last year's growth was to burn them. This practice cleared the land for another season's growth. Throughout the ages men have continued to burn trash off the land whenever there was enough of it to make the later work inconvenient. Indeed, despite full knowledge that such burning is treachery of the worst sort, many farmers still burn what they cannot conveniently plow in. Though they know that the world's great desert wastes were caused chiefly by prehistoric burning over the land, that knowledge doesn't stay the match.

Early man's real troubles, though, came from green, growing plants which inconveniently continued to spring up and threaten to shade his planted crops. These were not easy to cope with, but the moldboard plow proved itself capable of giving real relief from this menace. It did so by neatly inverting the sod.

As long as the bulk of decaying material in a soil is high, as long as a soil remains black, granulated, and highly productive, there is little choice among the various soil-stirring implements for breaking the land. Such fertile, black, mellow, highly biological soil continues to grow big crops regularly until its color begins to shade off to the tint of the native rock of which it was originally made. That shading off, of course, registers definite loss of organic matter, and just as certainly a corresponding loss of biological activity, for all the multitude of living organisms within the soil must rely (just as you and I must) on organic matter for food.

The faded-out soil no longer supports a heavy growth of vegetation. Sods, if any, are shallow-rooted in such a soil, root growth being confined to the upper few inches. "Deep" plowing in a soil of that kind is a crime against the crop for which preparation is being made, for deep plowing will remove the remaining small amount of organic matter to depths far beyond the rooting ability of many farm crops to salvage (before leaching has removed all the decay products). Since most soils on American farms today are in some stage of fading out—losing their organic matter—the hard words said in *Plowman's Folly* about the moldboard plow had reference to the effect of that implement upon substandard soil. In better soils, air can penetrate easily to plow depth; but not so in poor soils, especially clays. Hence in rich soils aerobic decay (well aerated) can continue after plowing; in poor soils the decay may become anaerobic (lacking air), because of the lesser supply of air. Thus the plow may injure poor land while not noticeably damaging fertile land.

The distinction between aerobic and anaerobic activity is far more important on the farm than in the laboratory. The technician in the laboratory will continue getting his salary whether the decay organisms he works with are aerobic or anaerobic. The farmer's tenure on his land may hinge upon the difference between these two types of decay, for, unless he wishes to purchase nitrogen for his crops, he is solely dependent upon aerobic decay (and/or upon the growing and sacrificing of legumes) for the supply of nitrogen his crops must have. Unless the farmer's crops have free access to a poundage of nitrogen greater than the total weight of all the mineral elements his crops will use, he has no chance to grow maximum crops until nitrogen has been provided. This explains why so much organic matter must be in the soil all the time. Yet the mere presence of organic matter means nothing in itself. As a source of food for a continuously high population of bacteria and other organisms it is invaluable. And, since decay proceeds continuously while the organic matter lasts (and the organisms then die), it should be evident that if we are to maintain continuously the necessary high populations of wrecking organisms, the organic supply must be replenished by frequent new additions within or upon the surface, preferably within.

Failure to maintain such conditions within his soil may easily mean that the neglectful farmer will eventually lose his land—at least as a productive source of revenue. When organic activity ceases, the farmer must "feed his land in order that it may feed him," or give up farming altogether. "Feeding the land!" The very expression is an offense against Original Design. Nothing of the sort was contemplated in the beginning; delinquent soil is so only when it has lost its ability to feed enough organisms.

When this low state has been reached, the moldboard plow, as used ordinarily, is incapable of promptly reestablishing organic activity. Its action moves organic matter *from* aerobic *to* anaerobic conditions, not the other way around. Thus, plowing worsens the situation. Whenever there is no longer a smudge of black color, the necessity for aerobic decay has become imperative, but the moldboard plow is powerless to help out. The virtues of the plow aside, its very design prevents it from contributing to improvement in aerobic activity within the soil—unless it is used in an unusual way. *Plowing twice,* the second time somewhat deeper than the first, is one way to plow beneficially. *Plowing shallow* enough that the subsequent disking will cut through the entire plowed layer is another. A third way is to *plow after a serious and partially successful attempt has been made to mix in a heavy green manure crop, a big crop of corn stalks, or other organic matter*. Some of these ways were mentioned and carefully described in *Plowman's Folly,* but were almost universally overlooked by its readers, to judge by comments of some reviewers and correspondents.

Plowing is the best procedure, as a rule, where deep sod is to be broken. Please note that *deep* sod is specified —not just sod in general. Wherever the blackening effect of the grass roots extends deeper than the plow will run, the sod is "deep" for plowing purposes, and you may safely plow; otherwise plowing will bring to the surface fresh clay or other inert subsoil, and that would be distinctly out of order. This should have been made clear in the first book. For that omission I have paid dearly, by personal replies to a thousand or more letters of inquiry as to what should be done about sod.

In this connection, however, we may properly question whether sods should ever be broken in ordinary farming. Our cropping system has made the plowing of sod a regular routine, but is there justification for the practice? We grow corn, follow with small grain, and follow that with clovers or grasses. But why? Our soils certainly have not benefitted from the practice. That is certain. As long as the land was black (fertile) the ordinary three-year rotation plan worked out well enough; but it should be evident to all by now that the manner in which rotations have been managed seems to have contributed to sterility of the soil, whereas soil was expected to be improved as a result of our following a regular crop rotation. If crop rotations had not lowered productiveness, farms where regular rotations have been practiced for more than a generation would be outstanding examples of soil maintenance. Instead, it is impossible to point to examples that can be credited to the faithful following of rotations. Rather, it is true that, regardless of the cropping system followed, most farms have lost productive ability within the past generation. Many supposedly well-managed farms have become badly eroded—also without regard to the particular cropping patterns their owners employed. The erosion came only because the manner in which the land was handled permitted gradual decline in organic activity in the soil.

Many agronomists, recognizing that crop rotation has not lived up to their fond expectations of a generation ago, now recommend to farmers that they lengthen their rotations, a consequence of which is less frequent plowing. This could result in improvement, but if so, the reason for the improvement would be neither the longer rotation nor the lesser number of plowings. It could result from the better chance grass would have to make headway by developing a larger and more vigorous root system. However, many farmers will not be able to lengthen rotations because they have too little land. For them some other plan must be thought up. These men will be compelled to learn how to recreate soil in the place where it is to be used, and will be unable to continue rotating crops at all. We may ask then: Why rotations anyhow?

The most plausible reason that farmers began to follow our most common crop-rotation pattern is that it allowed them to grow successive crops on the land *without* the heavy labor of extra plowings. A horse-drawn agriculture, remember, had to avoid at any cost overworking its motive power. Grain crops seeded after the corn crop saved a great deal of horsepower, when such practice could be managed. Seeding the hay crops in the wheat in the last days of winter or very early spring saved another plowing of the land. Thus the farmer reduced the work for his teams twice in three years, but failed to realize that he also missed two chances in the three years to add organic matter to the supply in the soil. For a generation or more the ordinary crop rotation worked passably, but the ultimate effects are not nice to see.

If farmers, before they heard of crop rotations, had kept on plowing the land each year—without straw or stalk destruction by fire—we might have avoided altogether our epidemic of erosion. Plowing would have been untidy, for few plows of that day could completely bury the usual bulk of straw or stalks. But the plowing, if followed up by planters and cultivators that could operate in trash, would have been far better than the practices we have developed. Since farmers could not cover all of the corn stalks, they burned most of them and plowed in the rest. This was true of wheat straw as well, unless it was used for bedding. Thus, with ever less organic matter in the soil, plowing became a tougher job, and that smart idea, *crop rotation*—growing crops in such lock-step succession that weeds had no chance to develop and make plowing necessary—seemed a big improvement.

Now that we have power which need not be babied, we no longer have to work the land according to power-saving methods. (Neither should we overwork it, which is just as bad—sometimes worse.) With better power we can plan our work according to cropping patterns that will greatly increase annual yields without in the slightest degree reducing the acreage we put to revenue crops each season. The same fields that grow our present rotation crops can grow continuously corn, wheat, and clover or grass; can grow bigger yields of these crops in each succeeding season; and can continue year after year growing high yields without fertilizers or lime. The recipe for this short-cut to high productiveness is easy: Precede each regular crop by a new batch of organic matter disked or otherwise mixed into the surface. This may be residues, a green manure crop, or both. Any one of the various ways of plowing mentioned earlier may be used for putting this organic matter into the ground, or it may be put in with one of the new rotary machines, if one is to be had.

If green manures are needed (they are likely to be in the early years of such improvement on very poor land), the problem of the crop to grow, and how to proceed with it, may be referred to local farmers, the county agent, or others who know the country. For each section of the country (unless the very northernmost part), crops that will follow corn and can be disked in the following spring are adapted. In like manner, wherever winter wheat is a rotation partner following the corn crop it can be paired with a summer-grown crop for manure.

From central Ohio, Indiana, and Illinois south, a fall-seeded, winter-growing crop such as rye can follow corn. On the richer lands of this section, however, a green manure crop may not be needed. Some ambitious farmers of the Corn Belt have reported trouble when they tried to mix in a big crop of corn stalks along with a crop of tall rye. The trouble was that their land was too rich to need so great a bulk of material put in at one time. When the land is already capable of high yields, the stalks alone, if mixed in thoroughly, are often enough new organic matter. Indeed, corn should produce heavier yields with the passing years if a bulky quantity of stalks is mixed in each spring.

One note of caution is important at this point: Before the corn is planted, the land should be carefully stirred several times to kill weeds.

Because of the greatly increased use of combine harvesters in rotation wheat fields (where grass or clover is coming along), trouble looms for the hay crops. It is serious enough to warrant eliminating in many sections the production of these two crops in the overlapping sequence which is followed in the usual rotation. Combine harvesting is done later by some weeks than binder harvesting. The stubble is cut higher by the combine, and the threshed straw is usually left clinging to the stubble in windrows. Each of these three characteristics of the combine harvesting tends to deprive the growing hay-crop plants of light they desperately need. At best, in growing wheat, the developing hay crop gets little enough light as a rule; and binder harvesting often brings relief just in the nick of time. Combining the grain crop prolongs the sunless agony, thus adding insult to the already somewhat light-starved plants.

If wheat were grown independently, it could follow itself each season on the same land. The necessary "re-fueling" of the soil for each succeeding year's production might be accomplished by simply disking in the combined straw, provided the latter had been well spread by the harvesting machine. If the land is thin, or the straw is used for bedding, summer-grown green manure crops are easily contrived. In many of the humid states, the soybean offers the ideal candidate for this purpose, since it already has made great strides in the same territory.

When hay is to follow hay continuously on the same land, the plants must be perennial, or additional seedings may have to be made from time to time. This is not always necessary, for legumes like red clover often come in voluntarily, or used to, and provide the needed hay. On farms where the "dream" of weedless corn production has become a reality, it will be possible to plan for hay harvest without having to worry about weeds in the corn. In that case, the hay can be cut on time—when it is at its very best. Under such conditions, timothy, inferior as hay when cut late, can be cut before full bloom and cured into hay nearly as good as alfalfa; and when so managed, timothy is apt to continue perennially, instead of dying out in a few years.

Likewise, orchard grass, never considered important on American farms, might also become an exceptional hay crop. Cut too late, orchard grass is even less interesting to hungry animals than is late-cut timothy; but cut early, it is choice hay. In fact, in some countries farmers depend more upon orchard grass than upon any other plant for their hay.

Legumes, most of which are not perennials, have a way of filling in when the grass thins out either in pasture or in meadow. Plans which place dependence upon grasses only are apt to become complicated by intrusions of red clover, white clover, alsike, or even alfalfa or sweet clover, if these have ever been grown upon the land. In any case these plants will be helpful. In fact, legumes are to be preferred to the grasses, except that they are not as a rule perennials, and consequently would have to be re-seeded frequently at considerable expense for seed.

Some adjustment in the cropping system probably can be made to advantage on most farms. Along with the combine harvester, which damages the developing hay crop, is the corn harvester, which has added to the farmer's wheat-seeding troubles. The accumulated effects of the two machines may be enough to make the common crop rotation obsolete without farmers' having to be told how rotation has contributed to the delinquency of their land.

If crop rotations should be abandoned, as these facts seem to suggest might be the case, unless better plans are developed for handling residues history is apt to repeat itself—just because it is so much easier to burn corn stalks and wheat straw than to make the extra effort necessary for properly mixing them into the soil surface. This sort of carelessness will be hardest to overcome in communities where the corn varieties still in use grow too tall and coarse for machine harvesting.

The necessity for better disposition of crop residues, green manure crops, and other growth has put many people into the mood for buying machinery that offers complete incorporation of the organic matter at one operation. Hundreds of people have written to ask about this machine or that. I can make no helpful reply to these questions. To begin with, I have not seen any of the machines put to test under the extreme conditions they would be likely to encounter on most farms. Also, inquirers usually have not indicated the kind of work they would expect of the machine in question if they should buy one. The only safe suggestion is that prospective buyers of these machines follow the rule I would follow in such case; refuse to spend any money until the machine has demonstrated on the farm it is being bought for that it can successfully meet the conditions of tough soil and bulky crop to be found there. All of this in addition to price considerations.

Following the appearance of *Plowman's Folly,* I was taken to task by the manufacturer of a rotary tillage machine because his outfit was not mentioned in the book. He knew it could not have been oversight, and assumed that his machine met completely all requirements for intermixing organic matter with the soil. I reminded him of two reasons why mention of his machine had been omitted: (1) Since the book was written with special application to soils already in distress, the extremely high cost of his machine put it out of reach of the farmers most in need of it; and (2) a few years before my book was written, I had tried several times, unsuccessfully, to get a demonstration of his machine cutting into the ground rye of heights above eighteen inches. The fact that this demonstration was not arranged for suggested that the manufacturer either was not sure his machine could do the work, or was sure it could not.

Whether such limitations applied then or apply now, to the various machines being manufactured, I do not know; but it will be only proper that a prospective purchaser of this kind of equipment insist that it perform successfully under conditions which his own farm presents before he makes a cash payment. And, because I cannot know the capacities of any machine of the type, I wish now to disclaim any implication that I have approved or encouraged its design or manufacture. Without doubt, under demonstration conditions, excellent work will be done by every type now being offered for sale; however, I can't forget the note I received a few weeks ago from a Kentucky correspondent who had bought one stating that that particular machine would not work in Kentucky soil. This man regretted his high investment, naturally.

As the situation now appears, the disk harrow, especially in the very heavy sizes which are becoming available, offers the best solution for the majority of the soils that can be cut into by disks. For stony soils, for sods that are not to be plowed, and for clays too tough for disking, the heavy cultivators now being used by, or attached to, tractors offer a way out, when equipped with chisel-form teeth. Scarifying the surface with such tools will, in many instances, soften clays to the point that disks will take hold; and deeper cutting of stony soils will make them penetrable by disks, which can then finish the operation.

For the main job, then, of recreating real soil where only substandard soil now exists there must be more frequent and more bulky addition of organic matter—not less frequent plowing, as is being advocated by some leading agronomists. The particular implement to be used may depend solely upon the choice of the farmer himself. Choice does not exclude the plow when it is properly used. The all-important point being, that, above all else, the soil needs food constantly for the uninterrupted maintenance of a high degree of biological activity within itself.

A Second Look at IX : Vanishing Pests

THE CHAPTER entitled "Exit Pests" in *Plowman's Folly* proved to be a stumbling block to many readers who could accept with reasonable reservations most of the rest of the text. To many thoughtful persons, this chapter seemed completely out of bounds and unworthy of serious consideration. The fatalistic view, that we cannot avoid insects and disease, and that we must make the best of a bad situation, is well nigh universal. Indeed, in some circles insects that prey upon our crops are considered to have the same kind of nuisance value as the fleas on a dog. In other words, the farmer is kept on his mettle by the necessity for action in order to preserve a portion of his crops for human consumption.

The universal fears of insects and diseases find support in our official experimental work, even though some scientific men know that crops growing under excellent conditions are less disturbed by pests than crops feeding in a poverty-stricken soil. An occasional fertilizer recommendation is accompanied by the information that the liberal use of fertilizers tends to reduce damage from pests. Yet no scientist, apparently, recognizes in this idea the germ for the bigger idea that, if soil conditions were made right, insects and diseases might disappear altogether. The conviction that by improving growing conditions one improves his chances of escaping serious infestation clings to much conventional teaching; yet few, if any, entomologists or pathologists believe that such an influence constitutes a margin of safety against attack. They believe with Cromwell: However much you may fertilize and otherwise improve growing conditions, you must still keep the sprayer ready for action.

Since they have not related scourges of insects and diseases to soil conditions, it is quite logical that in practice agronomists, soil technicians, and crops specialists should defer to entomologists and pathologists for guidance in their field work. However, when one of the country's leading students of soils had condensed the chapter, "Exit Pests," to seventeen words for study, he considered himself çapable of rendering this profound judgment: "This, of course, cannot be true." That statement probably would sum up the general view.

Late in 1945 I had the pleasure of talking to one of the country's leading orchard specialists who has for many years experimented with the use of heavy mulches under orchard trees. In orchard work mulching has proved notably satisfactory, which is entirely consistent with my belief that mulch on the surface will transform almost any soil into real soil, if the mulch is heavy enough. I inquired whether the professor had tried withholding spray from some of the experimental trees that were producing handsome returns under the mulching system. He had not, of course, because he depended upon entomologists and pathologists to attend to disease and insect control in the orchards with which he was experimenting.

We discussed incidents in the experience of each of us in which fruit from orchards growing in excellent soil but never sprayed was entirely free (or practically free) of blemishes of any kind. These experiences dated well into the past. As guides for orchard practices today they might properly be questioned. Yet there seems to be good reason for presuming that it might pay in these days to leave unsprayed a few trees among the mulch experiments. At least no such stone should be left unturned by experiment stations. If the unsprayed fruit proved worthless, as would be expected in the usual view, that fact would, of course, end the argument; but if, on the other hand, the unsprayed trees produced just as good fruit as those which had been sprayed, the information would be new and highly important.

Courtesy among scientists may keep us from learning much that we should know. In the orchard experiments referred to, the horticulturist, by courtesy if not by necessity, had depended upon soil specialists to suggest (or at least approve) his mulching program. Then for the maintenance of suitable defenses against pests in the orchard he called upon the entomologists and pathologists for help. Since the idea that pest attacks might depend upon soil conditions was foreign to each specialist concerned, nobody thought to test this idea by leaving a few mulched trees unsprayed. Perhaps in the next few years experimental work will have answered this highly important question.

My own experience and observation justifies, tentatively at least, this rule: *Destructiveness or lack of destructiveness by insects or diseases registers the status of growing conditions.* By this rule, if pests prove destructive, growing conditions are poor; if pests are absent or are not noticeably damaging, growing conditions are far above average. In theory, crops growing in real soils should be entirely free of pests. While I believe this, to date I have no complete proof of it, inasmuch as no soil I have worked with has been fully developed to the desired condition. Within the next few seasons I hope to have thoroughly proved or disproved the theory.

Weather is often thought of as the all-important factor in farming. In substandard soils this seems to be true. But real soils make crops behave differently. Even substandard soils that have been upgraded by one or more installments of organic matter tend to do the same thing. The behavior of many crops in upgraded soil suggests that drought will not be so damaging, and that damaging effects will not be felt so soon, as in less satisfactory soils. This ought to comfort non-farm people who try to grow crops for themselves or for sale. It is no small matter that insect or disease attacks may be delayed by days or even weeks, and that when attacks do occur the damage is usually negligible, as compared with that which results on near-by substandard soil. Such prospects as these may be eagerly welcomed.

Just think what it can mean to small gardeners who grow only their own food, and to farmers who like to eat apples they grew themselves, when they learn that properly managed soils may make it possible for them to produce practically perfect fruit without the necessity of complicated spraying programs. Not long ago a group of small gardeners were told by a fruit specialist that they should be extremely cautious about trying to grow their own fruit. The implications were that the professional grower is equipped to fight pests and that others should let him supply them with fruit. Though this particular fruit specialist has had many years of experience with mulched orchards, he has not tried risking a few unsprayed trees to see what would happen. The certainty of pests is axiomatic with him. While no official tests have established it as a fact, there is evidence to support the belief that perfect fruit would result on properly managed soil without spraying.

I remember well that, as a county agent in Kentucky thirty years ago, I helped with community fairs all over our county. Each year we invited displays of apples. In each but one of the six communities the apples were spoiled by blemishes of some kind. The exceptional community was far back in the hills, twenty miles away from paved roads or railways, but the apples produced there were as perfect as I had seen. I have never known how to account fully for this difference in the quality of apple displays. I suspect that in the backwoods community land was so plentiful that men who wished to grow fruit simply set their trees in freshly cleared areas, instead of (as is usually done) first wearing the land down until it no longer grew profitable crops, and then setting the orchard. Though this is assumption, it checks with known facts.

The theoretical problems inherent in this point of view are not to be cleared up by mere observations, regardless of how trustworthy the observations may be. The true scientist wants to know *why*. He must know why an unusual observation was possible before he can satisfy himself that he has solved the problem. While observation confirms the view that growing conditions are faithfully indexed by the behavior of pests, the background of reasoning to account for such behavior is an almost perfect blank. We know that plant sap differs appropriately from soil to soil, depending upon the abundance or scarcity of plant nutrient elements. Our sense of taste records the differences. The differences in taste between extremely good and extremely poor tomatoes are amazing; and these differences represent largely the differences in soil situation. But is this related to insect preference? I would like to know—wouldn't you?

There are other clues which may or may not lead to solution of this relationship. Here are two:

(1) Insects exert tremendous energy as they fly. Their energy output is enormously higher when they fly than when they walk, because they must neutralize the influence of gravity as well as move forward. Might this explain why many insects are drawn so strongly to sweets, which supply energy?

(2) Tissues of plants are less subject to injury, either by diseases or by insects, when the plants are growing in real soil, or even in soil in process of improvement. Why? May it be that the richer mineral solution available "ar-

mors" the cellular structure of the tissues against invasion by disease? This sounds logical in the case of attack by diseases. Some plants actually seem to develop heavier cell tissues in their leaf surfaces—enough heavier to be visible. This extra weight of tissue might not repel the chewing insects, presumably, but might it not be true that, if plant tissues contain greater percentages of minerals than normal, the insects would not have to consume as much tissue in order to supply their mineral needs? Also, if the tissues contain more minerals, the sap itself would be richer in minerals. Might insects which ordinarily live by chewing be able to satisfy their need for minerals by simply "drinking" the sap that flowed to them at a given point where they had broken into the tissue? Observation suggests this.

Whatever may be decided as to the above suggestions, many Americans would sleep better if Europeans had kept their corn borer at home. The worm has done a great deal of damage in this country, and probably will do a good deal more, but its worst damage has been psychological. Farmers who have never seen it live in dread of it. Yet this pest shows signs of "respecting" crops that grow in real soil, for it does noticeably less damage when the corn is growing in soil that has had plenty of organic matter mixed into the surface (or used as a thick mulch). I seriously doubt whether it need be feared at all under conditions of well-developed soil.

While I have not grown corn in recent years that was entirely free from this pest, I have not had any serious damage from it when the soil conditions were reasonably close to satisfactory. I feel sure that, as seems true in the case of other crop pests, soil condition is a major factor in achieving immunity to the dreaded corn borer. Wherever borers are present in great numbers, that fact should be taken as evidence that something is seriously wrong with growing conditions for the crop. In 1945 we grew sweet corn during some of the worst imaginable weather conditions (an important factor in total growing conditions, as anyone will agree); yet corn-borer damage was negligible. We had as many of the corn ear worm as of the much more dreaded borer; and, while neither was serious, the old-fashioned ear worm did more damage where it was present. I refuse to become hysterical about either; for each will yield to real soil conditions, I am confident.

Soil preparation for this 1945 corn patch had been sketchy. Because we had no tractor equipment, we hired a neighbor to level the waist-high growth that covered the one-third acre we expected to put into garden. "Level" was about all we gave him time to do with his disk harrow, since I knew that longer working with ordinary equipment would not justify the extra expense. We planted the trashy ground by hand. This was about June 25. Some rain fell in the next three weeks, but after July 15 there was no effective rainfall until September 7. By the latter date most of the stalks had definitely given up the effort to produce ears. Yet under these conditions such corn as developed was excellent. Only one damaged tassel was seen all season.

This record checks with previous corn-borer experience. Worry about it certainly seems unjustified, judging from the consistency with which we have been able to harvest practically perfect corn in spite of the borer's presence. Through proper soil preparation we shall hope to merit year after year a degree of immunity from the borer—as nearly complete immunity as it is possible to achieve in territory where the borer has become established. It may be possible to report complete immunity after a few years of grading the soil up toward the status of real soil. We certainly hope so.

In general, plant diseases (with certain notable exceptions) are easier to banish from the garden than insects. In fact, the only disease I can recall having trouble with after the soil had been properly supplied with decayable material is the bacterial wilt of cucumbers. This disease is carried to the cucumber plants by the striped cucumber beetle. I can remember but one time when we had no striped cucumber beetles whatever among our plants. That was in 1945, and during that season we also had no bacterial wilt. Evidently the disease had no means of being transported that season, otherwise it would have paid its usual visit.

It probably would not be strictly correct to say that we have had no vegetable diseases, though it is perfectly proper to claim no appreciable damage. Often the early leaves of tomatoes seem disposed to turn yellow and die back, but this happens as a rule before really suitable growing weather has arrived. As soon as warm nights have come, this trouble vanishes. It is not likely that any kind of chemical treatment would be justified against such minor difficulty.

Our potatoes in 1945 were planted from stock we bought from a farmer who had sold all his marketable sizes. We took cull sizes because we did not wish to bother with cutting. These were spread out on a barn floor to be exposed to mild light until planting time came. Thus the seed was well sprouted, and the sprouts were sufficiently short and tough that they would not break off during the planting. Among the seed were some tubers that showed signs of disease. These were tossed aside, but one which landed in a bean row, where it was cultivated along with the beans, yielded healthy potatoes in the fall. Not all diseased potatoes can be depended upon, but many do produce a crop. It is my belief that under the influence of real soil conditions diseased seed potatoes might in time grow a healthy crop. This result could not be expected in a single season, yet some progress appears to be made even in the first year. Occasional tubers from those we grew in 1945 now show some infection, though they appeared sound at digging time. We planted our 1946 potatoes from these, expecting that the crop would be less affected, which proved to be the case. In a few years, we hope, there will be no further disease in this stock.

These ideas are definitely unorthodox. Most commercial growers of potatoes, as of other crops, would be panicky if they could not depend upon an unfailing supply of insecticides, fungicides, and the appropriate equipment for applying them. Yet millions of people who grow fruits and vegetables here and in other countries have never conducted a pest campaign. Why is this? The secret may be that these people keep their land in better condition. It could be that simple.

This chapter would hardly be complete without the story of our 1945 potato patch, in which insects put on quite an act. It was really a show well worth watching. The planting, in the first place, was strictly distress procedure, for the potatoes had lain for weeks on a barn floor using up their energy growing the tough purple sprouts that develop in mild light. In order to speed up the planting we hastily mowed off the wild growth from a ten or twelve foot strip, scalped off the root-filled upper two or three inches, and planted the tubers in holes made with the corner of a hoe. These were spaced at one foot intervals each direction, putting about three times the usual number of plants on the area covered. This was a very crude way to plant potatoes. Nobody would argue that they were being pampered, surely; rather, they were being severely punished, judging by usual standards. Yet they survived to develop one of the finest examples I have ever seen of natural balance among insect populations.

A few weeks after the plants had emerged and started growing we saw the first adult beetles. Later, when it became evident that these adults were laying eggs, we discovered that almost every potato plant had as a tenant a lady beetle (both sexes—this is the bug's common name) nervously hunting for eggs of the potato beetle. In spite of all this voraciousness, a few clutches of potato beetle eggs hatched, and we could soon see the young larvae (black at this stage) working in the bud leaves of the plants. About this time other insects began to appear and take part in the proceedings. One of these resembled the old fashioned blister beetle (the kind you could drive out of the patch with a broom, and watch it follow you back). There were many others I could not recall by name, but all were using this potato patch as their happy hunting ground. For some weeks it was a continuous battle. In the end we discovered one day that the plants were again free of insects of any kind. The predators had eaten up their food supply and were forced to move on.

Please don't think I had no misgivings about what would happen to our potatoes during this siege. However, we were not able to note that serious damage had been done to any plant by the beetles. This sounds odd, even to me, for on the home farm we used to see potato plants stripped of leaves in a very short time when beetles were present in hot, dry weather. There was never a large population of potato beetles present, and some of them developed into adults without appreciable damage to the plants (impossible as that sounds). Commercial growers would have started the sprayer at the appearance of the first beetle, confident that otherwise the crop would be lost.

Under the better soil conditions we hope to have later, we expect to be bothered by potato beetles even less than in 1945. Conditions really favored the beetles that year. The tubers were planted hastily in soil that was neither well filled with organic matter nor granulated for the freer growth of roots and admission of air. The only organic matter was the grass and weed roots left in the soil after we had scalped off the top few inches. Moreover, the period during which rain would have helped most was almost rainless. Consequently this was a rather poor situation for growing potatoes in any case. In an upgraded soil—or even in the very spot where these potatoes grew, if mulch had been used—the 1945 results would probably have been better. It may never be possible to eliminate potato beetles completely, but we hope in the future to have even fewer of them than we had in 1945.

This chapter is a plea for the application of common sense, in addition to science, to the problems of insects and diseases. All experimental evidence is against the thesis I have presented. The divergence of experimental fact from the facts I have observed fully justified the professor quoted earlier in dismissing the matter. Yet, unless science ignores the obvious fact that spraying and dusting of crops the world over is very strictly limited in extent, there must be a real basis for such observations as I have made and here described. Nothing has been reported that cannot be verified—and duplicated. In all conscience, scientists ought to carry out investigations in this field which to them seems so bizarre.

A Second Look at : Tile Treachery

THE DISCUSSION of tile drainage in *Plowman's Folly* seems the most inept part of the book. While the argument as outlined was, and still is, correct it was improperly delimited. No proper attempt was made to explain the scope of the criticism directed at present-day use of tile. Indeed, the chapter contains almost no hint that its scope was limited. On this account many readers who failed to note near the end of the chapter that "except in swamps tile will be superfluous" decided that the author disapproved all drainage. It is no wonder, then, that many readers were ready to toss either the book or its author out the window.

As was true of most of the book, several preliminary forms of this chapter were written. When, on later reading, a chapter seemed unsuitable for use in the book manuscript, it was discarded and a new attempt was made. Russell Lord rewrote the introduction to one of the early versions and used it in *The Land*, Vol. II, No. 1. A somewhat fuller indication of the scope of the argument is seen in the following query quoted from that article: "Isn't it strange that land which needed no tile when the water table was high seems to need it now when the water table has dropped from ten to a hundred feet?" Yet this question, which reveals the anomalous situation against which the argument was written, closes the third paragraph of the article instead of leading off the first paragraph. I am not surprised that many readers were dissatisfied with this chapter.

Let me now account for the manner in which our land has been thoughtlessly overdrained:

It is significant that the first drain tile was laid in the United States in 1835. By this date many farms had already gone through the traditional routine of being cleared, skimmed of their early productiveness, and abandoned. Probably even then some of the older land had begun to develop those symptoms of improper land management, *wet spots,* in which water had not hitherto gathered after rains. Most American farm drainage of the past century was done as treatment for these "symptoms," and it was at this folly that the faulty chapter on "Tile Treachery" was aimed. No aspersion was intended against legitimate drainage projects of the past, present, or future.

Careful readers of the book got this impression, and approved the suggestions I made about remedies for wet spots. Some have reported that they now plug the tile lines after the spring rains have passed. At Malabar Farm, so splendidly depicted by Louis Bromfield in his *Pleasant Valley,* appropriate land treatment, including some attention to the prevention of undue water loss through tile lines, has restored old springs that had long since been forgotten. Indeed, Mr. Bromfield says that in some places old seepy spots have reappeared, sometimes causing trouble temporarily. This report indicates that Malabar Farm is gradually, if not speedily, being restored to the condition that may have prevailed on the farm of John Johnston (near Geneva, New York) before he needed to lay in the first drain tile to be placed on a farm in this country more than a century ago.

The outflow from springs, as well as temporary seepage water, often requires tile for its disposal. Fields are frequently separated by small streams when otherwise they might be worked together. Today, when tractor power must be planned for, such a situation calls for tile, if by the use of tile the fields can be thrown together. As a county agent I was often called upon to run levels for lines of tile, sometimes for help with complete farm drainage systems. Work on some of these projects proved extremely instructive to me as well as to the farmer involved.

One river bottom farm was difficult to operate profitably because of the manner in which its one tillable field was cut up. A stream from the upland flowed across it, passing through two swampy spots of considerable area and making a boggy swale of a broad strip between the lower swamp and the river into which the stream drained at the edge of this field. Little drain tile had been installed in the county at that time, and this farmer consequently knew nothing of how to deal with the problem that bulked so large in the management of his entire farm. Since a practical solution was educational work for other farmers of the county as well as for this man, draining the area was a legitimate county-agent activity. Hence I agreed to help the farmer carry out the required work.

First, I sent for an engineer (supplied then by the Office of Public Roads) to make the survey and set the stakes, thinking that service would be about the extent of my responsibility. The engineer came, made the survey for a single line of tile, set the stakes, and then explained to the farmer and to me how the work had to be done. That ended his duties, but not mine. The ditch bottom was soft mud, and water stood there at all times. To make matters worse, stakes were set to give variable slope to the tile at certain points. After the ditch had been dug, the farmer had still to have help in laying the tile. I therefore spent several days helping him lay it so it would really work. If this tile was to be a useful demonstration, it had to work properly; and I didn't dare risk what might happen if the tile were laid without constant supervision. Such was the justification for my work.

Having built the concrete-buttressed outlet at the river bank, the farmer could do no more than lay in the few hundred feet of tile that drained the lower bog. This was on a slope of four inches to each hundred feet. The next section of several hundred feet which crossed this bog had been planned at one inch to the hundred feet. This meant, of course, that it must be accurately laid and so anchored that it would not be moved afterward. Also, arrangements had to be made to prevent clogging the downstream tile with mud while the remainder of the line was being laid. All this we did, drawing through each tile as it was laid a swab which served to strain trash out of the water that went through it.

When the job was finished at last, we were gratified to

be able to hear the water flow through, even along the nearly level stretch across the lower bog. That meant success. It meant that now the entire trench could be filled with earth; and, more to the point, that in future this big field could be farmed as a single unit instead of as segregated spots with many "point rows." It would be an object lesson to every farmer who passed by, for the field lay along an important road leading to the county seat. Every farmer who had passed that way for decades had noticed this fine field that was ruined by bogs and ditches. Now the fact that it could be farmed as a single field with no obstructions would be noticed; and other farmers would begin to wonder whether they couldn't improve their own fields by the use of tile.

This story illustrates one of the many ways in which drain tile may be used beneficially, instead of being used merely to dispose of water which would not need to be removed if the land were properly managed.

Another instance in which a small investment in tile paid big dividends was the case of a farmer whose field, already narrow, was almost bisected by a bullrush bog more than one thousand feet long. The farmer doubted whether the slope was sufficient to permit drainage, and for that reason he had not done anything about it. However, he finally mentioned the problem to me, and asked whether anything could be done. After inquiry revealed that water did not actually stand in pools, I felt sure that there must be enough slope for drainage. I told him accordingly to expect me on a certain day to look the area over. Luckily, since the day selected was a school holiday, the teacher of vocational agriculture of the local high school was free and volunteered to go along. He and I were crew enough to manage a leveling instrument and rod that I had borrowed from the county engineer.

A preliminary leveling showed that there was a difference in elevation of three feet eight inches from source to mouth of the boggy strip. This was about four inches of slope for each one hundred feet, which is always enough. We proceeded, then, to set in stakes, so marking them that the farm owner could use them to gauge the depth of the ditch as he dug it. This done we returned to town, hoping the ditch would be completed and the tile laid, but none too sure that this farmer would have the energy to do the work.

I heard no more of this matter until a year later, when that farmer came to the office to tell me that he had grown enough tobacco in the former boggy strip to more than pay for the tile.

There have been thousands of cases in which the tile a farmer laid paid him enough extra returns in a few years to pay for his entire farm. Such stories used to be commonplace. But they are stories of the removal of water that had always interfered with proper use of the land. Such drainage is commendable as well as profitable, and was not the target of criticism in my earlier book. Objection was raised only against the thoughtless disposal of water that suddenly appears in unaccustomed places. Proper use of tile is quite necessary; only its misuse can properly be criticized.

When a farmer resorts to tile to clear away water so

he can get his plowing done earlier, he usually is thinking only of the present. Consideration of the past—of the causes that have changed the character of his soil—would force him to plan carefully for the future improvement of his soil, instead of simply removing today's wet spot. The very fact that water lies today where formerly it sank promptly should cause him to wonder why. Increased density of the soil is the only possible explanation. But why is the soil more dense today than it used to be?

In many parts of the country horses have been replaced almost entirely by tractors. Possibly these heavier sources of power, along with the weightier new implements they pull, may have packed the subsoil as the plowing was done. If so, such effects would be most marked at points where the subsoil was a little too moist when the plowing was done; and those spots would have been the lowest parts of the field, naturally. It is reasonable to believe that when fields are being plowed in early spring the tractor wheels puddle the subsoil under them while the moldboard is thoroughly troweling the about-to-be exposed surface of the furrow slice. (This is almost certain to happen unless the farmer is exceptionally careful to delay plowing until the lowest spots in his fields are ready. And how many farmers have that much courage when work is rushing them in the early spring?) This two-story compaction stops water on the surface, and later as it tries to pass through the plowsole into the subsoil. Some of the new, pick-up plows may appear not to trowel the landside and bottom of the furrow, but that puddling is done by the heavily burdened tractor wheels.

The likelihood that plowing will be done before the lowest parts of a field are ready is favored by the probability that rain may intervene if the work is delayed. Faced with these alternatives, few farmers dare delay plowing until each low spot has dried out deep enough not to be puddled by the passing plow.

Moreover, it seems never to occur to the plowman as he aches to get into action that the water which fills these low spots to the brim did not fall where it is now to be seen. Rainfall never stays where it falls. It must sink into the soil or run off. There is no other way. Gravity simply won't have it otherwise. Thus, in studying the situation, the farmer must realize that his formerly porous, spongy soil has become a roof, which fact accounts for the wet spots. If soil density were confined to the wet spots, the condition of the soil wouldn't be so bad, for then no water would be in the wet spots except what fell there. When water accumulates in depressions it does so because the surrounding slopes will not take it in. It has no recourse. That is why land develops wet spots which can delay plowing for weeks unless they are drained.

No farmer can be blamed for the fact that he tiles away the water from depressions. What he may properly be blamed for is his failure to think his problem through and apply the remedy that will prevent later embarrassment. More than one farmer has found a second pool of water gathered over the tile, after a few seasons have passed. And that isn't funny to those who have had it happen to them.

The best preventive for this embarrassment is the

restoration of the soil to such condition that it will again absorb rainfall. This can be done best and most conveniently by mixing into it all possible self-grown material. Even that isn't easy to do on land that has once settled together until it sheds water like a roof; but determination and persistence accomplish what otherwise would be impossible. Many farmers already have started work of this type on their land. Others will follow suit. Progress reports invariably indicate that water runs into the soil better, even the first season after treatment begins.

This assurance seems to justify a change of front about the necessity for terraces on some soils of the humid section of the country. Vast areas of our land should respond promptly to surface incorporation of organic matter—by improved porosity. On such land, terraces ought not be needed for controlling runoff. Some sands of the South and many loessal soils of the West are texturally different. Lacking the clay and colloidal material, these soils often move out in a hurry when enough rain has fallen to start moving over the surface. For these free-moving soils, terraces may be necessary to hold the soil in place long enough for it to grow the first few green manure crops. As mentioned before, these special soils lack the necessary fine material for "cementing" them together. Hence they must *always* retain some organic binder if they are to be safe from theft by wind or water. And, regardless of the textural qualities of soils, they are always safest when held together by roots or other organic binders.

Already Soil Conservation Service has done effective

work without terraces where formerly successful land use without them was thought impossible. Technicians of this service quickly sense helpful new practices and are anxious to help make the rehabilitation of soils as inexpensive as may be. Great strides have been made in cheapening the cost of soil restoration, but it seems to me that possibilities inherent in the surface incorporation of green manure crops surely will point the way to further major cost reductions.

The extent to which filling the surface soil with organic matter will change the soil's internal water relations probably is not very well known. We know that water will filter into the soil much more readily if its passage is aided by organic matter on or within the surface. We do not know how much water can be retained by the organic matter within those upper inches. We may be sure that, until the organic matter itself has been filled to capacity with water, it will release none to trickle into the deeper soil layers. When rainfall is light, therefore, most of the rainfall is likely to be held in the organic matter of the upper few inches of soil. The retention of rainfall in the root zone must necessarily decrease the loss of water from drains; and in this case we can be sure that less mineral nutrient elements will be leached out of a well-treated soil.

Root distribution will be tremendously increased under such conditions as have just been described. One good effect of this increased growth of plant roots is the more complete compensation for the continuous loss by decay of the soil's supply of organic matter; for these new plant roots also die as soon as they have completed their work of salvage, and can in turn be salvaged by a new set of roots established for that purpose. The ultimate effect of this increased organic activity is a start, at least, on the restoration of the original black color to the soil. The progressive building up of organic supply and consequent activity in the soil results in the retention of a greater volume of rainfall near the surface, instead of useless drainage into the subsoil. The retention of water in quantity in the surface inches logically should, and actually does, reduce the damaging effects of short droughts. Crops often develop precisely as if they were being irrigated, apparently oblivious to drought that is ruining other crops near by. They continue their growth days or weeks beyond the time when other crops begin to suffer drought effects. Eventually, of course, even this buffer effect is exhausted; but when rainfall does come it is apt to find the crop in better condition to benefit than if there had been no reserve of water in the upper inches of soil.

Conditions as here described begin to duplicate those that in the early years of tillage prevented wet spots on American farms at places where they now appear. The water in earlier times had no means of reaching the wet spot—no transportation. We have provided that "transportation" by allowing the upper soil to become compact. By making it porous again we will make sure that there will be no wet spots to demand attention before we plow—or disk.

A Second Look at XI : What We Eat

FOOD EXPERTS in the United States are in a tough spot. For a generation they have been making specific recommendations for food selection, including more or less definite rules that should help people eat the right foods in something approaching the right proportions. A quart of milk a day for every child has long been held forth as an ideal. That is one reason that G. I. Joe could grin down on the medical officer from a height of an inch or two greater than that of his father. There have been other fine results from the patient teachings of dieticians during the past generation. But there is no room for complacency yet in the nutritionists' camp.

One bugbear of the food expert's life is the way identical foods vary in the amounts of proteins, minerals, and vitamins they contain. It is not likely that this puzzle can be solved in the laboratory or kitchen. A good statement of the situation is given on page 962 of *Food and Life,* the Yearbook of the United States Department of Agriculture for 1939, as follows:

> In general it may be said that all plants have a composition which is inherent to that particular species or variety. If the soil contains in available form and in sufficient quantity all of the essential minerals for the growth of the plant and the climatic

conditions are favorable, the plants will have a normal composition and the further addition of essential minerals in the properly balanced proportions will generally affect but little the chemical composition of the plants. On the other hand, the deficiency in the soil of any element used by the plant is likely to result in a deficiency of that element in the plant. For this reason proper attention to the needs of the soil will go far toward assuring a normal composition of the plants and satisfactory nutrition of the livestock that consume the forage grown on the soil. The addition of calcium, phosphorus, nitrogen, and iodine to soils deficient in these elements has been shown to increase the contents of them in the forage. Presumably the same will occur when copper, iron, and cobalt are added to the soil, since deficiencies of these elements in the feed also have been traced to deficiencies in the soil.

Note that this paragraph, completely quoted, carries by implication the idea that our soils are substandard. The statement shows that plants require, if they are to be of normal composition, the right elements *"in available form and in sufficient quantity"* in the soil. No actual shortage of any element is presumed; only that the needed elements may not be present *in available form* in sufficient quantity. That, of course, is the true situation, as we have already shown. And, to have abundant fertility, we have but to rekindle the fires of decay and keep them constantly active.

The dilemma of the food expert begins with the parsimonious release of plant nutrient elements by substandard soils. Irregularities in this respect account for the variations (from food lot to food lot) in content of proteins, minerals, and vitamins. Each food becomes a special case. As a result, only the most general of dietary recommendations can be made; and even these may not, even though followed closely, provide an adequate diet.

Milk, the supposedly gilt-edged food, normally varies in fat between 3½ per cent and 5 per cent, which may or may not be important. But its vitamin A, of which milk is supposed to be a standard supplier, may vary sharply from lot to lot, the real situation depending upon several factors, chief of which is the diet of the cow. What she does not get in her feed she cannot pass on to her calf, or to you who "rob" her calf. It is regrettably true that in an era of substandard soils (deficient, if you insist) there can be no assurance that our foods will always be up to standard. Milk, which certainly will contain everything the mother of the calf is physically able to give to it, may be short in vitamin A when the cow is on a diet that provides too little of the necessary constituents.

The following additional quotation from *Food and Life,* p. 65, briefs the findings resulting from many experiments conducted to show what happens to the vitamin A of milk when cows are fed rations deficient in requirements:

> The amount of carotene (or of vitamin A) in a cow's ration has little or no effect on the milk yield, but it determines the vitamin-A potency of the butterfat. When the carotene received by the cow is less than a certain amount the calves are born abnormal; when it is reduced still more the cow herself becomes night blind; when the cow's milk has less than a certain vitamin-A potency the nursing calf becomes night blind.

Don't be alarmed! This merely describes experiments, not dairy farm conditions. Presumably, you can safely trust the milk you are using; but if symptoms of night blindness appear among your family, add butter, cream, carrots, or other yellow colored foods to their diet.

Milk is but one of our foods, though by any standard one of the best. If it may be deficient in the vitamin A, for which it is a standard source, what of the other foods?

Unfortunately, helpful information in this field is very sketchy in character and limited in supply. Food analysts have always been plagued by the lack of uniformity they find in samples of farm products tested for the various critical food requirements. This, of course, goes with deficiencies, and we might easily suppose deficient food is a modern thing. But that supposition is true only in the laboratory sense. Actually, the Chinese and Egyptians knew by 1500 B. C. that a man's eyesight in the dark improved after he ate liver. Thus perhaps even in Joseph's time famines may have resulted from soil deficiencies. If so, it has taken us a long time indeed to find out the true state of affairs.

Even today, though we have learned much about deficiencies caused by lack of vitamins, though many of the vitamins have been synthesized, no official investigation has been made into the possibility that if all our foods grew in real soil they would contain automatically enough of all the food requirements. Such investigation has been omitted, perhaps, because of the universal belief that crops exhaust soil, and that what is removed must be replaced. The current effort of bankers to get farmers to "keep faith" with their soils in this respect is perfectly consistent with currently accepted soil theories. It is easy to see that failure to check the possibilities inherent in the soil is to be expected, as indicated by this further brief item from *Food and Life*, p. 962:

> While deficiencies of minerals in the forage may be corrected by treatment of the soil, it is often more satisfactory as well as more economical to administer or feed some kinds of minerals to the animal.

"Treatment of the soil" means fertilizing, of course. The thought that minerals might be elaborated from sources within the soil and literally "grown" into the feeds is entirely outside the thought frame in which this passage was written. It is quite evident, then, that our investigators have conscientiously followed laboratory lines of thought, overlooking this innate possibility. (Perhaps by now you may wish to own a copy of *Food and Life.* If so, write your Congressman for one. If his supply is exhausted, you can get a copy by sending $1.50 to the Superintendent of Documents, Washington, D. C. Obviously, only brief quotations have been attempted here, and a more complete perusal by the reader will develop much of value. Its 1,165 pages are packed with material of interest to anyone who is curious about foods. Seventy-five pages are devoted to information on the one subject of vitamins, some of which may be out of date by now; but mastery of this book will equip one to catch up later with the newest developments in foods and nutrition.)

A reasonable suspicion exists that few of us these days ever eat a meal that doesn't consist chiefly of foods that are deficient in one or more essentials. If it were otherwise, how would we rationalize the extent to which people are ill or "below par" physically? Our most plentiful foods, corn, wheat, potatoes, etc., which are also our cheapest, are lacking in proteins and must be "supplemented" by meats, eggs, cheese, etc. People who must count their pennies at the restaurant can buy little except the cheapest foods. Yet this phase of our food situation has been a "blind spot" in our analysis of food facts—at least as far as action is concerned. A choice example of sidestepping this issue is a speech I once heard a representative of the War Food Administration make to a group of victory garden leaders. In substance it was this:

> It seems not to matter what we teach people to eat; they still follow their old habits and buy the same foods at the restaurant—just as if they didn't know better. As I watched the line in a cafeteria the other day I counted but three or four portions of meat on the first dozen or so trays.

He moralized from this that the promotion of victory gardens would give these people a chance to learn what they were missing by not buying the "protective foods." I fully agreed that victory gardens should be grown by everybody who could do so, but for a different reason. That term "protective foods" waves a red flag. It presumes a security that may not exist, as we have shown in connection with milk. Other foods that wear that badge are equally dependent upon basic soil conditions for their ability to deliver the "protection" the customer has been taught to expect. The victory gardener, if properly advised, might elevate some of the ordinary foods to a better nutritive status and thereby achieve a measure of freedom from the usual ills that go with malnutrition.

The worst worries of the nutritionist, however, stem from something deeper than mere variations in composition of the common foods. Our system of food production poses problems that make it virtually impossible for *everybody* to be properly nourished. We grow too much of the cheap, deficient foods; too little of those which "protect" the consumer against the poorer items. If you have sufficient money, you can be well nourished (at least so long as there are not too many others who also have enough money for food). But the supply of what are called "protective" foods would disappear as if by magic soon after *everybody* found enough money to enable him to buy regularly meals that are completely nutritive.

In other words, our eating habits are not altogether the result of either whimsey or poverty. There is a far more fundamental reason. We simply do not grow enough of the highly nourishing foods. People limit their meat consumption because of the cost, true enough; but the cost is higher than it otherwise would be because of our farming habits. Farmers like to use machinery as fully as possible in their work. The growing of row crops, grain crops, and hay gives most opportunity for exercise of this preference. Power farming, even though the power be horses or oxen, is much easier than the muscular exercise that otherwise would be necessary. Besides, because of his use of machinery, the American farmer can lord it over farmers elsewhere in the world, though he fails to note the accompanying soil degradation.

This penchant for power farming is not of itself significant, but crops that fit most easily into power operations happen to be (or have been developed into) the crops that contain least protein. Wouldn't you like to know whether the low-protein status of corn, wheat, and potatoes is natural to these crops, or is caused by our manipulations of our substandard soils in growing them? I would like to know too.

Perhaps for reasons of pride, we lower still further the food values of these crops before they reach our tables as corn flakes, grits, white flour, or mashed potatoes. Another crime against nutrition.

The suggestion that the protein content of our crops may be made abnormally low by our management of the land probably sounds far-fetched. It can be rationalized without unreasonable presumption, thus:

Cultivation, by keeping dry the upper few inches of the soil, prevents crop roots from invading this zone. Thus roots are entirely deprived of decay products they might obtain in this zone. Decay products in this upper zone might be richer in proteins or protein-making constituents than those that exist at lower levels, where oxygen and nitrogen cannot enter so freely.

So far as I know, this suggestion has never been made officially, which leads me to believe that this possibility, like others cited, may not have been investigated. The privilege of developing roots in this zone of soil should result in crops of better protein and mineral composition. Experience favors this conclusion, for even these crops, if grown in real soil or something approaching real soil, are richer in flavor than when grown on substandard soils. It seems reasonable that the real soil would provide better aeration, and therefore would permit more proteins to be developed, as well as favoring the release of more minerals from the crystalline form. If tests should reveal more minerals and more proteins, that fact would account for the enhanced flavor of food crops grown in such soil. To determine the facts in this matter, chemical tests are badly needed.

Among the so-called "protective" foods are some that cannot be cared for by machine methods; or, rather, there are several such crops which do best if mulched, and mulching is not done by machinery. Some of these crops are characterized by prominent flavors which tend to become insipid under cultivation. I was told recently by a man familiar with citrus production that one grower of his acquaintance discovered that his family picked for their own use the fruit of two or three trees growing in an isolated area that could not be reached by the cultivating tools. He decided to have this fruit analyzed. The tests indicated more of both minerals and sugar than is usual—suggesting that the root pruning done by cultivation, plus the destruction of organic matter in the root zone, had reduced the quality of fruit produced on trees given more care. This grower has since begun to mulch as much as possible of his citrus orchard. Non-citrus fruits seem to respond in the same way to improved methods of handling the soil. The only bearing apricot trees I know of in the humid section of this country are growing where cultivation would be impracticable or impossible. More and more emphasis is being placed upon the use of mulches in apple orchards. Blueberries refuse to grow and bear well under cultivation.

As a simple matter of economics, our more plentiful, cheaply grown corn and wheat, and our usually abundant potatoes, rank among the least expensive items of food. Differences in cost between the common foods and the less abundant "protective" foods often are so great that only wealthy people can afford the latter. In such a case, the suggestion that everybody drink a pint of milk daily and eat liberally of such expensive viands as nuts, cheese, fruits, butter, yellow and green vegetables, etc. can but fall on deaf ears among people whose incomes prohibit such "extravagance." For most of us, the cheapness of the plentiful foods is a fortunate circumstance. We might feel better about the whole thing if there were no suspicion that *we get even less than we pay for* (except obesity) when we buy foods that are short in proteins, minerals, and/or vitamins. This country needs desperately to make the really nutritious foods cheap enough for everybody.

Until the point has been disproved by appropriate tests, I shall believe that vegetables and other crops grown under mulch, or in real soil, are more nutritious than are the same food crops grown in the usual way—barring, of course, exceptional circumstances. If tests should prove this view correct, the way to have these richer foods at prices everybody can pay may have been found. One class of foods that has long had the full approval of dieticians is the fruits. And fruits develop at their best only in an undisturbed soil. Perhaps there is a moral in this fact. If fruits were less insistent upon having correct soil conditions, they might be as deficient in food essentials as the most plentiful of our foods.

It is high time, in my opinion, that we revise our thinking in several directions with respect to the health of our entire population. Instead of scolding people because they do not buy food they can't afford, *we need to grow a balanced diet on American farms,* and to cheapen all foods so that the poor as well as the rich may be well-fed. There is no other solution to the multitude of dietary ills from which our people suffer.

Reducing costs is not the impossible task most farmers assume. They little realize how unnecessary are many of the expensive practices they now follow. They must be taught that high-quality crops are possible in real soil, that real soil requires no fertilizers, and that crops so grown are practically free of pests. Relieved of the costs of fertilizers, lime, legumes for crop nitrogen, and the equipment and materials for pest campaigns, the farmer will be able to grow the finest conceivable vegetables, grains, fruits, and meats at costs that everybody will be able to pay.

When we have made the appropriate changes in our farming system, it will then be possible for the poorest to eat the very best food. If, after this has been done, people still shun the foods they ought to eat, it will be time for reprimanding them. Until that time, it is incumbent upon us to devote all necessary attention to developing a system of farming based upon human needs, rather than upon the ease and convenience with which crops can be grown.

A Second Look at XII : Real Food

AN EMPHATIC SUPERIORITY in taste and quality marks the difference between real food and the kind we ordinarily eat. To many of you, this will be a tall story unless, or until, you have actually tasted some real food; and relatively few people who depend upon market supplies have had that opportunity.

Having grown up in the market gardening business, I should have known the taste of first-quality vegetables. We grew in those days the best that were produced in our neighborhood, but I can't recall ever tasting as rich flavors as greeted my first experience with vegetables grown in soil that had been partially developed toward real soil. Knowing that my opinion in this matter was subject to personal bias, I was greatly relieved when in 1940 customers who bought our vegetables began praising them voluntarily, even though they were paying prices above the general market. This spontaneous approval by consumers whose business interest would have been better served by condemnation clinched the point.

Again in 1945 we had a garden intended solely for our own food, but from which we sold a few baskets of beans. From this very limited sale two voluntary stories reached me which confirm the idea I have expressed.

When our town celebrated V-J Day, all the stores were to close at noon. Early in the morning I had sold a basket of beans to a grocer who had disposed of but two pounds and expected to have to keep the rest over to sell as wilted beans the next day. Just before he was to close the woman who had bought the two pounds came back to buy the rest of the basket. She had tasted them and learned how superior they were. Another grocer whose store I visited but once during the season asked me recently why I had not come back, adding that those beans were the best he had had all season. Compliments, it seems to me, ought to be received with pleasure, though not without restraint. However, I am convinced that these responses to a superior crop are significant.

The distinction is far deeper than mere taste. There must be a corresponding difference in health-promoting value. On this point the evidence is not clear-cut in an experimental sense, but there are unmistakable signs that much new information is involved here. Some experimental work in the United States has increased both the proteins and the minerals in the crops to which it has been applied, but I know of no follow-up experimental proof that these crops promoted better health in the consuming animals.

From this point on, the discussion will scarcely be a close-knit argument leading to a definite conclusion, but the material is all within the general field of the food-health relationship. The instances cited deserve study in this connection, and are from sources not often quoted in this country.

To begin with, we have in the United States a long list of what are known as deficiency diseases. It is now generally conceded that the existence of these diseases proves the existence of deficiencies in both the food and the soil which produced it (a matter which has been previously discussed). Deficiency diseases reflect what appears to be a *soil-food-disease* causal chain. I should like to show in this chapter the existence of an equally valid *soil-food-health* relationship. Let us put it this way: We have been living for years in a mental state more or less dominated by the *inevitability of disease.* Why may we not with equal propriety live in an environment of *health as a natural outgrowth of real food?* I know of no reason why we may not. Indeed, I am convinced that, if we choose that course, we shall arrive at a happier state of affairs.

American tourists are familiar with the differences between our way of life and that of other countries. Mentioning our "way of life" reminds me of an epigram I picked out of a letter from "Kernel" J. A. Simpson, a neighbor of former Vice President John Nance Garner at Uvalde, Texas. Simpson said: "Our way of life should not be so much of a way of death." With which we can all agree. ("Kernel" gets his title from admiring friends because of his intense interest in developing edible-nut trees, especially pecans). The "way of life" we so loudly defend here cannot be superior in all respects to other ways of life, for there are people elsewhere who live longer than we do, have fewer diseases, and enjoy other special blessings of health.

Dr. James Asa Shield finds differences in the deficiency diseases that exist in different parts of the world. In Northern China, he says, the people have none of the degenerative diseases of the blood vessels or the nervous system that characterize the peoples of Continental Europe, England, and America. This freedom exists despite the shortage of calcium, vitamins, and calories in their food. Of Korea he says: "although syphilis is as frequent as the common cold . . . tabes (locomotor ataxia) was not once diagnosed by Wilson, who practiced there thirty years."[1] Dr. Shield raises the question of the possible relationship between the manner in which the land is handled and the health of the people, a question that is destined to interest an increasing number of practicing physicians in this country as they learn more about how people live elsewhere in the world.

Dr. Robert McCarrison, a British physician who entered the Indian Medical Service soon after graduation from medical college, has made a great contribution to knowledge about the relation of food to health. Early in his work he displayed talent for research and was given a laboratory, staffed and equipped for the study of factors he thought might explain the outstanding health of the Hunza tribe, among whose people he lived. He says of this tribe:

> My own experience provides an example of a race unsurpassed in perfection of physique and in freedom from disease in general. I refer to the people of the state of Hunza, situated in the

[1] From *Southern Medicine and Surgery*, Vol. CVI, No. 11 (November, 1944). Address before the Tri-State Medical Association of the Carolinas and Virginia, February 28–29, 1944.

extreme northernmost point of India. . . . Amongst these people the span of life is extraordinarily long; and such service as I was able to render them during seven years I spent in their midst was confined chiefly to the treatment of accidental lesions, the removal of senile cataract, plastic operations for granular lids, or the treatment of maladies wholly unconnected with the food supply.[2]

This is high praise for a primitive tribe who knew nothing of the "blessings" of vitamin pills, nor of scientific nutrition.

In 1922 Dr. McCarrison was invited to Pittsburgh to address a group of American physicians. His subject was "Faulty Food in Relation to Gastro-Intestinal Disorder." One paragraph from that remarkable paper deserves quotation here:

I never saw a case of asthenic dyspepsia, of gastric or duodenal ulcer, of mucous colitis, of cancer. . . . Among these people the abdomen over-sensitive to nerve impressions, to fatigue, to anxiety or cold was unknown. The consciousness of the existence of this part of their anatomy was, as a rule, related solely to the feeling of hunger. Indeed, their buoyant abdominal health has, since my return to the west, provided a remarkable contrast with the dyspeptic and colonic lamentations of our highly civilized communities.[3]

We may wonder, excusably, why so remarkable a statement has never been given out to the American people, but can be found only in a British publication. It could

[2] Guy Theodore Wrench, M.D., *The Wheel of Health, A Study of a Very Healthy People,* (London, The C. W. Daniel Company, Ltd., 1941), 26.

[3] *Ibid.,* 27

not be that the existence of such a tribe within the British Empire would be of no interest to laymen seeking health in this country. Perhaps Dr. McCarrison's audience was frankly skeptical.

Dr. McCarrison's approach to the question of health factors was to feed groups of laboratory rats on diets similar to the diets of various human groups whose medical history he knew. Of the group fed the Hunza diet, Dr. McCarrison reported to the College of Surgeons in 1931:

> During the past two and a quarter years there has been no case of illness in this "universe" of albino rats, no death from natural causes in the adult stock, and, but for a few accidental deaths, no infant mortality. Both clinically and at post-mortem examination this stock has been shown to be remarkably free from disease. It may be that some of them have cryptic disease of one kind or another, but, if so, I have failed to find either clinical or macroscopical evidence of it.[4]

Dr. Wrench reports further on the results of other diets which compared with those of other peoples who were afflicted by diseases of various kinds:

> He took the customary diets of the poorer peoples of Bengal and Madras, consisting of rice, pulses, vegetables, condiments, perhaps a little milk. He gave these to the rats.
>
> Now, this diet immediately opened the lid of Pandora's box for the rats . . . and diseases and miseries of many kinds flew forth.[5]

Then follows almost a page of names of diseases (duplicates of human diseases common to Americans as well as

[4] *Ibid.*, 33
[5] *Ibid.*, 36

other civilized people) with which these rats, on post-mortem, were found to be afflicted. While Dr. McCarrison's study did not take into consideration the condition of the soil which produced the food, he has made an invaluable contribution to information on the relationship between food and health—or lack of health.

Dr. Weston A. Price of California, late of Cleveland, Ohio, was for many years a practicing dentist. His curiosity about decay in human teeth caused him to travel to remote regions of the world, to study the teeth of people who lived so far from civilization that they were not influenced by it. What he found is significant. In the most remote places he frequently found teeth that were practically 100 per cent perfect. And he found invariably more evidence of decay wherever the refined foods of civilization were reaching these primitive people. What was even more convincing was his discovery that when he could visit a tribe twice, once before, and then after the construction of highways or railroads to the community, he always found teeth in much worse condition within a few months after civilization invaded. His findings are reported in his book, *Nutrition and Physical Degeneration*, published in 1939 by Harper and Brothers. This book deserves a serious reading.

Another book in this field that should be better known is Sir Albert Howard's *An Agricultural Testament*, published by Oxford University Press, London, in 1940. Sir Albert was sent to the Far East soon after he had completed his training in agriculture. At his new station he became a convert to the value of compost as made and used by the natives. In order to find out the applicability of composting to farm areas, he requested and was furnished a farm on which to experiment. In operating this farm for several years he made some very important observations of interest to people seeking ways to health. Lady Eve B. Balfour, one of his numerous "Boswells," quotes his experience with hoof and mouth disease (against which the American practice is to destroy all infected animals and quarantine all others that have been exposed), showing, apparently, that the compost-grown produce of his experimental farm had made his animals immune:

> I then took steps to have my own oxen and to ascertain from first-hand experience the reaction of well-chosen and well-fed animals to diseases like rinderpest (cattle plague), Johne's disease and so forth which are common in India. After a short time my animals duly came into contact with other oxen suffering, among other things, from foot-and-mouth disease.
>
> I have myself seen my oxen rubbing noses with foot-and-mouth cases. Nothing happened. The healthy, well fed animal reacted towards this disease exactly as improved and properly cultivated crops did to insects and fungi—no infection occurred.
>
> These preliminary results suggested that the birthright of every crop and of every animal is health and that the correct method of dealing with disease is not to destroy the parasite but to make use of it for keeping agricultural practice up to the mark. . . . Everything possible was done to grow crops properly; everything possible was done for the livestock as regards food, hygiene and general management. The result was freedom from disease.[6]

[6] Eve B. Balfour, *The Living Soil,* (London, Faber and Faber, Ltd., 1943), 65–66.

It should be noted that Lady Balfour is herself in charge of agricultural experiments, and writes from a background of agricultural experience and training.

A few thinkers in the United States have been feeling their way towards the same point of view about the relation of food to health. Dr. Jonathan Forman, Professor of Nutrition at Ohio State University and Editor of *The Ohio State Medical Journal,* wrote several years ago a brief article called *Hidden Hunger* that should be read by every American. Here is the beginning of this excellent bit of writing:

> Children cannot get what they should from their teachers if they are hungry. I refer here not so much to apparent hunger as to hidden hunger. Deficiency in vital food elements is widespread among our children. This has been brought about by our insistence upon over-refining our foodstuffs and the depletion of our soils of their essential minerals through bad farming practices. It has never seemed sensible to me to spend large sums of money upon teachers, buildings, and school books and at the same time neglect the health and nutrition of pupils. Undernourished children lack the mental alertness necessary for learning.
>
> Too many of us think of health as a condition which merely keeps us out of the physician's office. True health isn't that at all. It is a condition of the human body in which there is a joy of living, a buoyancy, a robustness—health *plus.* When people are physically fit they are alert. They have endurance and do not tire easily; and what is usually not emphasized, they do not worry. They meet the social problems of life with common sense and make the necessary adjustments.[7]

Dr. Forman is a nutritionist—not a soil scientist. His

[7] Jonathan Forman, M.D., "Hidden Hunger," *The Land,* Vol. II, No. 1, 25.

emphasis on the overrefinement of our foods is a natural outgrowth of his nutritional studies; his linking faulty nutrition to the soil and its management is originality that might well be copied by soil scientists themselves.

Another American, Dr. William A. Albrecht, chairman of the Department of Soils, University of Missouri, emphasizes the relationship between food as cause and health or disease as effect in another article taken from *The Land*. The following paragraphs express a point of view all too rare among conventional thinkers in soils or health:

> Food bulk is registered by satiation and the relief of hunger. Food quality, when defective, remains unregistered by these means, but gives us the hidden hungers that may be lifetime torments.
>
> These hidden hungers originate in the soil and reach us by way of plants that also suffer hidden hungers. So, also animals suffer their hidden hungers, and so humans, in their turn, consuming the products of starved plants and animals, suffer. This whole series of torments is caused by nutrient shortages in the soil. It should be exposed and possibly cured by soil treatment.
>
> Proper nutrition is an enemy of "disease," in plants as in people. Fungus attacks on plants, the "damping off" disease, has been demonstrated as related to a hidden hunger for lime or calcium. More recently potato scab has suggested its connection with insufficient calcium in the soil fertility offered the potato plant.[8]

At the time Dr. Albrecht wrote this article, he was well in

[8] William A. Albrecht, "Soil and Livestock," *The Land*, Vol. II, No. 4, 298.

advance of the thinking of many of his colleagues; gradually, however, others have been catching up.

Here and there throughout the United States there are others who are thinking and talking, and writing as well as working toward the goal of better soil management. Individuals, groups, incorporated societies, and promoters of particular points of view—all have as their ultimate goal "saving" the soil. The "conservation" idea is gathering momentum, and is likely to keep going until the country has been rather completely included into the legal districts provided for by law in each of the states. But the ultimate idea, too seldom expressed, is the physical regeneration of man.

Most of these enthusiasts will benefit from learning how the earth beneath their feet actually and freely gives up its locked-in stores of plant nutrient elements to him who applies the "key" of abundant and continuous decomposition. Up to now "soil conservation" has required fertilizer and lime, and more fertilizer and lime. Nobody, apparently, had ever stopped to recall that before there was the first single cell (the first organic matter) the earth was fully capable of supplying the necessities of life to its first living guest, the single celled organism. Now that we know that the crystalline portion of the soil still retains all the locked-in elements it ever had, and that the unfailing "key" to that store is decay maintained continuously in the soil, the way is open for each of these organized conservation efforts to speed up its program while eliminating costs heretofore thought essential.

Even in England this same kind of situation prevails.

The House of Lords has recently taken time on two occasions to deliberate soil, food, health relationships. The idea is vital there, because England and Wales have less than one acre per person, including the space occupied by cities, roads, mountains, and wastelands. Britons are seriously trying to feed themselves fully from their own land and fisheries. They easily talk outside the thought-frame of fertilizers and lime that has conditioned our thinking and talk in this country for so long. The reason they can do this is that they have produced their food heretofore from land that is more nearly real soil than most land in the United States. They have not required any great amount of soil amendment, and they probably will find ways to develop their future food supply without resort to outside aid for their soil.

Yes, between the food we eat and real food a great gulf is fixed. It is man's obligation to cross it.

A Second Look at XIII : The Farmer's Income

SIGNIFICANT INCOME from tillage of the soil is almost an exclusive American monopoly. For the visitor from other lands, where every man must either be or hire his own gardener, the American farmer and his machines constitute the country's most eye-opening wonder. In few other countries is farming the big business that it is in the United States and Western Canada. Fewer still have such a "bread basket" area operated by individual farmers as private enterprise. To understand this unique financial eminence, it is necessary to know something of both the causes from which it developed and the effect that farm prosperity has had on the country as a whole. It goes almost without saying that only a brief outline can be given here.

In no other part of the world do so few people grow food for so many. Elsewhere a minority is fed by a majority growing the food. Peasants may have their small surpluses: cabbages, beans, grapes, mutton, honey, and poultry. They bring these to the public square of the nearest town, sit all day in the sunshine, and haggle with passers-by, selling or bartering for other products. No great income can result from such casual marketing, yet farmer income throughout most of the world is of this undependable character. Exception must be made for areas near large cities where gardening is on a commercial basis. But by and large the cash take of peasants the world over is scanty, unless home industries—those of Switzerland being notable examples—are developed.

But the moneyless condition of the peasant does not inconvenience him to the extent we might expect. While the tiller elsewhere may have little money, he also has almost no chance to spend it. The age of domestic handicraft is not yet over in other countries. Shoes and clothing are still being made in the home for family use in many lands. These are not economic conditions to which we would, or should, return, but it must be said, on the other hand, that those who lack our conveniences also escape some of the hazards of a machine civilization. They at least do not run the risk of complete destitution if a factory closes for a short or long period.

From cultures less complex than our own came many settlers who helped to develop American agriculture—some from cities, some from the country. All knew how to work, save the few typified by those who came with Captain John Smith and had to be taught the necessary connection between working and eating. Most had grown their own food. They sought here the large opportunity of living in peace and contentment. The New World was different from the Old in many respects, but most importantly it offered an abundance of land. This factor made possible for the newcomers ways of living and farming they had never known before. From an intensive agriculture, they moved to an extensive one. In time the combined influence of much land, scarcity of agricultural labor, and a ready market for all crops produced the machine agriculture with which we are familiar today.

In the beginning, much of the land was covered with trees. The first job for many settlers (along the Eastern Seaboard and in the North) was the clearing of trees, so that dwellings might be constructed; the second, obviously, was additional clearing for a garden. Conquering the acre or two that each family required for these purposes was enough to keep most men busy at least for the first season. But each succeeding winter offered opportunity for cutting more trees, and most men continued, year after year, increasing the size of the clearing about the cabins. This had one defensive value, if no other: it kept unfriendly Indians farther away.

The ever-increasing size of clearings began, in a few years, to pose problems for the settlers. The patches cleared first, unless they were used for crops, began to grow up to trees again. Unless preventive measures were taken, growth was remarkably fast. Gladly would the settlers have hired help for this job of keeping the land clear of trees, but there were few men to be hired.

The farmer's children, who were of great assistance while they were in their teens, inevitably selected mates and departed for more remote forest areas, there to open new clearings. The fever for land settlement was contagious, and permanent help was out of the question, since every man wanted his own land. Possession of an ax and title to the land (often dubious) constituted preparation for establishing a home in the wilderness. Such was the reality under which the earliest of American farmers worked.

Meanwhile the cultivated land grew amazing crops of wheat, oats, barley, rye, flax, cotton, tobacco, and sorghum. The pressing needs were for better ways of planting and harvesting these crops. Aye, there was the rub. Almost every man had more cleared land than he could take care of properly. In a sense, the more land he had the worse off he was. Any food crop could be sold. By today's inflated standards, the selling prices were not high, but whatever the farmer got from selling his crop was almost clear profit, for no expense save for seed and labor was involved. Planting and harvesting required too much time. There was too much land to permit the work to be done quickly enough with the European tools the settlers had brought with them. Clearly, something must be done to speed up planting and harvesting on farms that were already big but still growing.

In time inventive genius developed machines that helped greatly. The first simple models were improved over and over again until, with up-to-date equipment, one man could manage acreage ten to fifteen times the size of the average European farm. This, briefly, is how the American farmer came by so much land and the machines with which to cultivate it.

What happened to him psychologically is equally significant. There would have been no machinery for farming these large acreages had it not been for the convenient fact that there was a ready market for everything the farmer could grow, and at prices that left a big profit.

The world across the seas was hungry. The American farmer was its invisible producer of food. For many decades, ships from our ports carried farm products to markets everywhere on the globe. From these trips they brought back spices, rubber, and literally hundreds of essential manufactured items, or raw materials that we needed or wanted here in America. Our farmers prospered, as did all our people, but the secret of their prosperity was the expanding market for farm products at prices the buying peoples were glad to pay—in goods.

While all of this trading activity was going on—and the soil seemed able to keep up the pace forever—new acreage continued to be cleared. There seemed no reason why a farmer should not increase his acreage so he could share fully in the general prosperity. What if an occasional field did begin to show "bald" spots here and there? The hardwareman in town had just stocked some foul-smelling stuff in sacks that he said would help to produce bigger crops on the fields that had begun to lag. It seemed to be something worth trying. Of course there was always manure that might be used. Whether he admitted it or not, every farmer knew manure was really better; but the hardwareman's substitute would deliver the promised yields. Moreover, you could put it on and be ready to plant before half the stalls could be cleaned. This reasoning prompted many a farmer to take the easier and quicker way, even though it meant leaving valuable manure in the uncleaned stalls.

Year after year of such compromise bleached out the fertilizer-fed soil. Not that there were no warnings. Editors of farm papers and experiment station men risked getting a bad name for themselves by telling farmers how much better it would be if they would first use the manure that clogged entrance to the stables. Farmers retorted that it was easy for advisers to talk, since they didn't have to do the hauling. Louis Bromfield likes to tell visitors about the "riches" he has taken out of the barn and barn lot of one of the poverty-stricken farms he bought. The story contains an obvious moral, but tragedy lies in the fact that the same story could be told of thousands of American farms of the past several generations.

Profit-taking farmers of the prosperous past developed their practices under multiple influences. They had plenty of land—which explains their resort to quick and easy ways of keeping up production. They had the cash, moreover; so they really could choose between the time-consuming way of hauling out manure and the more expensive, though quicker, way of buying and applying fertilizers. Also, there was the fact, often not recognized by farmer critics, that, unless the manure was hauled out and put on the land in early spring, between the time the soil was broken for the intended crop and the final fitting, there might not be another good chance all season to clean out the stalls. In short, manure never has been a convenience on American farms. During the winter it often cannot conveniently be put where it should be used. The field may not have been plowed—and manure ought never be plowed in. Put on row crops after planting, manure clogs the cultivators. There really isn't an easy, proper disposal of this barnyard impediment. Dairy farmers, under the urban sanitary inspectors, have become notable exceptions to this general pattern, and haul out their manure daily for some sort of disposition.

While crop yields remained high enough to yield a profit, the American farmer neglected what was happening to his soil. Profits always had made it possible to buy fertilizers as substitutes for manure. So he didn't worry. The increasing tightness of the land made it harder to work (encouraging the device of crop rotations to decrease the frequency of plowings). Diseases and insects increased correspondingly in prevalence and destructiveness. Despite increased use of fertilizers, crop yields had become harder to maintain. Yet all these facts seemed to escape the notice of most farmers until dwindling profits or actual losses forced their attention. By that time disastrous erosion was just around the corner.

It may be said with some truth that the farmer's liberal income had betrayed him. While he had the cash he spent it freely for fertilizers, instead of using the manure his farm produced. Gradually disappearing organic matter delivered his soil to the mercies of a dogged tightening of its structure. Farming began to require more power for plowing than formerly. Everybody who studied the matter, apparently believed, or argued, that plowing effectively loosens and aerates soil—forgetting that, unless there is abundance of organic matter in the soil, no amount of ordinary mechanical loosening can be effective beyond the few days or weeks required for gravity and pelting rains to pull it together again. The tightened soil structure excluded nitrogen, which formerly had conspired with organic processes in the soil to keep the structure open and airy. This exclusion of nitrogen made it necessary to grow legume crops for their nitrogen-gathering effect. But before legumes would grow, lime must be added to reopen the pores of the soil, and the growing legumes, unless grown during an "off" season, occupied the land for a profitless season. In addition, increasing trouble with insects and diseases made the use of pest controls seem essential. In short, farmers were feeling keenly the effect of circulating their money when they should, instead, have kept in circulation the plant food values (and other biological values) contained in their farm manures.

To alleviate these troubles, farmers are advised to buy even more fertilizers, and to use lime in ever-increasing quantities; to grow—or try to grow—more legume crops, especially alfalfa; to use bigger and bigger plows; to buy nitrogen in greater quantities, often for plowing under with non-legume crops, for speeding green manure decay; to treat seeds that are, or may be, infected by disease; and to use dusts or sprays in an effort to lessen damage from insects and diseases which seem to be inevitable. These and scores more of "improved" practices are today being urged upon farmers to compensate for the degradation of their land, and the end is not yet in sight. Indeed, so far as anyone can now foresee—barring an unlikely vow to develop real soil on their farms—farmers in the future must use more and more of fertilizers, of lime, and of pest controls. So what?

At this point we can see how high income of the past has made high income for the future absolutely necessary.

For, of course, the fertilizers, lime, and other chemicals now axiomatically necessary in American farming must be paid for. They are supplied only by people who earn their living by making and distributing them. As farmers have made greater use of these things during the past two or three decades, hundreds of new firms have entered "farm service" fields. This means that, of the more than one hundred million Americans who grow little or no food for themselves, a few millions justify their existence by furnishing these various "aids" to farmers. These are perfectly legitimate businesses, of course; but if what has been set up in this book is true, they cannot longer be thought of as essential businesses, insofar as the farm trade is concerned. A billion or more food growers elsewhere in the world have never even heard of these so-called necessities, and if they should become convinced that fertilizers, lime, and other chemicals are necessary, they have no cash with which to buy them. Yet for thousands of years peasant farmers ignorantly have managed to grow food of fine quality without "essential aids."

This is but part of the story. Few people can know the full extent to which farm-earned cash is dissipated uneconomically by the "service industries." And since such "aids" are not necessary to successful farming, their elimination could turn small loss to profit. Many farmers might even manage with lower incomes. The economics of such industries as feed-mixing, the packing of meats, the manufacture and sale of farm machinery, and scores of others related to farming is unknown to me, and I am not aware that criticism frequently directed at them is justified. However, they, too, may be parties to the melon cutting of farmer income. Whatever is the true situation, a 25 to 35 per cent reduction in farm expense could still permit the farmer to make a profit at lower market prices. This, in turn, would lower living costs for others, and should justify lower prices for what farmers have to buy.

It is dizzying to enumerate the multitude of ways in which the farmer's products may be used. Canning, sugar refining, shoe manufacturing (if and when hides are used), textiles, clothing, flour milling, macaroni, shredded wheat, flakes of several cereals, puffed wheat and rice, potato chips, corn refinery products of an amazing variety, soy beans in nearly everything you can think of from paints to buttons, mucilage from sweet potatoes, imitation tapioca from recently developed waxy grains—all are ways in which farm products are refined (or exploited) for the ultimate consumer. In all of these businesses, American inventiveness has its chance to prove that the American public will buy anything if the advertising is attractive enough, and will pay prices that bear little or no relation either to costs or to real value. Virtually the only curb on such exploitation is competition, which in some lines has been excluded by effective patents. Some of the above products sell at reasonable prices, but others apparently bring whatever the customer can be induced to pay.

From all of this it should be clear that, despite Chamber of Commerce protestations, something resembling economic parasitism flourishes in this country on a grand scale. If that term needs definition, lump it off as "Willingness to live luxuriously at the expense of the poor." In the case of the farmer's income, it means that the general public pays *a little to the farmer,* for the raw materials, and *several times as much to processors* for the privilege of consuming farm products (in some special form) which may or may not have been improved by the processing. Bookkeeping details of such enterprises are known only to insiders.

Occasional efforts have been made by farm organizations to duplicate real services by co-operative effort. Some have succeeded, but some have encountered essential costs of operation which make it impossible for them to replace economically the businesses they were intended to replace, to stop the "robbing of the farmer." Co-operatives succeed or fail on merit, exactly as do other businesses. Net farmer income may or may not be increased by the wider use of co-operatives. Often a proposed co-operative venture is to be but one more unit in an already crowded distribution area. In that case it is doomed before it opens its doors. Promoters of such attempts to share in middlemen's profits should know all the pertinent facts about the proposed activity before they launch inexperienced workers into a hazardous field. The history of private business failures is far more lengthy than the history of successes. The same is true of co-operative enterprises. Before a new co-operative is to be started, its backers should make sure that those already in the field are not merely hanging onto a hopeless project.

The farmer's crops are, indeed, new riches from the earth. Few other producers in the field of natural resources can return annually to the source of their product and come away with as much as they got the preceding year—and continue to do so for forty centuries, as has been done by farmers in the older parts of the world. It is fitting, right, necessary, that farm products be transformed into the most beneficial forms. Hundreds of kinds of business are engaged in operations that fabricate, preserve, refine, or otherwise convert farm-produced raw materials into more serviceable items for the market. No idyllic, moneyless economies such as exist in the rural sections of every part of the world except America can match for excellence the enormously complicated rural-urban relationship we have created in the United States. Yet there are urgently needed reforms that ought to be made in our own system to make it fit better into the world-wide system of trade. Otherwise, peace, which every nation wishes, is apt to elude us because of our inability to trade on mutually satisfactory terms with nations small and large the world over.

Nobody can justify on economic grounds a number of American business practices which tend to keep our wages, prices, and general scale of economic value so high that our products are largely inaccessible to people of other parts of the world. Because money was plentiful in our country, and because nobody showed fight to prevent such developments, many of our most respectable businesses have developed practices which amount to parasitism. In many instances this may not be apparent, even to the executives of these businesses, because they are merely doing what others around them are doing. The circumstance of abundant and cheap money has encouraged developments which could not have occurred in any other country in the world. These bad habits need correction.

Among our bad habits are high-pressure advertising, installment selling of consumer goods, and artificially high prices. There are many other equally pernicious features of American business which add nothing whatever to what we think of ideally as the American Standard of Living—now easily translated into "The American High Cost of Living." Please don't forget as you read this that I'm 100 per cent for the American way of life. My point is that it costs us several times as much as it should. We could, I am sure, enjoy every benefit we now have at costs well below half what we pay. Also, if we will deliberately set about to rectify the situation, we can soon be in position to enjoy many times as much export trade as might be possible otherwise.

In all three of my books, *Plowman's Folly*, *Uneasy Money*, and *A Second Look*, I have shown that farmers may rely upon natural forces to do for them all that is now being done by the use of fertilizers, lime, and chemical pest controls. No counter evidence exists, because none of the experiment stations has based its rebuttal evidence on the conditions obtaining in real soil, as set forth in these books. Moreover, there are many farmers and gardeners of the country who have proved for themselves that the thesis of these books is correct. If this premise may be admitted, then for any reformation of the American economic system we shall need to find other markets for the products of these "service" industries, and relieve the farmer of their cost.

Many an industry converts farm products to new forms which cannot be justified on merit (the highly watered modifications of cheese, for example), and by effective forms of advertising virtually drives the better, original forms of these products out of the market. Exposure of such practices is strictly in line with the better business era we need to create.

Then there are the foods that are extensively advertised because of their "energy value." It so happens that if one eats in proper quantities the plentiful, cheaper foods, he cannot miss getting all the energy value he needs. High-pressure influence to get people to eat more corn, wheat, or potatoes in fancy, refined, and expensive forms is entirely out of keeping with the proposed lines of reform. This blatant violation of commercial decencies is possible from the consumer's standpoint only because people permit the advertiser to do their thinking for them; from the advertiser's standpoint, only the cheapness of his raw materials makes it possible to sell these superabundant carbohydrates, fats, and sugars within the ability of the consumer to pay. Recommendation that this "superior" product be eaten with plenty of milk or fruit (also expensive) scarcely makes up for the fact that the packaged food costs ten times as much as equivalent or better food can be obtained in other forms.

White flour and white sugar, because of their inferior nutritive qualities rather than because of cost, should be scrutinized in any widespread effort to improve the country's health standards. The raw materials from which these parts of our diet are refined are more nutritious, though neither as attractive in appearance nor as convenient to use.

And the vitamin business! When we begin to get our vitamins where Adam got his, we shall no longer need to buy vitamins in capsule form. Indeed, when all our foods and livestock feeds are grown in real soil, and our meat animals are fed such foods, we shall no longer need to resort to supplements for vitamins A and C, nor to any of the usual fugitive sources—wheat germ, bran, etc.—for vitamin B_1. All the other vitamins, similarly, will be found in any reasonable combination of foods we may choose to eat. Indeed, some foods doubtless will furnish many of the vitamins in abundance. Vitamin starvation will then be a dead issue. However, until we have reached that hoped-for time, don't break away from your doctor's orders in the use of vitamins.

The ultimate total effect on the redistribution of the farmer's income seems impossible to appraise. The truth is that an amazing proportion of our whole population, quite unconsciously, lives comfortably from its share of the farmer's income. Tens of millions of our people would be appalled by the suggestion that their particular occupation might suffer as a result of a sane reformation of farming practices. Consider some of the industries that would be affected:

Steel manufacturers supply raw materials to the farm machinery trade. Every steel worker, therefore, from the ore mining regions of Minnesota all along the line through the Great Lakes shipping crews, the tugboat men, the blast-furnace workers (from laborers to metallurgists), the open hearth or Bessemer process forces, the rolling-mill employees, the tinplate or galvanizing personnel, railway workers, truckmen at many stages in manufacture, transportation, and distribution operations, wholesalers, retailers, salesmen—all would be affected by the elimination of cultivation from the growing of farm and garden crops. Considering that this is just one of the groups that would be affected, it should be easy to see that many and serious dislocations may easily follow such changes as are here being suggested.

In short, there will be millions of people who will learn, to their surprise, that because farmer Jones and a few millions of his contemporaries have learned how to grow more and better crops without using the particular product their plant supplies, their working time will be reduced, say 10 per cent, until a replacement market can be found. And let no one imagine that such innovations will not be fought tooth and nail from many quarters, every opponent being but evidence that the law of self-preservation is not changed by the farmer's determination to revise his procedures. Nothing short of enlightened, stubborn determination to fight this campaign through to success will overcome the stout opposition that will be presented by those affected adversely for the time being.

The goal under the program here proposed is a reduction in the costs of farm operation. The total economic effect, however, is even larger, inasmuch as commodity costs as a whole—farm products included—may be expected to decline. In the leveling out process, the distribution of income, not solely among industries, but among individuals as well, should afford a more satisfactory outlook for everyone.

Economic waste of the kind described in this chapter must be eliminated—even at the cost of a temporary disruption of prices. Our long-term economic welfare is far more important than the maintenance of a system which has already shown signs of decay.

A Second Look at XIV : Future Farming

A MOST IMPORTANT ITEM of unfinished business now before the councils of the nations is that of assuring the people of the world against a repetition of the latest orgy of human slaughter. And the most hopeful aspect of the present effort is that provisions for an ample and certain food supply are on the agenda. The Food and Agriculture Organization Committee may in the end determine whether there shall be future wars. Its work is that important. May it work wisely!

Propaganda to the contrary nothwithstanding, there is a persistent suspicion that the actual motive of aggressors may be just what they represent it to be: The necessity for reaching a dependable food supply for an increasing population. No aggrieved nation can publicly admit this plaint of the aggressor, of course; for if it willingly shared its own limited rations with the aggressor, its own people would eventually also come to want. Wars are never fought on the clear-cut issue of the aggressor's need for more food-producing territory, but upon issues that will enable the aggrieved people to justify the conflict. Caesar invaded Gaul in order to bring back *frumentum*, grain. His predecessors throughout time had raided the food supplies of their neighbors for like reason. And, while the wars of recorded history do not usually reveal food shortages as motives, the suspicion that such causes are fundamental will not down.

The most recent war may be no exception. A survey of the available land areas of the principal participants reveals that among the Axis nations none had as much as two acres per person, including such waste areas as mountains, the land occupied by roads and railways, cities, army camps, and so on. Indeed, England, Scotland, and Wales altogether provide less than one and one-fourth acres per person, including the bleak northern coastal areas; and the southern portion (England and Wales) has but .89 acre per person. However, there is the empire upon which the home peoples can draw for food—giving the peoples of the empire as a whole access to 15.5 acres each. Of the other United Nations, Russia has an estimated 21 plus acres per person, China something more than 8, and the United States 15.5.

On the basis of these figures, we would not be able to rule out as a war motive the necessity for Japan, Germany, and Italy—each with less than two acres of land per person—to seek additional food sources. Obviously this did not provide the whole reason for the restlessness of these peoples, but the obvious contrast between the land possessions of the United Nations and the Axis countries remains as a strong motive. To attribute wars to national temperaments, to forms of government, or to other ideological and organizational causes may be begging the question, for who can dissociate these various influences from the influence of threatened hunger!

Who can doubt that to a Japanese, eternally plagued by hunger, California, with its 12 acres per person, looked like Heaven itself? And the rest of the United States, sharing 15.5 acres per person, might easily be resented by a people who notably make use of every square foot of their land for producing food. How must it have seemed to the Japanese to be excluded from this country of abundant land, when they could see that acres and acres of waste countryside waited only to be developed into highly productive gardens, vineyards, and orchards? And when they saw how ineptly Americans used the land under cultivation, they could scarcely have taken comfort.

There is obviously no easy settlement of a world situation so complicated. We do not wish to admit people who could perpetrate another Pearl Harbor, even if they face the alternative of starvation. Neither do we like the prospect of sharing land with Germans or Italians, who tried so desperately to overrun Europe and Africa. Yet we cannot deny their right to an ample food supply—even to a place to grow their food. The question is to find a place that is not already occupied. These are but the simplest outlines of the extremely complicated situation with which the Food and Agriculture Committee of the United Nations has to deal. The Committee needs wisdom indeed.

Here at home we have problems of our own, despite our 15.5 acres per person. The majority of our people have even less land than the almost landless Japanese. Between fifty and one hundred million depend in varying degree upon the surplus grown by a mere six million farms, most of which produce no surplus whatever. Thus even in this country we have problems of food supply that would seem insoluble save for the fact that they have developed so gradually that their solution has kept pace with need. How, indeed, would our people be fed if a sudden break-down in transportation, refrigeration, or handling should occur? Before we waste too much energy feeding the rest of the world we might well improve the nutrition of our own people, who are helplessly dependent upon the deficient products of our substandard soils.

This food dependency of our people seems to be a serious fault of our highly developed civilization. New York apartment dwellers live off the artificially watered desert land of California. Celery, cantaloupes, lemons, and many other California products are regularly part of the diet of people three thousand miles away. Much could happen to so tenuous a supply line if somebody should decide to put pressure on those dependent upon it. Of course, California is by no means the sole source of supply for most of these products. But for millions of our people the sea lanes and the railroads of this country are their vegetable garden paths. They have the advantage that they need never get their feet muddy, but this would be slight compensation in case of a complete tie-up of national transportation. They are dependent upon the outcome of periodic negotiations between the railroads and their employees.

These customers to whom the farmer never is introduced are entitled, however, to get from the food he sells them everything that food is supposed to supply. If they become ill because beets or onions or potatoes lack vital elements that healthy soils supply, the blame rests, in the final analysis, upon the farmer who grew the deficient items. And in such a case, can the farmer plead innocence? Innocence of intent, yes. But not for long can farmers plead innocence of knowledge that their land is ailing, and that, therefore, it simply cannot grow foods that are entirely satisfying to the consumer. Consumers themselves are not generally aware of the situation, but when they have learned how their health, their very lives, are in the hands of farmers hundreds or thousands of miles away, they will doubtless act to assure themselves a proper food supply.

Even now world events are ushering in for American consumers of bread new lessons in nutrition.[1] The necessity for supplying as much wheat as possible to Europe has made it necessary that nutrients we formerly fed to cows, hogs, and chickens be allowed to remain in the flour that supplies us with bread. Perhaps a few more months of this chance to taste real protein in "white" bread will help us to appreciate the situation the Russians were in when their soldiers refused to use American white flour for baking until it had been reinforced by the addition of soybean flour. The Russian eats habitually what we are pleased to call black bread. It is less appealing to the sensibilities of Americans, but far more nourishing than our bread ever has been. When the Russian soldier found that his stomach still was unsatisfied after he had con-

[1] This was written during the period when "emergency" flour was resorted to in this country, in order to stretch our supply of wheat and assist countries in short supply.

sumed an adequate quantity of white bread, he demanded that something be done about it. Perhaps our experience with the superior nutrients we have been relaying on to the cows will teach us to despise the "wallpaper paste" we have heretofore been using as bread-making material.

Influences such as these must be taken into account in planning the future farming of the United States. Too long have we striven for greater tonnages of production, without consideration of the quality of that production. We have increased production per acre sometimes by changing from one kind of crop to another; and of that practice Dr. William A. Albrecht truly says:

> When one agricultural plant variety no longer is highly productive, we search and supplant it with another only to boast of our success in production of tonnage of herbage. But we forget that when the first variety failed because of the declining store of soil nutrients, then the second or introduced variety that succeeds must be producing tonnage by taking relatively less from the soil. It must be making itself by taking more from air, water and sunshine, or what is above the soil. Its service to animals must then be one of providing packing for empty paunches more than of supplying soil-contributed nutrients required for animal body construction.[2]

We humans have even less chance than domestic animals to get from our foods everything we need, for human foods go through refining processes which make them more attractive but often less nutritious. Our white flour is the shining example of that folly.

[2] William A. Albrecht, "Health Depends on Soil," *The Land*, Vol. II, No. 2.

I have shown in previous chapters that the earth is self-sufficient, and that its failure to deliver to plants everything they need can be traced to the manner in which we handle the land. As has been suggested, deficiencies may arise in part from unnecessary disturbance of the upper layers of the soil, which otherwise would benefit from the intrusion of nitrogen in company with the oxygen of the air. These two elements promote and sustain the necessary decay which is designed to elaborate from the involved rock particles additional "plant rations" in mineral form. The classic example of a crop growing in undisturbed soil is grass. It refuses to grow in disturbed soil and thereby becomes the outstanding nutrient-rich plant on every farm. Farmers have been awkward in their management of grass. They have really paid little attention to it, and have under-valued it seriously because they have known so little about it.

One of the marvels of Nature is the way in which a cow can graze day after day in what looks almost like a dry lot, and still fill the milk pail at night. This phenomenon may be traced to the fact that the grass roots benefit from the aeration of an undisturbed soil, and to the further fact that the cow keeps her grazing area closely cropped, so that the grass blades she gets are short enough to contain virtually no bulky indigestible strengthening tissues. This protein-rich grass is coming to be appreciated more and more by discerning farmers. Many in the future will save both time and money by reverting to the production of more grass and less of the crops that require much labor and machinery.

An outstanding instance of such a change of policy is that revealed in the work of Arthur Adams of Kansas, who is known as the "brome king" because he has eight hundred acres devoted to this nutritious grass. In all, he is said to have three thousand acres in grass. He does not bother to grow corn but rents his corn land to neighbors. He has what seem to me excellent reasons for all this, as related in the April, 1946, issue of the *Farm Journal.* In introducing the story, the editor remarks: "*Farm Journal* presents this story for consideration in long-time farm planning—not necessarily as a guide for this spring. The U. S. Department of Agriculture is urging increased production of corn and wheat this year." Other examples of excellent grass management are given in the Winter, 1946, issue of *Country Book.*

Whether it is used for milk or beef, grass is a short-cut to better nutrition. Completely grass-fed beef animals, provided the grass is kept always in the highly nutritious short stage that characterizes a heavily grazed pasture, can often times go to market in prime condition. Rarely do the cuts from such animals exhibit the unwanted "halo" of fat so frequently seen on cuts from corn-fed animals. Cattle grazed on pastures that are not cared for correctly can produce as poor beef as you will ever see; but judicious use of the mower at times when the grass threatens to become stemmy helps to make it possible for the animals always to find the nutritious short growth that is so essential for producing prime beef. I am speaking here of small pastures, obviously not of the vast Western ranges.

The extra use of mowers and other machinery which

may be found necessary in such an expanded program of grass management would compensate the machinery manufacturers somewhat for the loss of sales resulting from the abandonment of certain soil-stirring operations. I suspect that no rearrangement of farm plans would be so beneficial as a partial or complete elimination of grain growing on many farms. Both corn and wheat will be produced in tremendous surplus within a short time after foreign agriculture has been re-established on a sound basis. In advance of this eventuality, it will be fortunate for the country if a few farmers in each county where more grain is produced than is needed for local use would drop these crops from their plans and substitute grass or other needed crops. Pasture is the first and most logical substitute crop, for use with any and all kinds of livestock and poultry.

Men who would be interested in making such changes in their plans should consult the local representatives of Soil Conservation Service or other agricultural authorities, county agents, experiment station or college specialists, or Smith-Hughes teachers of agriculture regarding details of suitable grasses and legumes for such use. Ohio residents can get from the Ohio Experiment Station, Wooster, Ohio, the benefit of recent work in the seeding of alfalfa by methods that are both inexpensive and highly effective. Other experiment stations may be able to provide similar information. Ask for instructions in the seeding of alfalfa.

When real soil has been developed again on our farms, we shall be in position to grow new crops, or to grow again some of the crops that have been driven off by the degradation of our land. One crop that many of our forefathers grew is flax. Before cotton became plentiful, farmers grew flax for fiber, then later some of these same people grew a little cotton, which they used for weaving and knitting. As far north as my boyhood home in Kentucky, a hundred miles or more from the Cotton Belt, natives grew their own cotton, which they carded and spun into yarn for various uses. Flax, however, had disappeared from our section long before my time.

Flax for fiber is not a crop that can easily be introduced, because of the difficulty of separating the fiber from the rest of the plant. Flax for seed is less of a problem, and it is adaptable to wider distribution. Yet no one should try to grow seed flax until he has obtained trustworthy information about the requirements of the crop, and has made the necessary preparation for growing it. Good sources of such information are the experiment stations in the sections where seed flax is grown: the Minnesota Experiment Station, University Farm, St. Paul 8, Minn.; the Montana Experiment Station, Bozeman, Mont.; or the North Dakota Experiment Station, State College Station, Fargo, N. D. Where seed flax is adapted, it is said to be more profitable than wheat, as a rule. In the Northwestern area, where it has done best, it interchanges to some extent with spring wheat.

The manner in which women clear imported linens off the shelves as fast as they can be obtained from abroad suggests that fiber flax also may be worth a trial again. Its production now is confined almost wholly to the far

Northwest in this country. Flax is said to be very sensitive to soil deficiencies. The fact that wilt strikes it down mercilessly when soils have begun to deteriorate proves this. When we have restored our soils to something approaching their original quality, it seems that farmers who are willing to equip for it might grow flax profitably in many sections. Then our women might have a chance to own as much fine linen as they want. This seems worth consideration as a future farming possibility.

One special flax industry now operating in western North Carolina makes fine paper from seed-flax straw. Though it has been established only a decade or so, it already supplies part of the cigarette paper demand, replacing importations formerly obtained from France. This mill is a portent of an industry that may later prove attractive to farmers, since the sale of both straw and seed from flax would provide two incomes from this crop. This, too, is worth looking into.

Then there is the sweet-potato crop. It is a "natural" for the South, but it can also be grown in most of the states. Farmers who make a point of having weed-free soil have in this crop a chance for additional profit from land no longer needed for corn or wheat. In parts of the country where the rainfall is not excessive, this crop may produce exceptionally fine roots which can be kept in storage without the necessity for previous heat curing. The high rainfall of the South results in a potato so moist that it must be kiln dried before permanent winter storage is safe; but it is known that in less humid areas this is less true. However, the crop requires plenty of heat at the right time, and our northern latitudes may not provide enough heat in some seasons. Because of this possibility, farmers ought not risk too large areas to this crop, and should see to it that conditions are otherwise quite favorable before venturing into it.

And what about fruits of all kinds? The nutritionists are always urging us to eat more fruit. We don't do so because of the cost. With real soil available again, we will find that we can grow fruit without serious menace from diseases and insects. This will make it possible for everybody who has the necessary space to use some of it for fruit growing. Even if he has not taken the trouble to develop real soil, the fruit grower can compensate for that omission by keeping the soil well covered continuously with mulch material—deep enough that it is moist at the ground surface all the time. The mulch itself will recreate the real soil in a season or two.

Many farmers who grow corn or wheat would do well to consider devoting part of their small-grain lands to fruit culture—after conditioning the soil for the latter purpose. If many farmers should plan to do this, there would be a more plentiful supply of fruit for the market. It would not have cost so much to grow, since pest controls would not have been necessary. Thus the growers could afford to sell their products at lower prices than now prevail. Lower prices would increase the use of fruits by everybody; and, in the end, the people who grew the fruit would make a profit most seasons. Great possibilities for improving agricultural income, as well as public health, lie in such a change from our usual farming routines.

The thought that pest-free fruit could be grown will seem bizarre to people who have fought apple scab, aphis, curculio, codling moth, and a score of other fruit pests. In the main, the outcome of the fight is never the complete control of the marauder. The best that usually can be hoped for is that enough of the fruit will be acceptable in the market to yield a profit to the grower. Men who have had this experience will be extremely skeptical about the possibility of growing worm-free apples without spraying. But we might profit from the experience of an eminent English agriculturist. Sir Albert Howard bought in 1934 an orchard that, according to his report quoted by Lady Eve Balfour:

> was completely worn out through no fault of the previous owner. It was a veritable pathological museum—the fruit trees, in particular, were smothered with every kind of blight. Steps were taken to convert all the vegetable wastes into humus with the help of stable litter. Even after one year the pests began to retreat. In three years all had disappeared, the wooly aphis on one apple tree being the last to leave. During this period no insecticides or fungicides were used and no diseased material was ever destroyed. It was all converted into humus.[3]

If the production of pest-free fruit were not possible without chemicals, Sir Albert could not have achieved this result without their use. I have seen, as previously related, perfect fruit specimens displayed in community fairs in isolated sections where no one knew of the neces-

[3] Lady Eve B. Balfour, *The Living Soil* (London, Faber and Faber, 1943), 114.

sity for pest controls. So I know it is possible to avoid the presumed necessity and the expense of chemical treatments, and to come through with a good crop of fruit.

When ordinary substandard soil has been converted to real soil, or even while it is in process of conversion, it will support some crops that recent generations of farmers seem to have despaired of. One such is the blueberry, already mentioned. Another fruit crop for which I have hope of success is the apricot. Orchardists have long since abandoned efforts to grow apricots except in special areas. Killing of the fruit buds, by frosts that occur in spring after the quick-blooming tree has opened its blossoms, is usually blamed for failure of the crop. There is reason to believe that mulch culture of apricots may prove a double-edged remedy for this condition; however, proof positive is yet to be demonstrated. It is known that throughout the areas where apricots have long been off the orchard list an occasional tree which bears regularly is to be found. Usually, if not always, such a tree grows where it is impracticable to give it any cultivation. Many producing trees are on lawns of old homesteads. Some have ash heaps around them. In many cases near-by buildings offer wind protection. But the important point is that these trees produce a crop almost every season. Why?

The circumstances under which bearing apricot trees have been found outside their generally approved range suggest that "neglect" may be more helpful than care, for few of these trees get any special care. As a matter of theory, I have decided that this fruit deserves thorough testing under mulch conditions. The heavy, continuous mulch will result in providing the trees with a richer sap than they would have if they grew in soil without organic matter (a cultivated soil is one that usually is almost without organic matter in its surface); and, because of the mulch that covers the soil to a few inches depth, blooming should be retarded slightly in spring, thus enabling the tree to pass through some of the late frosts in dormant condition. The combination of later blooming with less dilute sap seems a probable solution for the traditional damage by late frosts.

In this connection it should be remembered that the use of nitrogen fertilizers under dormant fruit trees has been recommended for the purpose of increasing the sap density of the tree, so that the fruit buds will endure successfully a few degrees lower temperature. It is my belief that a well-maintained mulch will do this just as certainly as the fertilizer; and that it will avoid any possible mineral unbalance that may result from the use of the chemical. But, as stated above, this is still to be proved by demonstration. I now have a few small apricot trees growing under mulch conditions.

Edible nuts offer another important new crop possibility. Nuts provide good returns for a minimum of care, since they do not even have to be picked. As a dietary matter, nuts in abundance would be a boon to the American people. Because prices have been extremely high in recent years, nut production within the climatic possibilities for the locality ought to prove profitable to the grower. Peanuts for the South, as well as pecans and most of the other edible nuts; for northern latitudes, selected strains of thin-shelled, easy-cracking walnuts, hickory nuts, and possibly (in real soil) native chestnuts. I mention chestnuts despite their having been almost completely destroyed in recent years by blight, because I suspect that with the right soil conditions chestnuts may again become a dependable nut crop for much of the temperate zone. This, of course, is merely a matter of opinion; but it is notable that in the years immediately prior to their destruction by blight, chestnut trees were so much infested by worms that it was almost impossible to find one free of these pests. Such infestation has been found to indicate poor growing conditions in cultivated crops. Why might this not also be true of the chestnut?

Evidence on this point is by no means clear, but it is known that under forest conditions chestnut trees were crowded out of the better soils by tulip poplar, walnut, oak, ash, maple, and other trees. Along the Appalachian range, chestnuts were among the first trees to be logged out for saw timber, because of their extremely straight grain, which made the lumber easily workable for many purposes. The removal of these—they were sometimes giants three or more feet in diameter—fifty years ago left only the smaller, less thrifty specimens. Those remaining (all now dead) were to be found almost exclusively near the tops of the ridges, along with the pines and cedars. Gradual lowering of the water table has made growing conditions impossible for chestnuts, which like the moist conditions of the shady coves where the other hardwood trees crowd them out. Such reasoning justifies curiosity as to whether chestnuts might not again thrive in this country if they were given appropriate growing conditions, including real soil.

Over and beyond such changes in cropping pattern, farmers as a group ought to protect themselves against economic uncertainties by growing for themselves as much as they can of their own food requirements. This may seem to be a step backward, since all of our development in the recent past has been in the direction of specialization. The suggestion should be taken quite frankly with a "grain of salt." Certainly no farmer should devote to production for home use time that he is sure can be profitably spent growing market crops or animals. But in the years to come there are likely to be times when no man can know whether he will be able to sell what he can grow. In such times labor spent for subsistence crops and animals will pay dividends with a certainty that could not be expected of time spent otherwise. And home-produced foods are to be preferred to any government subsidy or other payment in lieu of what one should have grown. Neglect in this regard may quite properly be considered unpatriotic if and when the hard days come.

If growing one's own food in an age of specialization is thought to be a backward step, the sting may be partly removed, I suspect, when precaution proves itself to be a lifesaver. And, beyond that, the discovery that one can grow foods that are immeasurably better in flavor than those usually available in the market will be further compensation.

These are a few of the ways in which the farm of the future may well be different from that of today's pattern.

In general, we shall grow a greater abundance of everything we need. We shall grow everything at reduced cost. And we shall have a greater variety of crops in each locality, since we shall grow for use as well as for market.

About Island Press

Island Press, a nonprofit organization, publishes, markets, and distributes the most advanced thinking on the conservation of our natural resources—books about soil, land, water, forests, wildlife, and hazardous and toxic wastes. These books are practical tools used by public officials, business and industry leaders, natural resource managers, and concerned citizens working to solve both local and global resource problems.

Founded in 1978, Island Press reorganized in 1984 to meet the increasing demand for substantive books on all resource-related issues. Island Press publishes and distributes under its own imprint and offers these services to other nonprofit organizations.

Funding to support Island Press is provided by The Mary Reynolds Babcock Foundation, The William H. Donner Foundation, Inc., The Ford Foundation, The George Gund Foundation, The William and Flora Hewlett Foundation, The Joyce Foundation, The Andrew W. Mellon Foundation, Northwest Area Foundation, The J.N. Pew, Jr. Charitable Trust, Rockefeller Brothers Fund, and The Tides Foundation.

Island Press Board of Directors